VOICES OF OPPORTUNITY

In this book, the vital role of language in shaping the life chances of children from contrasting ends of the social ladder is explored. Grounded in the latest research and the contemporary experiences of educators, it highlights how oracy is a key driver of upward social mobility, especially for the most disadvantaged children.

Drawing on case studies, classroom practice and academic research, the book examines the widening language divide that emerges in early childhood and continues to grow throughout the educational journey. It contrasts the experiences of children from language-rich upbringings with those from language-poor backgrounds, showing how these differences affect access to learning, emotional well-being and future life opportunities. Topics include the emerging word gap for under-threes, the importance of vocabulary development, the power of oracy for emotional regulation and the barriers to career choices that result from poor language skills. The book also unpacks the evolving policy landscape, highlights organisations championing oracy nationwide and reflects the growing optimism surrounding language development for the future.

This book is valuable for educators and school leaders seeking to understand the connection between oracy and social mobility. It offers practical strategies, tangible actions and clear next steps for embedding oracy into schools.

Michael Gardner is the founder of The Oracy Shift, an organisation dedicated to elevating oracy in education. An experienced teacher, he is the Teaching and Learning Lead at Maritime Academy Trust, supporting professional development across 13 primary schools.

VOICES OF OPPORTUNITY

Oracy for Social Mobility in Education

Michael Gardner

LONDON AND NEW YORK

Designed cover image: Zagoruyko / Getty Images ®

First published 2026
by Routledge
4 Park Square, Milton Park, Abingdon, Oxon OX14 4RN

and by Routledge
605 Third Avenue, New York, NY 10158

Routledge is an imprint of the Taylor & Francis Group, an informa business

© 2026 Michael Gardner

The right of Michael Gardner to be identified as author of this work has been asserted in accordance with sections 77 and 78 of the Copyright, Designs and Patents Act 1988.

All rights reserved. No part of this book may be reprinted or reproduced or utilised in any form or by any electronic, mechanical, or other means, now known or hereafter invented, including photocopying and recording, or in any information storage or retrieval system, without permission in writing from the publishers.

For Product Safety Concerns and Information please contact our EU representative GPSR@taylorandfrancis.com. Taylor & Francis Verlag GmbH, Kaufingerstraße 24, 80331 München, Germany.

Trademark notice: Product or corporate names may be trademarks or registered trademarks, and are used only for identification and explanation without intent to infringe.

British Library Cataloguing-in-Publication Data
A catalogue record for this book is available from the British Library

ISBN: 978-1-003-86394-6 (hbk)
ISBN: 978-1-003-86389-2 (pbk)
ISBN: 978-1-003-60759-5 (ebk)

DOI: 10.4324/9781003607595

Typeset in Interstate
by Newgen Publishing UK

To my son, know that you have a voice and your words can make a difference in this world'

CONTENTS

	Introduction	1
1	Demystifying Oracy	6
2	Defining Social Mobility	17
3	From Birth to Age 3	29
4	Entering EYFS: The 'School Readiness' Divide	43
5	Closing Gaps in EYFS	52
6	Time to Intervene	62
7	The Key to Unlocking Learning	67
8	The Vocabulary Gap	86
9	The Fourth R	99
10	Oracy for Well-being	108
11	Leveraging Oracy for Well-being	119
12	Barriers to the Workplace	137
13	Workplace of the Future	150
14	Fostering an Oracy Culture	157

15	**Taking Action**	170
16	**Case Studies**	179
17	**Conclusion**	192
	Index	196

Introduction

Why Oracy, Why Now?

The past decade has seen turbulent changes nationally and internationally; from austerity to the fallout of Brexit, the COVID-19 pandemic to rising inflation, society has faced many new and unforeseen challenges. These social and economic shifts have affected everyone yet the negative impact has been most sharply felt by those at the lowest end of the social ladder. These major changes are not solely to blame for the widening gap between the rich and poor, yet they have certainly accelerated this growing divide. Upwards social mobility has become far less prevalent, with communities at both ends of the spectrum finding themselves stuck in place.

As more and more families fall below the poverty line, or are even classed as *'in-work poor'*, there has been a renewed focus upon the actions needed to narrow this gap. In an attempt to address this growing concern, successive governments have set up reviews and commissions to identify the levers for social equity, attempting to adapt and implement policies to facilitate meaningful change. These policies and initiatives are wide reaching, covering aspects of everyday life including economic, social, cultural, work and education. It is within the domain of education that oracy has appeared as both a barrier – as well as a driver – for upwards mobility for the most disadvantaged communities.

The Widening Oracy Divide

Oracy is commonly defined as the combination of *'learning to talk'* and *'learning through talk'*. Academics such as Vygotsky and Bruner have long championed the essential use of language in the learning process, and oracy is now valued as a central priority within the education sector. Yet, the acquisition and application of language also holds many benefits to a child's development that reach beyond pure academic achievement. The well-being, emotional regulation, confidence and self efficacy of a child can be significantly influenced by their power over the spoken word. This mastery of language affects a child's life trajectories from birth through to adulthood, with the most deprived communities hindered.

Language shapes life chances. Children from disadvantaged backgrounds often come from language-poor home environments, entering school with underdeveloped vocabulary and behind their more affluent peers in terms of basic language skills. This language gap exists upon entry into education and impacts the child's journey through school. Data from national tests – such as phonics screening and key stage assessments – show the oracy gap to be persistent and systemic. Research shows how oral language ability in Early years is connected to reading fluency and then onto academic prowess. Socioeconomic status is a strong predictor of academic success and a poor start to life can compound the inequality of opportunity from an early age. In essence, disadvantaged children start behind peers and fall further behind across the duration of their schooling.

As they move through secondary school, towards university or the working world, a young adult's grasp of language can affect their chances of successful entry into higher education or certain career paths. Whilst academic attainment matters, an individual's ability to build rapport, confidently engage in dialogue and read non-verbal cues are key communication skills needed at interview and into the workplace.

Schools Must Be the Great Equalisers

Schools are under increasing pressure in terms of funding, staff recruitment/retention and a mounting SEND crisis. State schools are treading water, barely managing to survive from one academic year to the next. Often the schools in the most challenging areas are facing harsh realities which impact the most vulnerable pupils directly; this includes reductions in support staff, limited enrichment opportunities, lack of resources and increasing numbers of severe needs of children entering their early years settings.

As a result of these challenges, the pupils in most need of oracy intervention are the ones with the least opportunities. These pupils have the most to gain from high-quality talk in class, and schools need to be the great equalisers. Where home environments are language-poor, schools need to set themselves up to be as language-rich as possible. This requires significant change over time, involving all stakeholders to work together to ensure oracy becomes a priority in school and at home.

In this book, the role of schools in shifting oracy to the heart of education will be explored, taking into account the roles of school leaders, teachers and support staff.

A National Conversation

The growing focus upon oracy as a lever for social change has led to the establishment of various government reviews, including:

- Various Ofsted and DfE reports on literacy and oracy
- Oracy All Party Parliamentary Group
- Oracy Education Commission (co-led with Voice 21)

This proliferation of reviews recognised spoken language as a core pillar of education, underpinning literacy, learning, well-being and employability. Many have called for oracy to be seen as *'The Fourth R'* alongside reading, writing and arithmetic. However, it is not only national government acting within the oracy space; organisations such as Voice 21, the Education Endowment Foundation (EEF) and Oracy Cambridge are advocates for change.

They are leading on large-scale research studies, pilots, trials and the development of evidence-based resources for schools to use.

This combination of government and third sector bodies has raised awareness around oracy and brought it into the national conversation.

Knowledge Is Power

As research studies and case studies have evolved over the past decade, we have a far greater understanding of language in education. Schools can now access resources and strategies that are grounded in evidence. Pedagogical models for oracy have been developed and aligned to the theories of language development. The Oracy Framework developed by Voice 21 is a fine example of scoping oracy domains, from cognitive to linguistic, in a format that is accessible for teachers to use.

However, as an education community, many are still standing at the foothills of oracy implementation, finding our bearings for the way ahead. Only a minority of schools have named a designated oracy lead, and many schools' development plans integrate oracy under the broader umbrella of literacy. Whilst many school leaders will have a growing interest and comprehension of oracy, there are still many who are yet to take steps towards truly embedding oracy into their school practice. There is a hope that the active push by government and oracy-advocating organisations will encourage more schools to embrace oracy fully.

Knowledge may be powerful but putting knowledge of oracy into purposeful action is what is needed now in the education sector.

Omnipresent Oracy

Experienced teachers will know that new ideas come in and out of favour in schools every few years. What appears to be a new, fresh concept to try is often a rediscovered approach from previous generations that has found a new purpose. Simultaneously, many new initiatives are seen as fads that lack real intent or depth; too often, they do not survive the academic year cycle, especially when something newer and shinier arrives. Many teachers may assume that oracy is one of these fads and may question, *"Haven't we been teaching language for decades?"* or *"Surely I have been getting my pupils to talk to each other already so what is new?"* These are valid challenges to ask of oracy but it is important that teachers understand the foundations of oracy and the potential benefits it can bring.

Talk Is Not a **Side Dish**

Even though oracy has clear ties to English and literacy, it is vital that it is not pigeon-holed into this curriculum domain. Oracy spans all aspects of schooling regardless of subject or age. From reasoning in maths to inquiring in science, language is (or at least should be) a fundamental component of every lesson. Language is an enabler for learning; those without it often struggle to engage or access learning. Therefore, it is very important that educators address any misconceptions about where oracy belongs and who it is for. If we want our pupils to master the art of learning, they need to first master the ability to use language. This ranges from active listening to problem solving, articulating to hypothesising.

Where schools have ringfenced oracy into the English curriculum, there will be substantial, unrealised benefits that do not reach the pupils who need it most. Yet, where schools recognise the need for oracy to thread it's way across the curriculum, pupils from all backgrounds will benefit and flourish. For pupils from the most socially underprivileged upbringings, having multiple opportunities across the timetable to observe quality talk, and rehearse themselves, is an extremely valuable part of their learning experience.

A Shift in Culture

Change in schools must be a combination of top-down and bottom-up, with all stakeholders engaged and bought into the journey. School leaders need to ensure that oracy is valued by forming a vision for their school that is connected to the school's priorities. Once a vision has been co-created with staff and families, leaders must start to review their existing policies and practices to identify where oracy exists and where it is urgently needed. This can range from review of Teaching and Learning policies through to examining the behaviour policies to ensure spoken language is explicitly incorporated. Cultural change takes time, patience and consistency – policies and procedures are a good starting place to kickstart change.

Change in schools is most effective when the staff at the *'coalface'* – teaching daily in class – are leading the way. Ensuring teachers are championing the change is fundamental; they need to be ready, willing and able to bring oracy to life through their teaching practice. To make this happen, teachers need quality continuous professional development (CPD) over a sustained period of time to equip themselves with the necessary skills and knowledge around oracy. Implementation can fall short when the teaching community is underskilled and undersupported.

A Roadmap for Change

This book examines the influence and impact of oracy from birth through to adulthood. Each stage of childhood development and education is explored, contrasting the trajectories of children raised at different ends of the social ladder. Each chapter focuses on a specific stage of education, whether academic or *'whole child'*, and reviews the benefits strong oracy can have upon a child's progress versus the barriers facing children who lack the language skills of their peers. Whilst educators tend to specialise in a specific age phase, there are lessons to be learned for all teachers and school staff regardless of specialism.

The chapters blend academic research, government policies and leading practices to provide a holistic view of oracy and it's ability to boost upward mobility for our most disadvantaged children. There are numerous case studies and interviews with active practitioners, charity experts and leaders from the workplace, in which different perspectives are shared on the power of oracy to improve the life chances of all learners.

Even though this book leans heavily upon the pedagogical and theoretical end of educational literature, the audience of active teachers has been taken into consideration. Each chapter ends with:

- A set of reflection questions to challenge the reader as they think about their own settings.
- A practical project task linked to the chapter's core focus area, which can be conducted across any school/trust.

We hope you not only read this book but engage with it as a project that lives and breathes in your school.

References

Hart, B. and Risley, T.R. (1995) *Meaningful Differences in the Everyday Experience of Young American Children*. Baltimore: Paul H. Brookes Publishing.

Major, L.E. and Machin, S. (2018) *Social Mobility and its Enemies*. London: Pelican Books.

1 Demystifying Oracy

The Origins of Oracy: From Concept to Classroom

The Concept of Oracy Defined

To an outsider, the modern classroom is full of mysterious, confusing acronyms, jargon and teaching terminology. Many pedagogical concepts that cross the *'no man's land'* between the theoretical world of research into the classroom are just as perplexing for teachers too. New concepts such as retrieval practice, adaptive teaching and schemata have gradually become integrated into teaching lexicon. In a similar way, the concept of oracy has stepped into the educational spotlight and teachers are grappling with it's definition, scope and implementation.

However, oracy is by no means the *'New kid on the block'*. Rewind 60 years and the first use of the word *'oracy'* was coined by Andrew Wilkinson in his paper *'The Concept of Oracy'* (Wilkinson, 1965). Wilkinson stresses the need to place oracy on par with both reading and writing, defining it as: *'the ability to use the oral skills of speaking and listening'*.

Wilkinson highlighted the need for speaking and listening to form a more explicit component of teaching practice. Whilst he acknowledged that Government guidance called for *'speech training'* in schools, the tangible strategies and direction for oracy were vague and lacking any real substance.

The Social Constructivist Influence

Although his studies predate that of Wilkinson's, Lev Vygotsky's works regarding oracy (albeit not by that specific name) played a crucial role in the initial definition of this concept.

Vygotsky emphasised the importance of both culture and language in a learner's cognitive development. He describes the process through which we experience the world and communicate in it via the dual frameworks of language and culture. Vygotsky (1978, p. 98) says, *'I do not see the world simply in color and shape but also as a world with sense and meaning. I do not merely see something round and black with two hands; I see a clock …'*

Vygotsky disagreed with the narrow perception of oracy held by peers such as Piaget. He argued that more focus was needed upon the social component of language. For a learner to move from *actual development* (what they had already achieved) towards *potential development* (the level at which learning takes place), they needed the opportunity to communicate and interact with others. In essence, learning does not take place in a vacuum – oracy and dialogue are the vehicles for the human mind to absorb, comprehend and connect new and existing learning.

> **Definitions**
>
> **Actual development:** the area where a learner has proven they can achieve something.
>
> **Potential development:** the area where a learner has not yet mastered something but can do so with support.
>
> **Schema**: the cognitive structures in which the known information is organised in the mind. This network of previously gained knowledge affects how new information is processed.

Vygotsky laid the groundwork for research into the effectiveness of social interaction in learning. This included the evolution of collaborative learning and dialogic teaching. As part of his legacy, Vygotsky developed a model known as *'Zone of Proximal Development'* (ZPD), where he conceptualises the space in which potential learning occurs (see Figure 1.1).

The zone of proximal development is the goldilocks space between a learner's comfort zone and what they find too challenging to grasp.

However, in the time since Vygotsky introduced his social constructivist theories, his model of ZPD has been criticised for being too generic. For example, why do some children still fail to learn even with significant adult support in place. Some argue that we should see it as an overarching model that incorporates more specific cognitive learning theories within its broad scope. With advances in science, researchers have a far greater understanding of cognitive development, neuroscience, genetics and other areas of the learning mind that were hidden from Vygotsky's perspective.

So what does this mean for the modern day teacher?

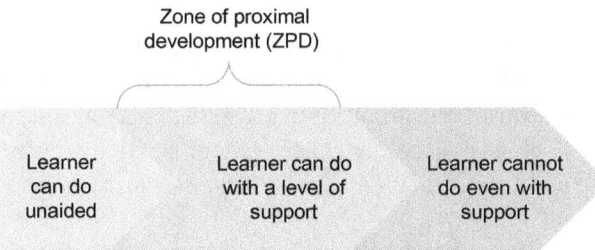

Figure 1.1 Zone of proximal development.

Most student teachers will have studied the learning theories of Vygotsky, Piaget and others along the path to becoming a fully fledged teaching professional. Whilst many of these earlier theories have been challenged or adapted as a result of evolving research, it is important to understand their core principles. Learning requires social interaction to fully engage the learner's mind and help them to fulfil their potential. Therefore, when considering ways to improve oracy, we must simultaneously evaluate how social interaction becomes embedded into the classroom too.

Bruner Builds on Vygotsky

With the foundations of oracy laid out by Vygotsky and Wilkinson, it was further developed by Jerome Bruner, an American Psychologist, whose research advanced cognitive learning theories. Just like Vygotksy, Bruner recognised the significance of socialisation within the learning process. Bruner's social interactionist theory of language development highlights the relationship between learners and the world around them. Through close interaction between a developing child and linguistically-mature adults, the scope for language development was far greater.

Bruner points out that all children are *'born with the innate ability to acquire language'* but social interaction is fundamental in enabling this acquisition to take place (Bruner, 1983). In his theory, he developed the model of *'Language Acquisition Support System'* (LASS) in which he outlines ways in which a child should be actively engaged in language. This included:

- Adapting language used to communicate with a younger child. This is often referred to as *Child-Directed Speech* (CDS) and involves immediate family adjusting their tone, expression, prosody and vocabulary when speaking directly to a child.
- Collaborative learning whereby adults introduce the child to new concepts and aspects of everyday life. A good example is shared reading, when the adult explains new terms or vocabulary to the child directly.
- Modelling examples through the use of phrases and stem sentences. This is an important method for demonstrating suitable language application in real world contexts. For example, prompting a child to say 'Good Morning' when they greet their grandparents at the door.
- Motivating and encouraging positive attempts at oracy to help reinforce language use. Praising then rephrasing the language will help to establish a safe environment for the child to interact within.

Bruner and Vygotsky's theories for language development both begin a long time before a child enters formal education. Their models examine oracy from birth, when the baby mind is a sponge for language acquisition, through into early childhood. As educators, even though our influence truly commences once the child sets foot inside the classroom, it is equally important to understand the foundations of language development and social interaction that comes beforehand.

Defining Oracy: An Evolution of Ideas

The Language of Learning

In the decades following the research of Piaget and Vygotsky, other academics have built further on the links between language and learning. As research evolved, the word *'oracy'* became a more familiar part of the educational vernacular. Frameworks for defining oracy became more formal and the focus shifted towards a broader view. One such academic who started to expand the definition was James Britton.

Britton, an influential educational theorist, emphasised the crucial role of language in cognitive development and learning. His work illustrates the point that oracy is not simply a means of communication but is an essential ingredient of cognitive development. In his book 'Language and Learning' (Britton, 1970), Britton outlines the various ways in which language and learning are intertwined together. These points include:

- **Language as a tool for learning:** Britton states that learning needs language so pupils can make sense of their experiences and organise their thoughts. Language helps to bridge personal experience with academic knowledge.
- **Language as part of cognitive development:** His work links the application of oracy with the mind's natural cognitive growth. Whether through talking, questioning, testing ideas or reflecting on learning, Britton believed that all these oral activities promote deeper thinking and cognitive growth.
- **Exploratory talk:** Britton highlights the importance of what he called *'exploratory talk'*, in which learners are given the freedom to experiment with their ideas and understanding. For this to work, he stresses the need to remove the pressure of *'correctness'*.
- **Three functions of language for learning:** Britton distinguishes between three forms of language that play differing roles in the learning process. They are:
    - Expressive language – the ability to express needs and wants
    - Transactional language – for clear purposeful communication
    - Poetic language – encourages creative expression

Definitions

Exploratory Talk: a dialogue style marked by open-ended questions, active listening and openness to new ideas and perspectives.

Dialogic Teaching: an interactive approach where teachers and students engage in structured dialogue to deepen understanding, encourage critical thinking and promote active learning.

Dialogic Teaching – Learning to Talk and Learning through Talk

Whilst Britton defines the various functions of language for learning, academics such as Robin Alexander have been pivotal in advancing the role of talk in learning. Since the early 2000s, Alexander has developed the concept of *'dialogic teaching'* (Alexander, 2008). By Alexander's definition, dialogic teaching harnesses the power of effective talk in class, enabling learning to become more interactive.

To understand how dialogic teaching fits within oracy, it can be helpful for us to view oracy as being formed of two main parts:

- **Learning to talk (Oracy Education)** – Instructing students on the physical, linguistic, cognitive, social and emotional aspects of spoken language and communication.
- **Learning through talk (Dialogic Teaching)** – Using talk in the classroom to deepen understanding through dialogue with teachers and peers (Figure 1.2).

Many schools will spend a significant amount of time and effort focused upon *'learning how to talk'*. This can be seen in the drive for improving phonics teaching and outcomes, enhancing communication and language within early years or supporting children with SEND needs. At a national level as well as at a school level, systems and structures have been built over recent years to improve the literacy levels of our youngest learners. Frameworks for assessing progress in these areas (such as the phonics screening check and Early Years 'Good Level of Development') have evolved to help benchmark language outcomes across the UK.

Has the other circle of the Venn diagram received as much attention? And if not, why not?

The focus on *'learning through talk'* is harder to see within the majority of our schools at present. This is possibly due to several reasons, including:

- The theoretical nature of dialogic teaching requires a greater depth of understanding and expertise by all staff.

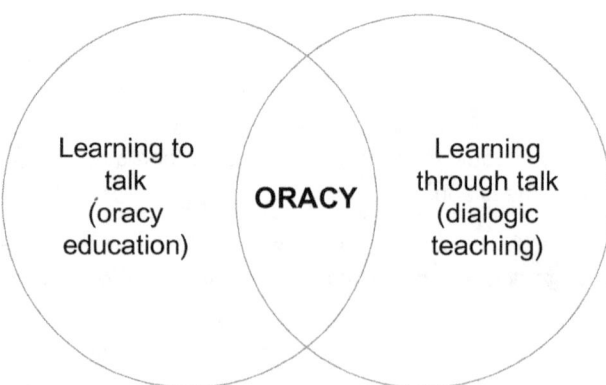

Figure 1.2 Oracy as learning to and through talk.

- A less quantifiable and measurable output in lessons, i.e. it is easier to screen a phonics assessment with a raw score than it is to measure the quality of talk taking place across a timetable.
- Oracy needs to be integrated across all aspects of the curriculum and school ethos to learning. This requires a long term, cultural shift with staff buy-in to the aims and purpose of embedding talk into the ways we teach and learn.
- Opening up lessons to learner-led talk can cause anxiety amongst teaching staff, especially those new to the profession.

Challenging the Venn: Two Sides to the Coin

This Venn diagram places oracy in the overlapping intersection between *'learning to talk'* and *'learning through talk'*. This model has been challenged by Professor Neil Mercer, who argues that oracy should not be confined to the shared space. He claims that, if both aspects of learning to and through talk are considered part of oracy, then both circles sit fully under the oracy umbrella.

So, if the Venn is not quite right, what can replace it as a conceptual model for oracy?

Mercer reframes the two areas as two sides of the same coin (Mercer, 2000). This alternative model emphasises the overarching nature of oracy, showing just how far reaching it spans across the learning spectrum. Mercer is also keen to highlight that there is an over-emphasis on *'talk'* in these definitions of oracy. Many educators will see *'talk'* as covering both speaking and listening, but it is easy to find an imbalance in focus towards the speaking element. However, as we will later explore, oracy has multiple facets beyond merely the ability to speak; listening being an essential skill for the mastery of oracy. A great speaker does not necessarily equate to a great listener.

A Broader Scope beyond the Academics

Oracy's impact upon learning development has been well-documented by the likes of Vygotsky, Bruner, Mercer and others. As research into educational psychology, behavioural development and childhood growth have evolved, more attention has been placed on the role oracy plays. Key studies in psychology and education have demonstrated how oracy fosters self-regulation, emotional intelligence and social competence.

Anyone who has been a teacher knows that their responsibilities are by no means restricted to teaching in lessons. Teachers wear many hats, from counsellor to nurse, career advisor to family support worker. It is for this reason that understanding of the non-academic benefits of stronger oracy is even more important.

Emotional Development and Oracy

The ability to talk gives someone the capacity to express their emotions to others. The correlation between a child's oracy and their emotional regulation can be clear to see in many classroom situations. How many times have children been told to *'use words not actions'* to express a whole range of emotions, whether it is anger, frustration, anxiety or confusion?

Catherine Snow is well recognised for her research into early language development, especially within social settings such as the home environment. Her studies identified the impact that healthy conversations between parents and children had upon the child's emotional resilience and empathy. She found that children who were encouraged to express their thoughts and feelings within a safe environment were able to regulate their emotional state better (Snow, 1993). It is helpful to imagine oracy as a tool that we want our children to possess so they are better equipped to better navigate challenging situations.

Further studies by Hart and Risley reinforce Snow's findings that better oracy impacts emotional well-being in a positive way. Even though their study primarily centred on vocabulary, they were able to connect early language exposure to emotional security (Hart and Risley, 1995). They found that children growing up in positive, language-rich homes possessed better emotional well-being when compared against peers from language-poor home lives.

Behavioural Influences

Vygotsky (1987) put forward the idea of *'inner speech'* as an internal mechanism with which we can reason, moderate and regulate our behaviours. He stresses that this internal dialogue is not innately possessed but matures over time and is influenced by the world around us. Vygotsky claims that inner speech is not consistent between individuals but can vary substantially. This difference can derive from a person's upbringing, cultural background, social settings and other surrounding factors.

He believed our earliest language experiences are fundamental in forming our inner dialogue and can help us in:

- **Self-regulation**: managing emotions, inhibiting impulsive actions and enabling concentration and willpower
- **Forward planning**: thinking ahead to prepare for change or new challenges
- **Problem solving**: considering next steps and potential consequences
- **Empathy towards others**: identifying feelings of others and comprehending the thoughts, actions and interactions of people around them

What Vygotsky makes clear is that oracy is not restricted to the spoken words that we produce and hear from others. Oracy is also that internalised speech that we use to rationalise, justify, make sense of and contemplate everyday situations we encounter. Now consider how limited inner speech could impact a child's presented behaviour. Without this internal oracy in place, the capacity to self-regulate exhibited behaviours can become far more difficult for these individuals. Later on in the book, we will explore the impact of limited oracy upon the behaviours for learning (as well as general social behaviours) seen in classrooms and homes today.

Conversations and Contexts

Another perspective of the impact oracy can have upon an individual child's behaviour comes from Deborah Tannen. A well renowned sociolinguist, Tannen studied the conversational styles and interpersonal dynamics of language amongst young children. Her research shows how individuals can interpret language differently as a result of their cultural, social and personal differences (Tannen, 2005). For children without sufficient awareness and exposure to the conversation styles of others, it can lead to social misinterpretations. Inadvertently, these mismatches can create tension and uneasiness between individuals.

Whilst this may sound theoretical, it is easy enough to connect this with the reality of school life. Reflect back on those playground incidents between pupils. How many of them were a result of misunderstanding or misreading of messages between those involved? Consider how often teachers try to resolve these situations with the advice to *'use your words'*. Naturally, teachers are trying to model the socially acceptable norms for managing conflict, with oracy acting as the vehicle for resolving differences.

Redefining Oracy for the Modern Classroom

The Rise of Oracy Champions

With recent shifts in the educational landscape, there has arisen several organisations (whether governmental or charity sector) that are focused on the development of oracy in education. These bodies have evolved and grown into nationwide beings that have started to:

- Refine the concept and definition of oracy to fit the modern education system
- Construct frameworks in which oracy can be measured against
- Invest in research (including pilots and school-based trials) to better understand the science behind oracy
- Develop toolkits and strategies for effective oral interventions
- Lobby Government for funding and support with oracy initiatives

As research continues to reinforce the impact that oracy can have upon both academic and holistic child development, these organisations have grown in recognition and status.

See Table 1.1 for some of the most established oracy-related bodies in the UK (as of 2025):

A Framework for Oracy

As the leading body for oracy in the UK, Voice 21 and Oracy Cambridge are responsible for the creation of an *'Oracy Framework'*. The purpose of this framework is to lay out what 'good looks like' for all aspects of oracy. They divide oracy into four key strands of development that are separate yet interconnected.

The four strands are:

- **Physical:** use of the voice and body language for communication
- **Linguistic:** use of vocabulary, style of language and nuanced expressions
- **Cognitive:** the ability to understand and respond to language effectively
- **Social and Emotional:** the capacity to socially interact with others (Figure 1.3)

Throughout this book, the framework will be used as a means of defining the scope of oracy and also assessing different aspects of childhood development against the strands. By broadening the definition of oracy to go beyond merely *'speaking and listening'*, the

14 Voices of Opportunity

Table 1.1 Oracy-based organisations in the UK

Organisation	Oracy focus
Voice 21	Voice 21 are dedicated to integrating oracy into every UK school's curriculum, with a focus upon teacher training and school-wide support. Voice 21 are known for their 'Oracy Framework' (introduced later in this chapter)
The Education Endowment Foundation (EEF)	The EEF conducts and funds research to evaluate the effectiveness of educational interventions, including oracy programmes. Its focus is on creating evidence-based recommendations to improve oracy outcomes, especially for disadvantaged pupils
Oracy Cambridge	Oracy Cambridge, co-founded by Professor Neil Mercer, focuses on research-driven approaches to oracy. It aims to build evidence-based practices for effective oracy teaching, with an emphasis on dialogic teaching and enhancing students' reasoning and critical thinking skills
National Literacy Trust	Known primarily for promoting literacy, the National Literacy Trust also champions oracy by highlighting its role in improving language, communication skills and overall literacy. It supports initiatives to reduce the language gap among disadvantaged pupils through speaking and listening initiatives
The Communication Trust	Focused on supporting children with speech, language, and communication needs, the Communication Trust promotes oracy as a vital part of development. It works to provide resources and advocacy for improved speech and language support in education

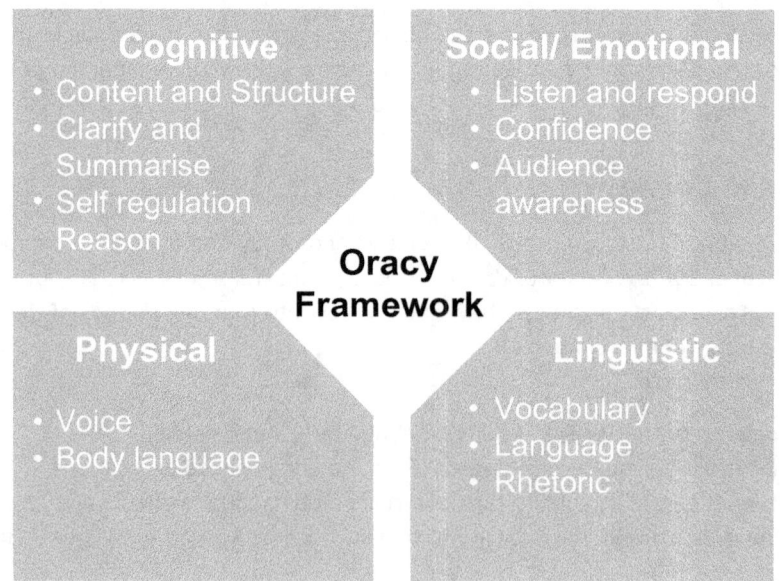

Figure 1.3 The oracy framework (Voice 21 and Oracy Cambridge).

framework helps to open up the discussion around how far reaching the impact of strong (and weak) oracy can have upon a child.

Chapter Summary

- Oracy has evolved over the last 60 years, shifting beyond its initial definition of speaking and listening towards a broader scope of language development.
- Social interaction is a central aspect and enabler of oracy, supporting cognitive growth within the *'Zone of Proximal Development'*.
- Research has expanded the range of conceptual models for oracy, such as dialogic teaching, exploratory talk and inner speech.
- Beyond academic benefits, improving oracy levels has been proven to positively impact a child's socioemotional development.
- The oracy framework defines four strands: physical, linguistic, cognitive and social-emotional; this has helped to establish a consistent structure for educators and academics to use for benchmarking oracy.

Reflection Questions

- How knowledgeable are you (and your staff) on the pedagogy and origins of oracy?
- Can you/they provide a definition of what oracy is and why it is important for learning?
- To what extent is oracy considered during your planning process? Is it an explicit expectation for all lessons to incorporate oral strategies?

Time to Take Action

Using Voice 21's Oracy Framework, conduct a brief analysis of your current class/school approach to oracy. Considering the four strands, identify areas of strength as well as development (Table 1.2).

Table 1.2 Audit of the four strands of oracy

Strand	Strengths	Development areas
Physical		
Linguistic		
Cognitive		
Socio-emotional		

References

Alexander, R. (2008) *Towards Dialogic Teaching: Rethinking Classroom Talk*. 4th ed. York: Dialogos.
Britton, J. (1970) *Language and Learning*. Miami: University of Miami Press.
Bruner, J. (1983) *Child's Talk: Learning to Use Language*. Oxford: Oxford University Press.
Hart, B. and Risley, T.R. (1995) *Meaningful Differences in the Everyday Experience of Young American Children*. Baltimore: Paul H. Brookes Publishing.
Mercer, N. (2000) *Words and Minds: How We Use Language to Think Together*. London: Routledge.
Snow, C.E. (1993) *Linguistics and Education: Goals, Approaches, and Outcomes*. New York: Oxford University Press.
Tannen, D. (2005) *Conversational Style: Analyzing Talk Among Friends*. Oxford: Oxford University Press.
Voice 21 (2025) *The Oracy Framework*. Available at: https://voice21.org/wp-content/uploads/2022/09/The-Oracy-Framework-2021-1-1.pdf (Accessed: 4 June 2025)
Vygotsky, L.S. (1978) *Mind in Society: The Development of Higher Psychological Processes*. Cambridge, MA: Harvard University Press.
Wilkinson, A. (1965) 'The Concept of Oracy', *English in Education*, 51(3), pp. 3-5.

2 Defining Social Mobility

Making Sense of Social Mobility

A Traditional Perspective

In this book, we'll explore how oracy links to social mobility. To understand this connection, it's essential to first define what we mean by *'social mobility'*. This term has evolved from a traditional idea to a more complex concept, with evolving measures and interpretations.

The Social Mobility Commission, in its recent *'State of the Nation'* report, provides an updated definition of social mobility for the UK Parliament, describing it as when someone experiences *'different life outcomes than their parents'* (Social Mobility Commission, 2024). These outcomes may include changes in:

- Income levels
- Occupational class
- Educational qualifications
- Housing situations

The simplest example of mobility is when someone is working in a professional occupation yet their own parents worked in manual labour. Or if someone is earning a considerably higher income compared to their parents at the same age. While we often think of social mobility as moving upward, it's important to recognise that mobility can also go downward. Although, as we will later discover, downward mobility is a far rarer occurrence.

A Legacy of Social Classes

For social mobility to exist, there needs to be a structure of social classes for individuals to move between. In the United Kingdom, the hierarchy of social classification originates from centuries ago. Even as far back as the Middle Ages, citizens were categorised by their occupations, economic status and education.

Traditionally, the United Kingdom had three levels of social class:

- **Upper class**: consisting of the aristocracy, landed gentry and nobility. These families had vast wealth and strong influence over the political and economic spheres of power. Through intergenerational wealth and power transfer, these families have maintained

their positioning at the top echelons of society. The most obvious of these families would be the British Royal Family.
- **Middle class**: Over centuries, this class has expanded in size and has even been divided further into upper-middle, middle and lower-middle classes. Still seen as financially well off, this covers a wide range of occupations from doctors to lawyers, architects to bankers. Maintaining a balance between educational progress and financial freedom is important for keeping on the middle rungs of this social ladder.
- **Lower class**: Whilst certain blue collar occupations, such as manual workers and drivers, have migrated into the lower-middle class, the lower classes are those who are merely surviving. Living paycheck to paycheck, these individuals and families have minimal financial security and are often unemployed and requiring government assistance.

However, with societal change has come a shifting perspective of how we categorise our social class system. As the economy has evolved, Britain is no longer simply separated into a three-tier social hierarchy. The definition of social class has become far more complex and the criteria for identifying your own social classification have become less well defined.

Evolving Definitions

The Great British Class Survey (GCBS) was a nationwide survey that gathered insights and data from over 325,000 adults across the country (Savage et al., 2013). The aim of the survey was to develop a new model for social class that mirrored the realities of 21st Century Britain. The survey defined seven new classes based upon economic, cultural and social capital.

Definitions

Highbrow cultural capital = This type of cultural capital is associated with upper-class individuals and traditional cultural domains such as art galleries and museums.

Emerging cultural capital = This type of cultural capital is associated with younger people and their social interests, such as social media, clubs and sports.

Economic capital = Associated with income and assets owned

Social capital = Associated with the quantity and social status of an individual's family, friends and known contacts

---

This table outlines the seven classes and how they measured for the three forms of capital.

Traditionally, social mobility has been viewed as improving one's life outcomes in financial and economic terms. Being the first in a family to attend university, enter a professional career path or land a high-paying job were classic milestones of social mobility success. Sonia Blandford (2019), however, suggests a rethink is needed in defining what *'good'* social mobility looks like. She argues that common benchmarks – like attending a prestigious university – are too narrow to fully judge how mobile an individual truly is.

Blandford goes on to claim how social mobility should not be seen as migrating to another class but about enhancing life chances for all and promoting equality of opportunity within each class. This view contrasts with the traditional concept of social mobility as a ladder that everyone aims to climb. Suggesting that only upward movement improves life outcomes can inadvertently imply that the quality of life is inherently limited for those lower on the ladder.

A broader definition of social mobility is needed – one that stresses expanding opportunities within all social classes and across geographic areas. Success in social mobility should not be measured only by economic and financial markers, but by the quality of life options available to all communities.

The Ladder Is Not Linear!

The image of a ladder, representing various levels within the social hierarchy, can be a useful way to illustrate the challenges of social mobility. With a widening gap between society's 'haves' and 'have-nots,' the rungs of this ladder are growing increasingly distant, making upward progress substantially harder for individuals.

However, this traditional metaphor of a linear, up-and-down ladder has been contested by academics who argue that mobility is not merely a one-dimensional climb. Gideon Calder (2016), for example, challenges the idea of a single measure of social positioning. He advocates for a multidimensional view of social mobility, considering economic, cultural, and social capital (see Table 2.1). Calder states that an individual may experience upward mobility through a highly paid profession (economic capital) while remaining lower in terms of social and cultural capital. For instance, their job might align with a higher social class than that of their parents but they lack the associated social or cultural advantages.

Table 2.1 The seven social classes according to the Great British Social Class Survey

Class	Economic	Social	Cultural
Elite	Very high	High	Very high highbrow
Established middle class	High	High mean of social contacts	High highbrow and emerging
Technical middle class	High	Very high mean of social contact	Moderate
New affluent workers	Moderately good	Moderately poor mean	Moderate highbrow but good emerging
Traditional working class	Moderately poor (though with reasonable house price)	Few social contacts	Low highbrow and emerging
Emergent service workers	Moderately poor (though with reasonable household income)	Moderate social contacts	High emerging but low highbrow
Precariat	Poor	Lowest	Lowest

Source: Savage et al. (2013).

The 'Stickiness' of the Ladder

Since the Great British Class Survey redefined the UK class system into seven distinct classes, academics have increasingly based their research on this newer model. Using the ladder metaphor, Major and Machin (2018) describe the uppermost and lowermost rungs as being particularly *'sticky.'* Their studies indicate that mobility tends to occur mostly within the middle rungs, largely due to the social and economic capital gained from attending university.

However, movement at the top and bottom ends of the spectrum has remained limited. Those on the lowest rungs face significant barriers to upward mobility, while the elite at the top are well-insulated from moving downward. Despite all good intentions and efforts to progress, many remain stuck to the lower end due to external factors out of their control.

As educators, we encounter children from families positioned at different points on this mobility ladder. Our role isn't to move them up the ladder directly but to equip them with the knowledge, skills and capital – both social and human – to make the most of opportunities as they arise.

Absolute versus Relative Mobility

Defining mobility is not as simple as visualising a ladder upon which everyone is climbing, falling or stuck. Mobility can be categorised as being either absolute or relative. Whilst both forms of mobility see individuals advancing beyond the lifestyles of their parents, they are not equal in relation to social justice and fairness.

> **Definitions**
>
> **Absolute mobility:** When everyone improves their position compared to previous generations, but their relative social rankings remain the same.
>
> **Relative mobility:** When individuals' positions shift relative to one another, often reducing social and economic gaps by allowing those from lower positions to catch up to higher ones.

In the Social Mobility Commission's 2022 *'State of the Nation'* (2022), they use the analogy of an escalator to demonstrate the difference between absolute and relative mobility. If everyone is in a queue for just one escalator, those at the front will advance upwards sooner than those lower down the order. The positioning will stay consistent with no opportunity for those at the back to move up the line. Whilst everyone will eventually move upwards from their starting position, the gaps between social classes will never close due to limited opportunity. This is **absolute** mobility (Figure 2.1).

However, if more escalators become operational, there will be more chances for individuals to break free from the linear queue and accelerate, even take over, those in front of them. This is **relative** mobility.

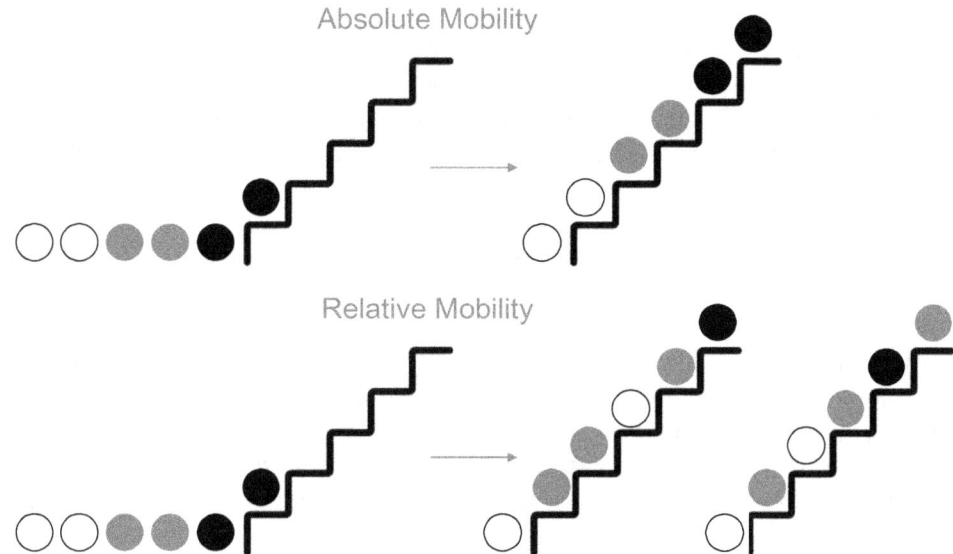

Figure 2.1 The escalator analogy.

Another analogy is to imagine a marathon where all runners are trying to reach a finish line that keeps moving further out. *Absolute mobility* is when all the runners are picking up speed and getting faster over time; everyone makes progress, but they maintain their relative positions, with the fastest runners still leading and the slower ones keeping behind.

Relative mobility, however, would be if the slower runners received an extra boost, allowing them to move closer to the front runners, while the fastest ones maintained their pace. In this case, not only are all runners moving forward, but the slower ones are closing the distance with those ahead, ultimately reducing the gap between the leading and trailing groups.

Absolute mobility tends to be measured by the percentage of people whose income is higher than their parents at the same age. However, relative mobility is measuring the chances various groups have of reaching a particular outcome. It is possible for absolute mobility to increase between generations, especially with a changing educational system where more young people are entering university and then heading into higher occupational positions compared to the prior generation. Yet *'if people from advantaged backgrounds are still more likely to get the top positions than those from lower socio-economic backgrounds, relative mobility would stay static'* (Social Mobility Commission, 2022).

Benchmarking the UK versus Rest of the World

The Poor Relative: Understanding Why the UK Is Lagging Behind

Social mobility is not isolated to the British Isles. It is a worldwide issue that many Governments, charities and schools are tackling as the disparity between the wealthiest and most vulnerable grows wider and wider.

So, is the UK alone in it's social challenges?

Whilst many other developed nations experience similar challenges regarding social mobility, recent reports have ranked the UK poorly compared to other nations. In 2005, a report from London School of Economics (LSE) showed the UK as being significantly lower than other developed countries for social mobility. In this report, Blanden et al. (2005, p. 19) found that the UK's social mobility was on par with the United States but fell substantially below that of Canada, Australia and our Scandinavian neighbours. They focused on the connection between family income and educational attainment, stating: *'The strong relationship between family income and educational attainment is at the heart of Britain's low mobility culture'*

Through analysing mobility between the rungs of the ladder, they noted that only 9.6% of those growing up in the bottom quintile (lowest 20%) of family income were able to move into the top quintile by adulthood. To explain this simply, less than one in ten people from the bottom 20% of household incomes make the move up into the top 20%. Compare this to 13.5% in Canada, for example, and it is clear to see that the UK has a more ingrained mobility problem to address.

The World Economic Forum (WEF) released their *'Global Social Mobility Index'* (2020) in which they assessed 82 global economies across different continents. In relation to the UK's performance they found:

- The UK lagged behind regional peers for overall education quality and equity because of high pupil-to-teacher ratios (especially in pre-primary education where the ratio is among the highest in the OECD)
- Significant disparities in educational quality between schools
- Fair wages were ranked very low in relation to European counterparts

All of these studies indicate a widening chasm between the social classes of the UK population. Income inequality and educational disparities are ranked worse than other similarly developed nations and the gap continues to widen.

Public Perception of Social Mobility: A UK-Wide View

Academic reports have measured the quantifiable impact of social immobility. However, for the person in the street, they feel the impact in a far more tangible way. Whether it is the squeeze on their finances, the sense of social inequality or the perceived lack of opportunity, the person on the street is seeing, feeling and experiencing the challenges of social mobility everyday.

The Sutton Trust (Latham, 2024) surveyed the British public and found:

- 83% believed there is a large class gap in the UK today (63% said the divide is greater than 50 years ago)
- A significant majority said children from wealthier families had better opportunities in schools (62%), universities (62%), pre-school education (59%) and jobs (54%)

- 50% of younger adults (18 to 24 years old) believe it is harder to move from working to middle class today
- 81% thought it was the government's role to ensure fair access to all educational opportunities and 69% for job opportunities.

In summarising their findings, they state that: *'In terms of absolute social mobility, a former golden age of upward mobility had been replaced by a modern era of declining opportunities and more limited upward mobility'* (Latham, 2024, p. 2).

Not only is it important for all stakeholders (whether Government, business, schools or the general public) to acknowledge the *'stickiness'* of the UK's social mobility, it is just as crucial to understand the factors driving this gap.

Recent Drivers in the UK

Understanding why the UK's social divide has grown further apart is complex and multifaceted. A cocktail of global, national and regional events have influenced the trajectory of the country's socio-economic progress. Each factor could fill up a full chapter of analysis by itself, although here we will outline the high-level drivers for social 'stickiness'.

They include:

Economic Troubles

The lasting impact of economic recession and austerity since 2008, in which the gap between rich and poor grew wider. During the start of Government-driven austerity, Prime Minister David Cameron claimed that, *'We're all in the same boat'* when referring to the need for shared responsibility for weathering the economic storm. This political optimism contrasts with the quote that *we are not in the same boat, but we are in the same storm.*

Austerity hit the poorest in society the most, with higher unemployment, a crackdown on social spending and the removal of support facilities for the most vulnerable. Of course the UK was not solely to blame for the global recession but the Government's approach to reduce spending certainly impacted our disadvantaged communities the most. The Social Mobility Commission (2024) noted how the percentage of children living in relative poverty in the UK has risen since 2012 and is at about 30%. Alongside austerity, the fallout from Brexit has further shackled the economic growth in the UK.

Post-Pandemic Fallout

The impact of Covid lockdowns and restrictions are still being felt across the nation in 2025 and will continue to adversely affect those stuck at the lower end of the social ladder for years to come. Financially, many lower paid workers experienced reduced hours and job losses during the numerous lockdowns. They were also in customer-facing roles where they were heavily exposed to covid transmission resulting in higher numbers affected more seriously by the infection.

In educational terms, children from disadvantaged backgrounds suffered a loss of learning due to the *'digital divide'*. Less reliable internet access, fewer devices to share (if any) and less adult support at home widened the learning gap relative to their middle class peers.

Regional Variations

In 2017, the then Secretary for Education, Justine Greening claimed at a Sutton Trust Summit that Britain had *'cold spots'* where disparities were far easier to spot. The UK economy has historically been very *'London-centric'*, and this remains the case today. Despite the numerous Government attempts at 'levelling up' and bridging the North-South divide, there is clearly a measurable difference between London and the South East versus other areas of the nation.

This variation is compounded by a range of factors. From international investment focusing heavily upon London to a lack of infrastructure and Government spending outside the capital, this regional disparity appears to be spreading, not shrinking. Opportunities for younger generations, in terms of jobs, apprenticeships and Higher Education are found in the South Easternmost region of the UK. Graduates looking to move up the social ladder into the higher paid professional jobs have far more opportunities in the capital's job market, even with attempts to grow the business sectors of the *'Northern Powerhouses'*.

A Nationwide Approach

Recognising the Impact on Child Development

In 2016, Theresa May gave her *'Great Meritocracy'* speech in which she proclaimed that, *'talent and hard work'* matter. Whilst few would argue against this statement, Blandford (2019) states that this perspective ignores the various barriers facing children from disadvantaged upbringings. Blandford describes how, despite talent and ability, many children and young adults are falling at the first hurdle due to factors out of their control such as prejudice, social capital, limited networks and financial restrictions.

Acknowledging how social mobility directly affects a child's development, and therefore future prospects, is vital to tackle the problem at hand. In June 2010, David Cameron commissioned Frank Field MP to carry out an independent review on the impact that poverty had upon children's life chances. Field's in depth report shows that life chances fall into three distinct categories: child, parent and environmental. He refers to these as *'life chance indicators'* through which we can measure annual progress on a range of factors that influence every child's future outcomes (Table 2.2).

From his summary, Field (2010, p. 5) identifies these key indicators as being heavily influential upon a child's prospects, stating: *'We have found overwhelming evidence that children's life chances are most heavily predicated on their development in the first five years of life.'*

Further into this book, we will examine the importance of the initial stages of upbringing from birth up to starting school; Field's indicators will be a helpful set of measures in this analysis.

Field goes on to highlight how, *'later interventions to help poorly performing children can be effective but, in general, the most effective and cost-effective way to help and support*

Table 2.2 Life chance indicators

Child factors (at around age three)	Parent factors	Environmental factors
Cognitive development (inc. language and communication)	Home learning environment	Quality of nursery care
	Positive parenting	
Behavioural and social emotional development	Maternal mental health	
Physical development	Mother's age at birth of first child	
	Mother's educational qualifications	

Source: Field (2010).

young families is in the earliest years of a child's life.' For the families struggling at the lower end of the social class system, many of these life indicators are not being met for a whole range of economic, financial and social reasons.

Other studies reinforce Field's acknowledgement of the significant impact of social mobility upon a child's future outcomes. These reports maintain that:

- The greatest point of leverage is 0 to 3 years old. A government report, *'Seven truths about social mobility 2012'*, identified emotional well-being, resilience and social skills as being critically developed in this window (Blandford, 2019).
- Class and income inequality are massive multipliers and accelerators of these impacts on child development (Calder, 2016).
- Socioeconomic status affected a child's trajectory and development more than measured ability. Leo Feinstein's PhD research found that an academically gifted child from a working class family would fail to keep pace with less academic middle class peers over the longer term (Major and Machin, 2018).

Any teacher who has worked in the UK state school system will be able to testify to the importance of strong foundations for children as they enter the school gates for the first time. However, the challenge to support the most disadvantaged pupils cannot be fixed solely by quality first teaching and targeted interventions. A child's development starts at Day One – therefore, support needs to extend earlier then what schools traditionally offer.

Government Initiatives in Recent Years

Over the last several Conservative and Labour governments, there has been a concerted effort to tackle the gap between rich and poor. Yet, with the austerity drive, the post-Brexit impact and global pressures, the impact of national efforts has been weak and inconsistent.

Since 2011, over £9 billion has been spent on pupil premium funding. Intended to empower schools to provide targeted support for the most disadvantaged pupils, pupil premium has seen some successful steps forwards with school-level support. However, as pointed out by the Social Mobility and Child Poverty Commission, the more recent efforts have been *'uncoordinated, confused and patchy'* (Calder, 2016).

Furthermore, the Social Mobility Commission recommends a 100% increase in pupil premium funding for early years. As Blandford (2019) outlines, £1 invested into improving early years education equates to the same impact as £7 spent on Key Stage 1 and beyond. Targeting funding to the earliest possible stages of childhood development has the greatest influence on a child's trajectory.

With the arrival of the new Labour Government in July 2024 came a manifesto of pledges including the commitment to *'building a country where background is no barrier to opportunity'*. Bridget Phillipson, the Secretary for Education, has set out ambitious plans to boost investment in early years and schools in order to address inequalities in the schools. At time of writing, this government is still in its infancy, so the impact of new initiatives remains to be realised.

As governments come and go, schools have remained at the coalface of society's biggest challenges. Even though successive governments have attempted to address the social imbalance, our educators have continued to positively impact the prospects of the children under our care. Schools will never be the full answer to the social mobility crisis but they can certainly do their part in raising attainment and progress of our most vulnerable learners.

Chapter Summary

- Social mobility encompasses more than upward climbing in class; it requires broadening opportunities across all classes and addressing systemic barriers like entrenched income inequality and the *'stickiness'* at the top and bottom of the social ladder.
- While absolute mobility ensures general progress for all, relative mobility reduces social and economic gaps, offering a fairer distribution of opportunities across generations.
- Economic austerity, regional disparities and the pandemic have deepened inequality, with disadvantaged groups disproportionately affected in education, health and career prospects.
- Research highlights the importance of early childhood development, particularly in the first 3 years, as the most effective way to improve life chances.
- While initiatives like pupil premium funding have aimed to address educational disparities, their impact has been inconsistent and underfunded.

Reflection Questions

- How can schools better collaborate with families and communities to address the early developmental challenges faced by disadvantaged children before they enter formal education?
- How effective is your pupil premium funding in supporting the intended pupils? What tangible outcomes can you identify that derive from this funding?

> **Time to Take Action**
>
> Conduct a social mobility analysis of your local catchment area. By researching and analysing the key demographics of your local community, you will have a greater understanding and empathy of your families and pupils. Without this knowledge, addressing the specific needs of your school community will be challenging and uninformed.
>
> - How does your school compare to National and regional benchmarks?
> - What other factors would you need to consider to understand social mobility for your families? (i.e. employment levels, local deprivation rating, levels of social housing)
> - From Table 2.3, what is the biggest barrier to your local school community?

Table 2.3 Social mobility audit (using DfE's schools, pupils and their characteristics, 2023/24)

Metric	National	School
Free school meal (FSM) Eligibility	**24.6%** North East: 31.2% West Midlands: 28.9% North West: 27.7% Yorkshire & Humber: 26.% London: 26.6% East Midlands: 24.1% South West: 20.5% East of England: 20.1% South East: 19.7%	
Minority ethnic background	**37.0%** Primary: 37.4% Secondary: 35.4% Special needs: 31.7% Alternative provision: 25.4%	
English as additional language (EAL)	**20.8%**	
Young carers	**0.6%** Primary: 0.5% Secondary: 0.9%	
Class size	Infant (Rec & KS1): 26.6 Primary: 26.6 Secondary: 22.4	

References

Blanden, J., Gregg, P. and Machin, S. (2005) *Social Mobility in Britain: Low and Falling*. London: Centre for Economic Performance: London School of Economics.

Blandford, S. (2019) *Born to Fail? Social Mobility: A Working Class View*. John Catt Educational.

Calder, G. (2016) *How Inequality Runs in Families*. Bristol: Policy Press.
Field, F. (2010) *The Foundation Years: Preventing Poor Children Becoming Poor Adults*. Poverty and Social Exclusion (PSE). Available at: www.poverty.ac.uk/report-poverty-measurement-life-chances-children-parenting-uk-government-policy/field-review (Accessed: 29 May 2025).
Latham, K. (2024) *Social Mobility and Opportunity: What the Public Thinks*. London: The Sutton Trust.
Major, L.E. and Machin, S. (2018) *Social Mobility and its Enemies*. London: Pelican Books.
Savage, M., Devine, F., Cunningham, N., Taylor, M., Li, Y., Hjellbrekke, J., Le Roux, B., Friedman, S. and Miles, A. (2013) 'A New Model of Social Class? Findings from the BBC's Great British Class Survey Experiment', *Sociology*, 47(2).
Social Mobility Commission (2022) *State of the Nation 2022*. Available at: https://assets.publishing.service.gov.uk/media/62b2e45b8fa8f5357a677f29/State_of_the_Nation_2022_A_fresh_approach_to_social_mobility.pdf (Accessed: 29 May 2025).
Social Mobility Commission (2024) *State of the Nation 2024: Local to National, Mapping Opportunities for All*. Available at: https://assets.publishing.service.gov.uk/media/66f68e33e84ae1fd8592ea6b/SOTN-2024.pdf (Accessed: 29 May 2025).

3 From Birth to Age 3

The Most Crucial Years

Why the Baby Stage Matters

It's easy to assume that language development in babies occurs naturally as they grow. Historically, this belief was reinforced by the idea that language acquisition was purely genetic – well-spoken parents produced well-spoken offspring. However, this oversimplified view overlooks the vital role of social and environmental influences in shaping a child's early linguistic abilities.

Norman (1992) debunked the genetic myth, demonstrating that language acquisition from birth to age five relies heavily on specific conditions, including:

- **Social interaction**: just as Bruner identified, language is developed through social exchanges and meaningful interactions with others
- **Active participation**: adults play a role in a child's language development from birth, helping to shape, scaffold and stretch their linguistic abilities
- **Contextual learning**: children need to connect words to tangible, concrete examples around them for them to possess meaning
- **The pleasure principle:** joy in language use helps to nurture engagement and learning
- **A sense of cultural belonging**: identity and belonging are formed through shared communication with those in their immediate circle of influence

The World Health Organisation (WHO) identifies infancy and early childhood as unique windows of development, during which the brain is highly receptive to linguistic and social input. While a baby's communication may seem limited, they are actually absorbing language and social cues like '*sponges*'. This makes the quality of language and interaction around them from day one vitally important.

Greenwood et al. (2020) emphasise that adult–child interactions during these critical years profoundly shape a child's future life outcomes, determining whether their journey into adolescence and adulthood is one of opportunity or limitation.

The urgency of early intervention is starkly illustrated by Blandford's (2019) findings on the early impacts of oracy across socioeconomic groups. By 3 years old, a developmental gap of 23% already separates the richest and poorest children in the UK. By five, this gap has widened to 27%. These disparities mean that before children even enter school, those from disadvantaged backgrounds are already significantly behind their peers.

As we'll explore throughout this chapter, embedding oracy into home life from birth is essential for cognitive, social and linguistic development. Like dominoes, early language acquisition sets off a chain reaction that influences academic success, social-emotional well-being and life opportunities. Yet, certain barriers facing the least socially secure families can hinder their children's progress and outcomes. Addressing these challenges is not just a matter of equity, it is a foundation for future success.

Building Blocks of Oracy

If we were to reverse-engineer, the journey of a successful young adult back to their earliest years, we could uncover the *'domino effect'* of learning – where each developmental stage builds on the previous one. This sequential process highlights how the foundational skills of oracy pave the way for academic achievement and lifelong success.

For a young adult to flourish in a successful occupation, they would have needed (in reverse order):

- **Professional Communication Skills**: Confidence in building rapport with interviewers, using persuasive language, positive body language and active listening to take advantage of opportunities.
- **Academic Competence**: The ability to apply literacy skills to reason, articulate and respond effectively in higher education or training programs.
- **Engagement with Learning**: A secure foundation in secondary school that enables comprehension, critical thinking and connections between new and prior knowledge (schema).
- **Fluent Reading and Writing**: The ability to expand vocabulary and articulate thoughts effectively during Key Stage Two.
- **Comprehension Confidence**: Proficiency in interpreting meaning and making inferences with little effort.
- **Fluent Reading Ability**: By Key Stage One, the capability to read unfamiliar texts fluently and create meaning through a well-developed vocabulary schema.
- **Oral Expression**: Early Years development of clear speech, the ability to share thoughts and express emotions effectively.
- **Active Listening Skills**: From infancy, learning to interpret tone, prosody and expression in social interactions.

The Predictive Power of Oracy

Research consistently highlights the predictive qualities of early oral language skills for future academic success. For example:

- **Oral Language at Age Three**: Strong oral language skills at age 3 predict reading ability at age 5 and reading comprehension at age 8 (Alvarez, 2019).
- **Vocabulary at 30 Months**: The rate of vocabulary acquisition at 30 months can indicate later academic success, particularly in literacy (Rowe et al., 2012).

UK schools often rely on academic targets linked to previous assessments – Key Stage 1 outcomes predict Key Stage 2 SATs, which inform GCSE and A-level targets. While this approach has its merits, it overlooks oracy as a critical early indicator of success.

By integrating language development measures into these predictions, schools could identify and support children who are at risk of falling behind earlier in their academic journey. Rethinking our approach to oracy could better equip disadvantaged learners, helping them to overcome barriers and achieve long-term success.

The Language-Rich Environment

One of the most influential factors shaping a child's linguistic development is the environment they are born into. As Norman (1992) established, language acquisition depends on a variety of external components, including social interaction, contextual framing of new vocabulary and two-way communication. These elements mean that children worldwide experience a spectrum of language environments, some rich and stimulating, others limited and restrictive. This variance marks the early conception of what we now call the language gap.

The 30 Million Word Gap

Hart and Risley's landmark study (1995) introduced one of the most recognised concepts in the study of early language acquisition: the **30 Million Word Gap**. Their research analysed the home lives of 42 American families from welfare dependent, working class and professional backgrounds, focusing on the number of words children heard between the ages of 12 and 36 months.

Their findings were stark:

- **Welfare-dependent families**: Children heard **620 words per hour**, totalling approximately **13 million words** by age 4.
- **Working-class families**: Children heard **1,250 words per hour**, totalling about **26 million words** by age 4.
- **Professional families**: Children heard **2,150 words per hour**, resulting in **45 million words** by age 4.

This 30-million-word gulf between children from professional and welfare-dependent families highlights the substantial disparities in linguistic exposure based on socio-economic status (Figure 3.1). These early differences have become cornerstones for the study of oracy and its links to social mobility.

While Hart and Risley's findings are widely cited, subsequent research has challenged their findings. For example, Gilkerson et al. (2017) employed the Language Environment Analysis (LENA) system, an objective tool for measuring parent-child talk in the home without relying on manual transcription. Their study found a smaller – but still significant – 4 million word gap between the lowest and highest socio-economic classes by age 4.

Regardless of the specific figures, the overarching conclusion is consistent: Our most disadvantaged children are already falling behind their more privileged peers by the age of 3. Despite the ability of all young children to absorb language, some are exposed to significantly fewer linguistic opportunities than others, with long-term consequences for their cognitive and social development.

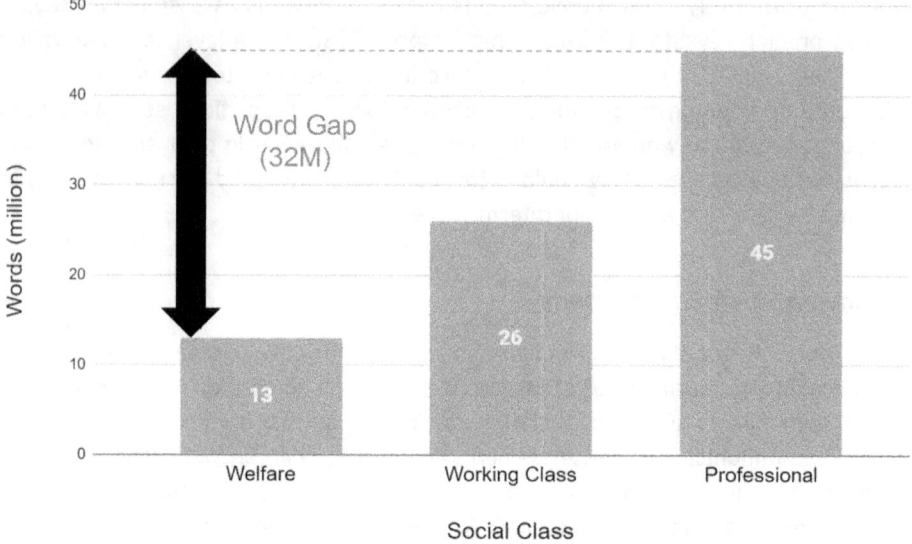

Figure 3.1 The 30 million word gap.

Definitions

Language-Rich Environment: a setting where children are consistently exposed to a diverse and frequent use of spoken and written language through meaningful interactions, conversations, storytelling and access to books and other literacy resources.

Language-Poor Environment: a setting where children have limited exposure to spoken and written language, with minimal meaningful interactions, conversations or access to literacy resources, hindering their language and cognitive development.

Quality, not just quantity

Since the introduction of the *'30 Million Word Gap'*, researchers have expanded the conversation to consider not only the quantity of language a child hears but also its quality. For example:

- The richness of vocabulary, sentence complexity and conversational engagement all contribute to the depth of a child's linguistic development.
- Two-way interactions (conversational turns) are particularly crucial in fostering active engagement and understanding.
- Research has increasingly highlighted the importance of *how* words are spoken, emphasising the role of emotional tone, context and cultural relevance.

By shifting focus from word counts to meaningful interactions, educators and policymakers can better understand the holistic nature of a language-rich environment and its pivotal role in addressing the social mobility gap.

We will explore the various strategies that can simultaneously boost the quantity as well as the quality of language a young child must be immersed in for the first years of life. Whilst it appears obvious to claim that a child's oral development will accelerate if they are surrounded by high quality language, empowering and equipping all families to achieve this is a far greater challenge. Many barriers to nurturing a language-rich home are facing our most disadvantaged families; further into this chapter, we will examine these in more detail.

Not Every Start in Life Is Equal

Socio-Economic Barriers

Children from disadvantaged families face unique barriers that restrict their opportunities for healthy language development. This starts from birth, some may even argue earlier. Within the first 3 years, these children have fallen behind peers with diminishing chances of catching up. This perpetuates the ongoing cycle of social inequality and division; in other words those trapped in the *'stickier'* lower end of the social ladder are stuck there across generations.

Time Poverty

The first few years of a child's life are crucial in their social, emotional, cognitive and linguistic development. As outlined by Norman (1992), this is a time for parents and caregivers to immerse their child in a language-rich environment, full of quality dialogue, vocabulary and social interaction between adult and child. However, for many families at the lower end of the social ladder, other stress factors prevent them from spending this quality time with their own children. They are *'time poor'* (Figure 3.2).

Regardless of effort and determination to bolster their child's language development at a young age, these demanding external factors significantly influence the opportunities for high quality, adult-led oral interactions. With increasing economic pressures, from global crises to rising inflation, more families are falling below the poverty line; as financial demands rise, many families will become more *'time poor'*, impacting the levels of support and quality time they can spend communicating with their children.

Maslow's Hierarchy

As outlined with regards to time poverty, oracy can be shackled by the more basic needs of human survival. Experienced teachers will recognise how learning cannot effectively happen unless a child is feeling safe, calm and comfortable. A child who missed breakfast or didn't sleep well will often struggle to concentrate and progress through the school day. In a similar manner, preschool-age children need to have their most basic needs met for them to thrive – not just survive.

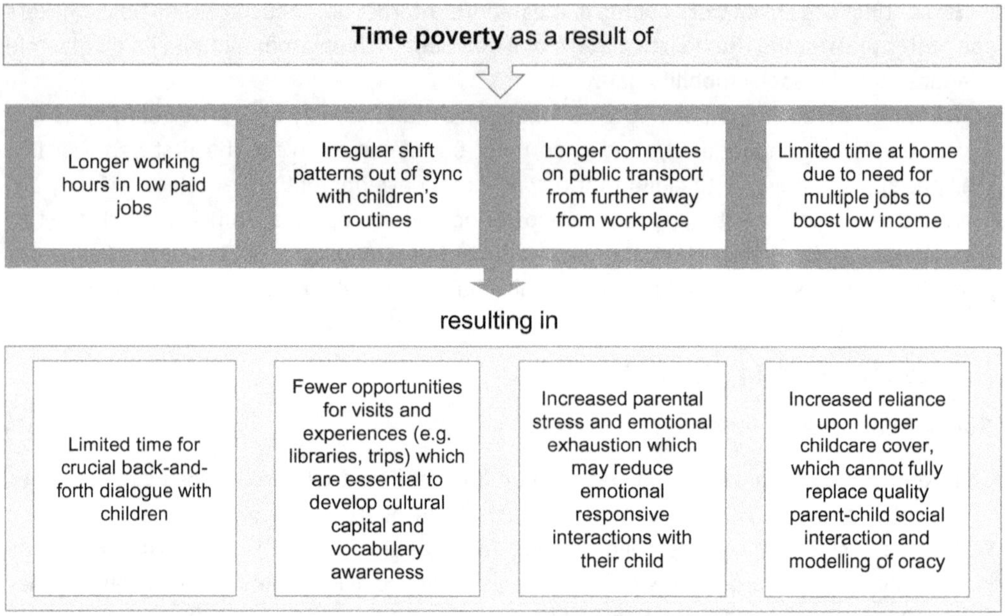

Time poverty as a result of

- Longer working hours in low paid jobs
- Irregular shift patterns out of sync with children's routines
- Longer commutes on public transport from further away from workplace
- Limited time at home due to need for multiple jobs to boost low income

resulting in

- Limited time for crucial back-and-forth dialogue with children
- Fewer opportunities for visits and experiences (e.g. libraries, trips) which are essential to develop cultural capital and vocabulary awareness
- Increased parental stress and emotional exhaustion which may reduce emotional responsive interactions with their child
- Increased reliance upon longer childcare cover, which cannot fully replace quality parent-child social interaction and modelling of oracy

Figure 3.2 The impact of time poverty.

Maslow's Hierarchy of Needs (1943) is a psychological framework proposed by Abraham Maslow in 1943, illustrating the stages of human motivation. The model is typically shown as a pyramid with five levels. Starting at the base with the most basic physiological needs, it progresses up to the pinnacle of self-actualisation. Maslow emphasised that unmet lower-tier needs can hinder progression to higher levels. For example, if a child is tired and cold, their mind is solely focused on improving their physical situation, therefore preventing them from progressing onto the next tier of development in which they can flourish (Figure 3.3).

For our lowest socio-economic families who are surviving day-to-day, their priority is on trying to meet the physiological needs of their children. Food, housing, heating and sleep are all on the top of this list and many families are even struggling to cover these fundamental needs on a daily basis (Table 3.1).

So how does this impact a young child's oracy growth in the long term?

Children living in economically disadvantaged home settings often experience disruption to their lower tier needs. This makes it difficult for them to reach the higher cognitive and linguistic milestones, such as expressive and receptive language, which are crucial for oracy development before they enter the education system.

The Power of Reading and Books at Home

With the array of challenges facing certain social classes, the opportunities for time and effort to be directed towards linguistically rich interactions between children and caregivers start to dwindle drastically. Yet, the spoken, conversational dialogue and modelling of language is only one facet of a child's holistic development. Access to literature and the shared

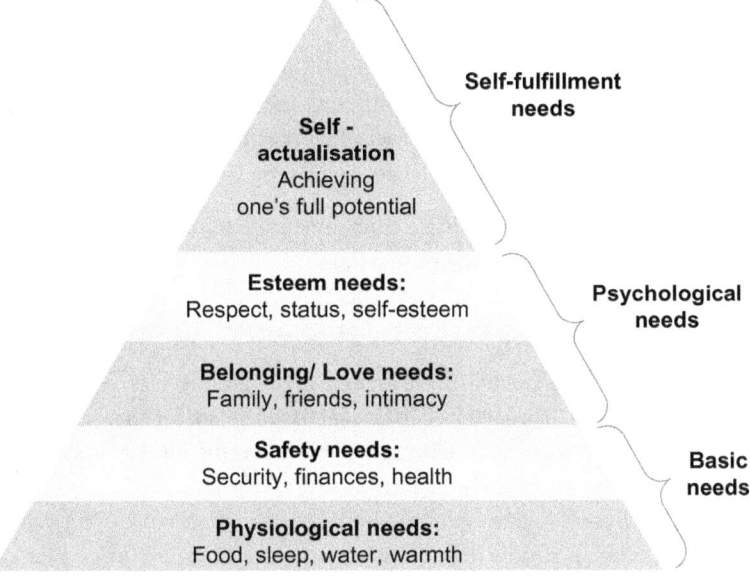

Figure 3.3 Maslow's hierarchy of needs.

Table 3.1 Unmet needs impacting oracy development

Unmet need	Impact on oracy
Physiological needs • Lack of nutritious food (or a general lack of sufficient food) • Lack of heating due to rising fuel costs • Lack of comfortable sleeping arrangements	Hunger, fatigue and discomfort detract from a child's ability to meaningfully engage with others in social settings Children lack the energy to concentrate upon stimulating language exchanges and lack the stamina to focus upon the language surrounding them
Safety needs • Housing uncertainty and instability • Financial insecurity • Unsafe/unhealthy living conditions	As a result of instability and insecurity, children can lack the emotional security needed for healthy interactions and relationships to those around them Caregivers experiencing high levels of stress can struggle to provide the rich, responsive language interactions needed for early oracy to develop
Belonging needs • Limited parent-child time due to multiple jobs, long hours and long commutes • Time poverty • Lack of child books and toys for play within the home environment	Time poverty and limited time spent with caregivers can limit the child's chance for meaningful, shared experiences, such as story time, library visits, role play and more The lack of space and resources to use for healthy exploratory play will restrict the opportunities for imaginative play, through which children build empathy and understanding of the world

experience of reading is a distinct medium through which children's vocabulary can widen beyond the everyday language.

Since 2019, The National Literacy Trust (Picton et al., 2024) has been conducting national surveys to assess the levels of engagement with children's literature at home. Their findings paint a bleak picture of reading, both generally and particularly for the most deprived children across the UK. In their latest report, their results show:

- 50.5% of parents read daily with their child, a decrease from 66% in 2019
- 46.4% did shared reading with their child daily
- 22.4% of families reported having fewer than ten children's books in their home
- 19.5% had not visited a library at all in the past 30 days

The overall trend shows a decline in levels of engagement with books and reading at home over the past 5 years. This trend appears across the social spectrum but the impact is felt far more within the lower socioeconomic families as this form of linguistic exposure is crucial for building vocabulary and cultural capital.

The correlation between reading and oracy may not seem as explicit but there is a strong evidence base that proves just how important access into literature is for a child's language development. Hayes and Ahrens (1988) found that children's books offer an especially rich source of exposure to advanced vocabulary that children might rarely, if ever, encounter in everyday conversations. These words fall under the tiers 2 and 3 of the vocabulary pyramid. While language directed at preschoolers tends to focus on simpler words, even as children grow older and caregivers use a wider range of language, the vocabulary often remains within a similar breadth as that used with younger children. This highlights the value of books in providing access to less commonly used and more complex words, which are crucial for expanding a child's language repertoire.

Furthermore, children who regularly engage in shared reading gain exposure to more mature linguistic vocabulary (Hart and Risley, 1995); those who don't fall further behind from an early stage. The language input young children absorb from stories directly affects their oracy, broadening their vocabulary schema and opening their eyes to the contextual meaning of new words.

The importance of reading and the need to provide access to high quality books can clearly be seen in the growth of local and national organisations dedicated to this social mission. Such examples include:

- National Literacy Trust
- Centre for Literacy in Primary Education (CLPE)
- BookTrust
- Bookmark Reading Charity

One Step Forward, Two Steps Back

Marmot et al. (2020) conducted a landmark review into the root causes of health inequalities across England, particularly amongst the most disadvantaged families. Their findings identified the importance of targeted, evidence-based strategies to reduce disparities between socio-economic groups. The report stressed that addressing inequalities requires interventions to support, 'children's access to positive early experiences. Later interventions, although important, are considerably less effective where good early foundations are lacking.'

So, have we seen positive change in the past 15 years since this report was published?

The original Marmot Review was published in 2010, during the early years of austerity and before the socio-political upheavals of Brexit, rising inflation and global conflicts. A decade later, in 2020, the report's findings were reassessed in the light of these new challenges. This **'10 Years On' review** reaffirmed the link between lower socio-economic status and the barriers faced by children in their earliest years. Despite some progress, several worrying trends were highlighted:

- **School readiness levels** had initially increased due to earlier child care interventions. However, since 2020, schools have reported growing worries about children entering early years settings with obvious developmental delays.
- **Child poverty has risen**, with an extra four million children living in poverty between 2010 and 2020 and growing further since.
- **Funding for Sure Start children's centres** was drastically cut, especially in the most deprived areas, reducing access to vital early support.
- **Child and youth services funding** in deprived areas declined more steeply than in more affluent areas of the country.
- The **childcare workforce** continues to experience low pay and limited access to qualifications, impacting the quality of early education.

These factors create significant barriers to young children's development, impacting their cognitive, linguistic, emotional and physical growth. Many children in disadvantaged families face challenges that are difficult, if not impossible, to overcome without systemic change.

The Marmot Review continues to advocate for strategies to level the playing field, making sure that all children, regardless of background, have a strong foundation for lifelong learning and success. The barriers identified in the report align closely with its recommended strategies, highlighting the critical link between early intervention and positive outcomes, particularly in oracy development (Table 3.2).

Addressing the Gap Early

The Role of Caregivers

Whilst many educators recognise the importance of language development in the first few years of childhood, their reach is traditionally limited to the moment at which the child walks into the school. By this point, some of our most disadvantaged children are already significantly behind their better off peers; the language gap is no longer in it's infancy.

It is therefore even more crucial to focus early support towards the caregivers, as they possess the necessary time and space to guide their own childrens' oral growth. They wear many hats as a young child's focal point in their microcosm; from modeller to play facilitator, storyteller to questioner, the demands upon them are extremely challenging. Without support and a chance to discuss the importance of oracy at home, many parents will feel ill-equipped to maximise the opportunities they have with their children.

Table 3.2 Matching barriers to their impact on oracy

Barrier	Impact on oracy	Recommended strategy (Marmot Review)
Increasing levels of child poverty	Limited access to language-rich resources and experiences (books, libraries) Lack of affordable, high quality childcare Poverty stress factors (housing instability, food insecurity, reduced time with parents) leading to a less-conducive home environment for positive language interactions	Government spending initiatives to target most deprived areas Investment in better quality childcare provision, targeted within the most deprived communities
Funding cuts for early childhood support (e.g. Sure Start centres)	These centres provided vital resources such as parent-child interaction programmes, speech and language therapy and access to books and structured play Without these, many disadvantaged families lost opportunities to foster their children's language skills during the critical early years, exacerbating the gap between socio-economic groups in oracy development	Increase the levels of early years spending (to be on par with OECD average) Improve quality and accessibility of early years services in all regions of England (e.g. Children's Centres)
Persistently low levels of pay and qualifications in the childcare workforce	Children attending nurseries with highly qualified staff are 10% more likely to achieve a good level of development (GLD) by the end of the Early Years Foundation Stage (Save the Children, 2016)	Increase the required levels of qualifications for childcare workers Raise the minimum pay thresholds for the childcare workforce

Speak More to your child – Child-Directed Speech

Academics have spent decades studying the way in which parents speak to their babies and toddlers – not simply in terms of words but also focusing upon the delivery of speech. Clearly, a baby cannot comprehend the direct meaning of words spoken to or around them but research shows they are far more capable of deciphering meaning, tone and emotion from the way the words are spoken.

'Child-directed speech' (CDS) refers to the way in which parents talk to their infants. Also known as 'motherese' or 'parentese', many studies have identified the features of this type of speech as being:

- Exaggerated in intonation and expression
- Repetitive in nature
- Simplified in terms of vocabulary choices
- Higher pitch than adult-to-adult dialogue

These adaptations to speech are claimed to make it easier for younger children to access the language and, over time, start to recall and use the words themselves. Some of the key studies exploring the impact of CDS include:

- Clarke-Stewart (1973): found that children whose mother's spoke more to them possessed larger vocabularies as they began to communicate.

Table 3.3 Putting child-directed speech (CDS) into action

CDS strategy	Action	Impact on oracy
Narrate everyday activities	Describe familiar daily activities as you complete them with your child "Now, we're putting your shoes on" "Let's stir this soup" "We need to wait for the receipt"	Exposes the child to vocabulary in real-world contexts, helping them to associate what they experience with the relevant words
Encourage conversational turns	Pause during interactions to allow the child time to respond (even if a baby who is babbling)	Fosters active engagement Teaches a child about the social norms of conversation
Use repetition and expansion	Repeat what the child has said back to them and expand with more detail. Child: "Dog!" Adult: " Yes, that's a big, black dog. It's wagging his tail"	Child can hear their own speech back to them Opportunity to model correct grammar and pronunciation Modelling how to add more description
Focus on warmth and expression	Adult speaks in a sing-song, melodic rhythm with a higher pitch tone Clear articulation and pronunciation is key	This way of speaking captures a child's attention, ensuring the interactions are enjoyable

- Brown, Cazden and Bellugi (1969): parents respond to the 'truth value' of what their child says rather than correcting the child's grammar e.g. a child saying 'there doggie' is responding with 'Yes, it is a dog' rather than 'No, we say "there is a dog!"'.

Through these ongoing, frequent parent–child interactions, children are able to grow their vocabulary and schema (their knowledge of the world). For example, when someone uses the word *'banana'* and points at a banana repeatedly, the child starts to form a mental connection between the concrete (the banana) and the abstract word. As the child continues to learn new words in real-world contexts their schema grows more complex and they can begin to attach more words e.g. they can add adjectives to describe the noun (the juicy, yellow banana).

In essence, CDS emphasises the need for caregivers to interact purposefully with their child to scaffold the journey through early oracy. This is even more critical for families from the lower end of the *'social ladder'* to mitigate the effects of the growing gap in language development. Table 3.3 outlines the possible actions that can be taken to incorporate CDS into the home setting.

Strategies for Oracy at Home

THE EPPSE study and the more recent SEED study (Melhuish and Gardiner, 2021) studied the home learning environment (HLE), and they looked at the range of childhood experiences that aid, or hinder, language development. They recognised that the more language-rich

40 *Voices of Opportunity*

Figure 3.4 Seven key aspects of the home learning environment (HLE).

experiences a child experiences during infancy, the better they perform academically. Reflecting on Marmot et al.'s (2020) barriers to such experiences for certain children, it is even more important for support to be in place to help families build these into their daily routines.

Seven key aspects of an effective HLE were listed by the EPPSE study. The common thread running through all seven is the need for adult interaction with the child, with language being the shared focus. In homes where there is stability, security and high degrees of parental engagement, the HLE can be nurtured and refined to meet the child's needs. But, in more volatile, insecure households, the HLE is negatively affected by an array of external factors (i.e. housing instability, limited parental time with children and lack of literature) (Figure 3.4).

The National Literacy Trust (Picton et al., 2024) found some alarming statistics that show an increasing need to re-engage parents regarding oracy at home. It also points to the challenges of time poverty facing many households. They found that:

- In 2024, only 78.1% of parents spoke to their child daily in the last week. This is a decrease from 90.3% in 2019.
- 56% of parents had played with their child daily in the last week. This is a decrease from 76.2% in 2019.

The tangible challenge for schools and educators across the country is how to best support families in establishing effective HLEs for children who are not yet part of the educational system.

Chapter Summary

- The first 3 years are pivotal for language development, as they shape cognitive, social, and academic outcomes through high-quality interactions.
- Children from low-income families face a language gap by age 3, limiting their vocabulary and chances of being *'school ready'*.
- Strong early oral language acts as a predictor of later academic and career success, reinforcing the need for early intervention.
- Rich, interactive language fosters growth, while oracy-poor environments deepen inequality; both quality and quantity of dialogue matter.
- Economic challenges limit disadvantaged families' access to books, quality childcare, and language-rich settings, worsening the gap even further.
- Literacy initiatives support caregivers with resources to create enriching language environments, helping to break cycles of inequality.

Reflection Questions

- What are the key barriers to quality language development for children aged 0–3 in your community, and how do socio-economic factors exacerbate these challenges?
- How can local initiatives, such as libraries, early childhood programmes or community resources, better support families in fostering language-rich environments for young children?

Time to Take Action

Take yourself through the journey from early oracy through to adulthood. Complete the following statements, specifically considering the pupils you serve.

1. Active listening by children supports their language development because…

   _____
   _____
   _____

2. Stronger language acquisition (receptive and expressive) helps with their reading fluency because…

   _____
   _____
   _____

3   Better reading fluency leads to reading comprehension because…

_____

_____

4   The mastery of reading supports learning development because…

_____

_____

References

Alvarez, C. (2019) *The Natural Laws of Children: Why Children Thrive When We Understand How Their Brains Are Wired*. Boulder: Shambhala Publications.

Brown, R., Cazden, C. and Bellugi, U. (1969) 'The child's grammar from I to III', *Minnesota Symposium on Child Psychology*, 2, pp. 100–154.

Clarke-Stewart, K. (1973) 'Interactions between mothers and their young children: Characteristics and consequences', *Monographs of the Society for Research in Child Development*, 38(6-7, Serial No 153), pp. 1–108.

Gilkerson, J., Richards, J., Warren, S., Montgomery, J., Greenwood, C., Oller, D., Hansen, J. and Paul, T. (2017) 'Mapping the early language environment using all-day recordings and automated analysis', *American Journal of Speech-Language Pathology*, 26(2), pp. 248–265.

Greenwood, C., Schnitz, A., Carta, J. and Wallisch, A. (2020) 'A systematic review of language intervention research with low-income families: A word gap prevention perspective', *Early Childhood Research Quarterly*, 50(1), pp. 230–245.

Hart, B. and Risley, T.R. (1995) *Meaningful Differences in the Everyday Experience of Young American Children*. Baltimore: Paul H. Brookes Publishing.

Hayes, D. and Ahrens, M. (1988) 'Vocabulary simplification for children: A special case of "motherese"?', *Journal of Child Language*, 15, pp. 395–410.

Marmot, M., Allen, J., Boyce, T., Goldblatt, P. and Morrison, J. (2020) *Health Equity in England: The Marmot Review 10 Years On*. The Institute of Health Equity.

Maslow, A. (1943) 'A theory of human motivation', *Psychological Review*, 50(4), pp. 370–396.

Melhuish, E. and Gardiner, J. (2021) *Study of Early Education and Development (SEED): Impact Study on Early Education Use and Child Outcomes up to Age Seven Years*. London: DfE Government Social Research.

Norman, K. (1992) *Thinking Voices: The Work of the National Oracy Project*. London: Hodder & Stoughton.

Picton, I., Moisi, I., Jackson, T. and Clark, C. (2024) *Parents Support for Young Children's Literacy at Home in 2024*. National Literacy Trust.

Rowe, M., Raudenbush, S. and Goldin-Meadow, S. (2012) 'The pace of vocabulary growth helps predict later vocabulary skill', *Child Development*, 83(2), pp. 508–525.

Save the Children (2016) *Untapped Potential: How England's Nursery Lottery is Failing Too Many Children*. London: Save the Children.

4 Entering EYFS
The 'School Readiness' Divide

Defining 'School Readiness'

A Framework for Early Years Success

In the last chapter, the increasing divide between the most disadvantaged young children and their better-off counterparts was clearly outlined. By age 3, a rising number of children across the UK are entering our Early Years settings unready for this important transition. In recent years, this has been measured under the term, *'school readiness'* and here this concept will be defined, analysed and connected to oral development.

A Definition from UNICEF

In 2012, UNICEF published a framework (Britto, 2012) for defining school readiness, constructed from three core dimensions:

- **Ready children:** focusing on a child's learning and development
- **Ready schools:** focusing on the school environment and the associated practices that foster smooth transition into primary school
- **Ready families:** focusing on parental and caregiver engagement and mindset in relation to the transition process into primary school

All three dimensions are equally important and require equal attention because school readiness is complex and requires the buy-in of children, families and educators.

In their framework, UNICEF identifies the aspects of child development that are important to an individual being considered *'school ready'*. As any Early Years practitioner will realise, UNICEF's scope of readiness mirrors the *'early learning goals'* of the EYFS Profile. As defined by UNICEF, they include:

- Physical development and well-being (e.g. motor skills)
- Socio-emotional (e.g. sustained attention, emotional regulation, following instructions and developing social relationships)
- Language and literacy (including oracy)
- Maths skills (e.g. understanding mathematical concepts, pre numeracy skills)
- Attitudes and behaviours towards learning (e.g. resilience, persistence, initiative, creativity and problem solving)

DOI: 10.4324/9781003607595-5

A UK Perspective: The EYFS Profile

The UK Early Years Foundation Stage (EYFS) Profile is a statutory assessment tool used to evaluate children's development at the end of the reception year (age 4-5). It covers 17 early learning goals across areas such as communication, language, literacy and mathematics, assessing their **school readiness** and identifying areas for support. Teachers gather observations and evidence to inform these assessments, which inform parents and shape educational strategies for future learning (Figure 4.1).

For each Early Learning Goal (ELG), a child is judged as to whether they meet the *'level of development expected at the end of the EYFS'* (DfE, 2024). In essence, being judged as *'expected'* for their age is equivalent to maintaining a level of *'school readiness'*. The 2-year journey through our early years provisions is the opportunity for children to become *'school ready'*. However, as will be explained, more and more children are entering EYFS far below the expected levels of development and leave EYFS 'unready' for Key Stage 1.

The Key Domains of Development

In many walks of life, being ready, willing and able are essential ingredients for smooth transition; whether it is entering a new occupation, joining a new team or taking on new responsibilities, successful transition depends on a range of factors. Let's take the example of a doctor. They need to be; ready to cope with the stresses and emotions of medical care; willing to show determination, perseverance and courage in their practice and able to perform the necessary medical treatments and diagnosis required of their role.

In a similar vein, the children walking through the doors of our Early Years settings need to be ready, willing and able to engage with learning; the absence of any of these factors can disrupt their smooth transition into EYFS. There are key developmental domains that every

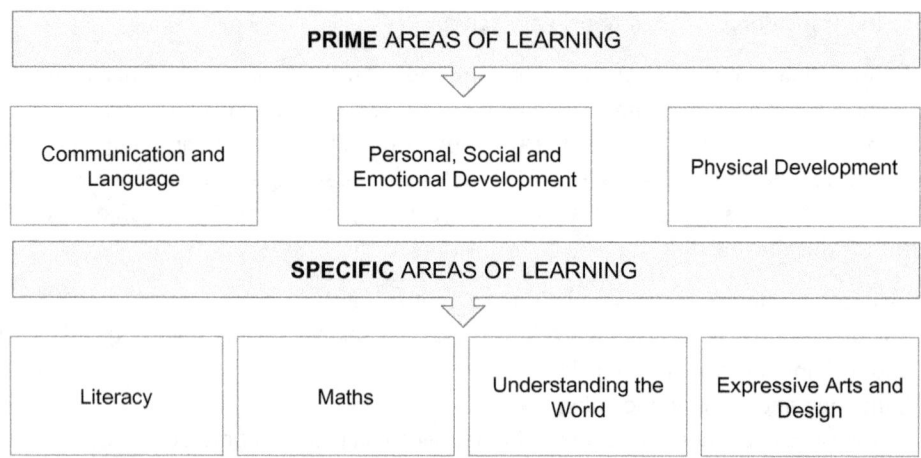

Figure 4.1 The seven areas of learning and development.

child is baselined against as they enter school and these can be used as a benchmark for *'school readiness'*.

Oracy Is the Cornerstone

As outlined in Table 4.1, oracy is integral to many aspects of a child's development within the early years. For a child who struggles to understand and communicate effectively, they will face many obstacles within these various domains. This isn't simply limited to academic progress but can significantly impact a child's social-emotional development too.

As we witness a decline in levels of *'school readiness'* for the children entering early years, this aligns to a growing concern around the communication and language needs being identified in recent cohorts. This correlation is not a coincidence – lower levels of oracy are part of the reason for this school readiness divide. It is therefore imperative that all stakeholders, including Government, schools and families, work closely together to boost the levels of oracy intervention across our early years settings.

Table 4.1 Linking oracy to early years developmental domains

Development domain	Skills	Impact on oracy
Cognitive	Problem solving	Ability to think and articulate solutions clearly
	Memory and attention	Following instructions and participate in shared activities
	Early numeracy/literacy	Ability to access early exposure to maths, oral sharing and early reading resources
Social-emotional	Emotional regulation	Manage emotions during separation from caregiver
	Peer relationships	Develop key skills for social interaction i.e. turn taking, empathy and social bonding
	Self-confidence	Build positive self-esteem and confidence to participate verbally within the group
Physical	Gross motor	Ability to safely use the outside space in readiness for playground interaction
	Fine motor	Ability to start purposeful mark making to express ideas, feelings and creative expression
	Hygiene and health	Understand routines e.g. handwashing, toileting and instructions to be followed
Communication and Language	Expressive language	Develop vocabulary to express emotions, thoughts and needs to others
	Receptive language	Ability to understand instructions and respond accordingly
	Listening and Conversational	Develop the active listening required to underpin collaborative learning

Tracking the Decline in *School Readiness*

A Worrying Trend

Whilst teachers nationwide are reporting a rise in *'school **un**readiness'* for their children in early years, it is important to support these commonly held opinions with quantifiable statistics. Children are seen as *'school ready'* if they are assessed as being able to achieve all the age-related expectations across the domains (see Table 4.1). This is often referred to as having a *'good level of development (GLD)'*.

If we compare the GLD for two separate cohorts in 2018 versus 2024, the growing divide in school readiness becomes more apparent. In 2018, 71.8% of children had a good level of development whereas, in 2024, this had dropped to 67.7%. Whilst 2024 showed a slight increase (+0.5%) on 2023's outcomes, there has been a significant decline in GLD since the COVID pandemic.

When comparing the most disadvantaged children (using Free School Meals (FSM) as a standard measure) to non-FSM peers, the gap in GLD has remained around 20% since 2021/22. The stark reality is that half of disadvantaged children are assessed as being unready to enter Key Stage One and this has knock-on effects to their future academic prospects (Figure 4.2).

Looking further into the GLD data trends, other significant disparities between social and geographical groups can be found (Child of the North, 2024). They include:

- Variability in outcomes between local authorities. For example, the percentage of school ready children in Manchester was 59% compared to 84% in London.

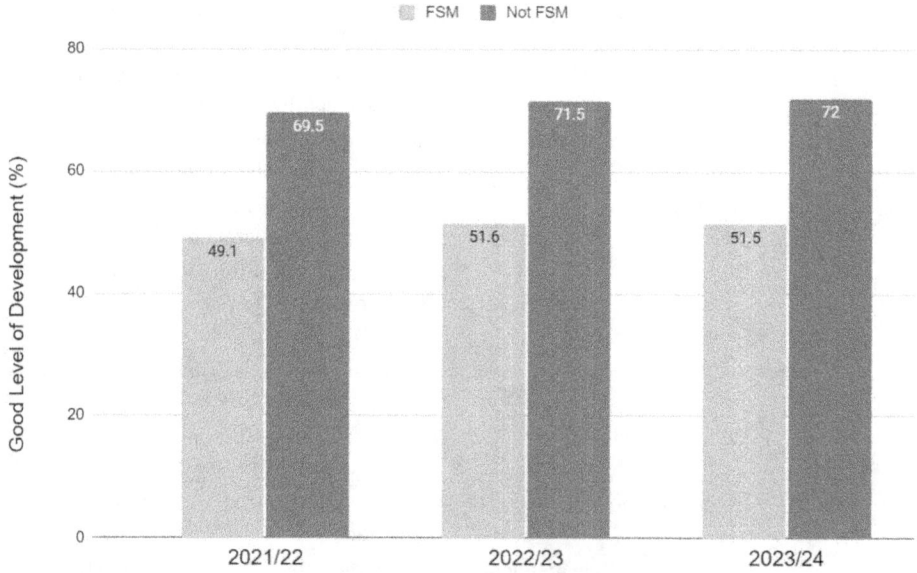

Figure 4.2 GLD trend.

- A 16 percentage point difference between children with English as an Additional Language (EAL) and those with English as their first language.
- Children deemed not ready were 2.5 times more like to be persistently absent than their peers.

This trend is supported by the latest *'State of the Nation'* report conducted by the Social Mobility Commission (2024). They found a strong correlation between GLD and levels of deprivation; the areas with the highest 10% of deprivation were also the areas with the lowest percentage of children at GLD. The GLD levels incrementally rise alongside the steps up the income deprivation deciles, reaching the highest GLD within the 10% least deprived neighbourhoods. In simpler terms, the poorer communities had higher levels of children not ready for education. The Social Mobility Commission does state that this is a correlation and a causal relationship cannot be assumed merely on this basis.

Aside from the clear statistical decline in school readiness, anecdotal evidence has shown a marked rise in concerns from Early Years specialists. Anne Longfield, Executive Chair of the Centre for Young Lives (Child of the North, 2024, p. 3) said: *'I have heard many concerning experiences from school staff about children arriving at Reception wearing nappies, still using buggies, and unable to communicate at the expected level or to socialise with other children.'*

A Lack of Oracy Readiness

As outlined in the previous chapter, many children are entering early years without the necessary oracy foundation skills to engage with their peer group and their learning. Oracy is interconnected with all areas of the early learning goals and without a secure grasp of language, a child will fall further behind on the journey through the foundation stage.

Academic Impact

Early years is known as the *'foundation stage'* because it helps establish the skills and behaviours required for learners to engage with the learning process as they progress through the school system. By examining the required skills and capabilities needed to be *'next Key Stage ready'*, we can reverse engineer the progression of skills development all the way to early years.

The Child of the North report (2024) highlights how good academic achievement can *'lay the foundations for later academic success'* and future employment prospects too. Their report found that over half of children deemed not to be *'school ready'* performed below age-related expectations in Key Stage 1 tests; compared to only 6% of *'school ready'* children, this stark contrast only serves to reinforce the importance of getting children prepared as early as possible.

How does poor oracy play a role in academic unreadiness?

- **Cognitive development:** those with poor vocabulary and language will struggle to understand instructions and explanations, hindering their ability to engage with learning
- **Delayed literacy skills:** oracy underpins early reading and writing. Weak language acquisition slows down the development of phonemic awareness, decoding and general progress towards literacy goals

- **Curriculum access:** Early Years learning is heavily scaffolded through verbal instructions and sharing. Children with limited language will find struggle to contribute in shared learning, collaborative tasks and problem solving

Social and emotional impact

Aside from academic progress, a substantial focus of early years is targeted upon the more holistic development of a child's character, well-being and self-efficacy. Watch a toddler throw a tantrum and it is easier to understand how underdeveloped language can result in emotional dysregulation and physical responses to convey feelings. As children age, they acquire language in a way that enables them to better express their emotions, explain their concerns and empathise with others. Conversely, children entering school with underdeveloped oral capacities struggle with the new social interactions and changes to their emotional state.

A lack of oracy can affect social and emotional development through:

- **Expression of emotion and need:** With weak oracy skills, children can struggle to communicate effectively with adults and peers. This can lead to frustration and emotional distress.
- **Relationship building:** To effectively interact with others, children rely upon communication. A lack of language can lead to social isolation or challenges with forming healthy friendships.
- **Self-esteem:** a child lacking language can often feel less confident and possess lower self-esteem. This can lead to anxiety around participation with group activities.

The Leuven Scale

Early years practitioners are constantly observing, recording and tracking progress of their children as they play, socialise and interact within the provision. The majority of the data focuses around a child's development towards the early learning goals. However, monitoring children's sense of well-being and engagement within the space is possible through use of 'The Leuven Scales'. This 5-point scale focuses on well-being and involvement levels and should form a key component of every EYFS setting's ongoing assessment cycle.

As identified by Maslow's hierarchy, children who feel confident, safe and happy will engage more effectively with learning and their peers. For many disadvantaged children, they enter their early years provisions with many unmet needs. It is important to use the Leuven scale, alongside a good understanding of the child's home life, to support their well-being and emotional state of mind. It can be helpful to consider:

- Can they communicate how they are feeling?
- Are they at the low end of involvement because they are lacking the social interaction skills needed for forming relationships?
- Do they exhibit physical reactions to express emotions? Is this due to a lack of expressive vocabulary? (Figure 4.3).

Entering EYFS 49

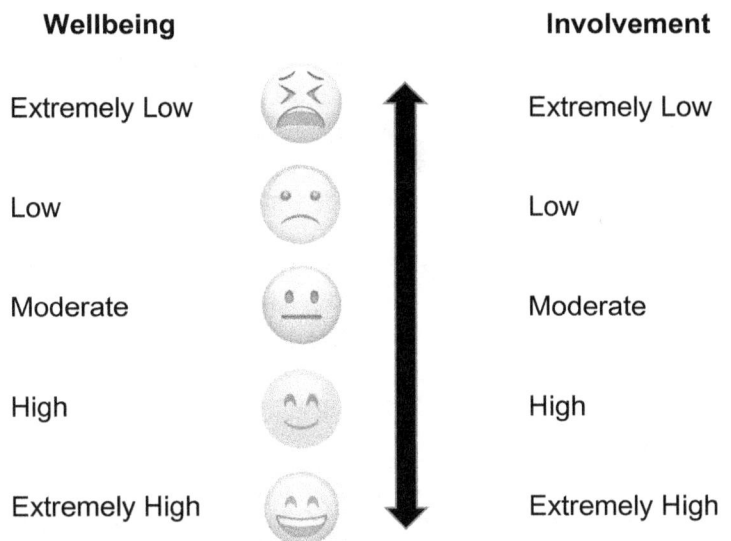

Figure 4.3 The Leuven scale for well-being and involvement.

Reassessing Priorities

The early years is undoubtedly the foundation for every child's jumpstart into their educational journey. The better a start a child can have, the smoother their transition into school can be. Conversely, a child leaving EYFS without a secure foundation in the age-related expectations will struggle to catch up to their 'school ready' peers for the rest of their schooling.

In order to increase the levels of *'school readiness'* amongst our most disadvantaged children, there needs to be a collaborative effort between families, early education providers and policy makers. It's essential that:

- Families are empowered with tools to support language and learning at home
- Early education providers are equipped to identify and bridge developmental gaps
- Policymakers address systemic inequalities impacting children's early years

By working collectively, we can ensure that all children, regardless of their background, are given the foundational skills needed to thrive in school and beyond, fostering a generation that is better prepared to meet the challenges of their educational journey.

Chapter Summary

- Oracy is central to a child's academic, social and emotional development in the early years. Poor communication skills can limit progress across all areas of learning and social interaction.

- A fall in children achieving a Good Level of Development (GLD) since 2018 highlights a growing readiness divide, with disadvantaged children being disproportionately affected.
- Limited oracy leads to struggles in cognitive, literacy and curriculum engagement, as well as challenges in emotional regulation, relationship building and self-esteem.
- Tools like the Leuven Scale help practitioners assess children's emotional state and involvement, essential for creating a supportive learning environment.

Reflection Questions

- How well do the developmental domains outlined in this chapter align with your current assessment practices in EYFS? Are there areas where your approach could be improved to better support school readiness?
- What specific strategies does your school employ to support oracy development for children entering EYFS with communication delays? How can these be enhanced to address the readiness gap?

Time to Take Action

Review your most recent reception cohort's GLD outcomes, comparing the difference between disadvantaged children and non-disadvantaged. Fill in the % achieving GLD in Table 4.2, then answer the following questions:

- Where are the most significant differences between the demographic groups?
- How are your early years teams adapting their provisions and curriculum planning to address these gaps?
- What oracy strategies will you try to incorporate into the provision to support the disadvantaged children close the gap?

Table 4.2 Comparing GLD

GLD area	Disadvantaged GLD %	Non-disadvantaged GLD %
Communication & Language		
Personal, Social and Emotional Development		

Table 4.2 (Continued)

GLD area	Disadvantaged GLD %	Non-disadvantaged GLD %
Physical Development		
Literacy		
Maths		
Understanding the World		
Expressive Art & Design		

References

Britto, P. (2012) *School Readiness. A Conceptual Framework*. New York: UNICEF.

Child of the North and Anne Longfield's Centre for Young Lives (2024) *An Evidence-Based Approach to Supporting Children in the Preschool Years*.

Department for Education (2024) *Early Foundation Profile Stage Handbook*. Available at: www.gov.uk/government/publications/early-years-foundation-stage-profile-handbook (Accessed: 29 May 2025).

Social Mobility Commission (2024) *State of the Nation 2024: Local to National, Mapping Opportunities for All*. Available at: https://assets.publishing.service.gov.uk/media/66f68e33e84ae1fd8592ea6b/SOTN-2024.pdf (Accessed: 29 May 2025).

5 Closing Gaps in EYFS

A Window of Opportunity

Flipping the Narrative: The Matthew Effect

> Whoever has will be given more, and they will have an abundance. Whoever does not have, even what they have will be taken from them.
>
> (Matthew 13:12)

Rigney (2010) explores the concept of *'The Matthew Effect'*, building upon the well-known biblical quote Matthew 13:12. Rigney's message is an urgent one; he claims that those possessing more advanced abilities will be better placed to access learning than those who have less developed skills. This further widens the gap between the *'haves'* and *'have nots'*. This argument can be applied to oracy, as the children who have benefited from a language-rich start to life are well positioned to progress through learning at school with relative ease. Conversely, children lacking the basic language skills will become more easily frustrated, disengaged and fall further behind with learning.

However, the early years stage is a key window of opportunity to prevent these gaps from widening at speed. Young children are primed ready to learn, absorb and embed language into their repertoire. Through targeted strategies, we have the chance to close the oracy gap before children enter formal education in Key Stage One. Instead of seeing the *'Matthew Effect'* as inevitable, schools need to prioritise support to those who need it most.

Definitions

The Matthew Effect = the concept that those who start with an advantage accumulate more advantage over time, whilst those at a starting disadvantage grow more disadvantaged over time. In effect, the rich get richers whilst the poor get poorer.

Closing Gaps in EYFS 53

Know Your Children, Know the Gaps, Know What Is Needed

As with any project, to have effective impact it is vital to understand the problem that needs to be addressed from the very beginning. As our children enter early years, they will be assessed to measure their starting points. Through rigorous baselining, we can identify:

- The individual **children** whose oracy skills are underdeveloped
- The **areas** of learning and development that need prioritising

Early years specialist, Alistair Bryce-Clegg (2015) advocates for the completion of a *'Gap and Strength Analysis'* (GSA) for each cohort upon entry into the Early Years provisions. Bryce-Clegg outlines the process for conducting a thorough GSA three times across an academic year starting with a baseline in Autumn term.

1. Using baseline assessments against the prime and specific areas of learning, identify the children who are **performing below age-related expectations (ARE)**. Also identify those performing above ARE so the provision can be adapted to challenge them further.
2. For the group deemed 'below ARE', count the areas of learning that they collectively fall below ARE in. This allows you to easily **rank the areas by largest need**, making prioritisation an easier process.
3. Choose the most significant areas of need and, as an EYFS team, **construct a plan** that aims to develop teaching, resources and the continuous provision.

The GSA can help focus attention on the most pressing concerns and the children most at risk of falling behind. Identifying children who possess weaker oracy from the start is crucial to providing them with language-rich opportunities during their time at school.

Being better informed about the specific needs of a cohort is fundamental for proactive change, but the trickier challenge is HOW to adapt the provision to close this gap. The rest of this chapter will lay out a range of strategies that can be introduced into Early Years in order to positively impact language development.

Building a Language-Rich Environment

Consciously fostering the development of a language-rich home environment is a key step in the healthy language development of preschool children. However, as social mobility research shows, many children are entering school from language-poor home lives in which they have experienced a deficit of up to *'thirty million words'* (Hart and Risley, 1995). For this reason, schools play an even more important role in providing a space that is laden with rich language for these children to hear, absorb, rehearse, and interact with.

Setting up the early years provision to develop opportunities for talk must be a priority for every setting. Bryce-Clegg (2015) explains the need for each setting to have a multitude of spaces that allow children to speak to peers, self-reflect, communicate with adults, shout, whisper, ask questions and role play.

Botrill (2018) advocates for teachers to deploy *'parent patter'* to fill the void of parent-child dialogue that has become a more gap in many households. Just like child-directed

Table 5.1 Strategies for a language-rich environment

Plan for...	To impact oracy by...
Interactive displays: Use of captions, labels and prompts on displays, enhanced areas and resources E.g. labelling found objects on a nature tuff tray	Encouraging children to engage with the written language alongside the physical resources, photos, artefacts Building familiarity with key words, sparking curiosity to ask what they say in relation to the tangible objects around them
Daily Talk Time: Schedule in opportunities for rich, purposeful conversation, modelled language and open topic discussion E.g. collective snack time can be a chance to discuss that day's activities, topic focus or even ask open-ended questions of each other	Providing consistent opportunities to model structured conversations, including turn talking To practice active listening and responding to each other's ideas and opinions Modelling social norms, such as manners
Vocabulary Walls Key vocabulary on display as part of ongoing topic focus or Early Learning Goals E.g. A *'Word of the Day'* display, with regular rotation of vocabulary	Building children's working lexicon over time Celebrating and shining a spotlight on the value of learning new words Reminding children and adults to use the newly learnt words in context within continuous provision
Adult-child interactions: Adults consciously model rich language during interactions whilst child play and learn in the provision. This can range from narrating actions, asking open-ended questions and modelling stem sentence	Helping children observe and hear modelled language, which they can then rehearse in their social interactions with peers Expanding upon children's attempts with further detail and description

speech (CDS), Botrill identifies the growing need for teachers to be the main language role models for many young children in early years (Table 5.1).

Storytelling Makes all the Difference!

During early years, stories and reading play a crucial role in supporting children's oracy development, particularly for those from disadvantaged backgrounds who may lack exposure to books at home. Research by Wells (in Norman, 1992) highlights that learning the structure of stories helps foster literacy and curiosity. Storytelling and narrative give children a framework to grasp language patterns and rehearse known *'story language'*. Knowing that fairy tales begin with *'Once upon a time...'* and end with *'they lived happily ever after'* is a perfect example of explicitly modelling storytelling in it's most basic form.

Alongside the need for oral storytelling is the importance of having books within the provision. Whilst young children are still unable (for the majority) to read, being immersed in an environment full of books has a significant impact upon their curiosity and engagement with literacy. Books offer exposure to more complex language structures that are not heard within everyday speech; this can include passive sentences, relative clauses and other grammatical structures (Dawson et al., 2021). Consistent exposure to stories and books helps broaden their linguistic understanding in the long term.

Furthermore, children's books often contain more complex sentence structures than typical child-directed speech (Cameron-Faulkner and Noble, 2013). This helps children develop a deeper understanding of syntax and sentence structure. However, children with limited vocabulary may struggle to deduce word meanings, which hinders comprehension and can lead to disengagement from reading over time (Alvarez, 2019).

By embedding storytelling and reading into early years settings, educators can bridge these gaps, boost vocabulary, and nurture the foundational language skills necessary for future academic success (Table 5.2).

Table 5.2 Strategies for storytelling in EYFS

Plan for...	To impact oracy by...
Story Circles: Ask the children to contribute to a shared story, taking turns to add their ideas on to each other. Adults can participate as a means of modelling quality extended sentences, inserting key vocabulary and reinforcing positive sharing behaviours (active listening, body language)	Providing an opportunity for all children to be heard (as and when they choose to) Building confidence in more reluctant speakers Allowing children to rehearse known story language and to observe peers sharing their schema
Acting out: Once a story has been read, encourage the children to physically act out the narrative, including gestures, expressions, emotions and movements	Immersing the children into the narrative, which creates excitement and drives engagement Making the story more memorable through the physical interaction alongside the verbal narration Connecting the spoken vocabulary to real world contexts e.g. emotions being shown, actions being performed
Story sacks: Once a story has been read, provide a bag of related items (puppets, toys, artefacts, images) that link to the story, characters and setting	Provides tangible props for children to reenact the story in their own play Helping to connect key concepts and vocabulary to real world contexts e.g. reading about a beach and then being able to feel sand in your toes and examine seashells Allowing the story to become part of continuous provision, extending the enhanced opportunities for children to rehearse and revisit the narrative repeatedly across a sustained period of time
Personal Storytelling: Encourage children to tell their own stories that involve their daily lives outside of school. E.g. sharing 'weekend news' Adults can model this personal approach, using rich vocabulary and extended sentences	Showing children that they have a voice that is valued by others Encouraging personal expression of their own interests Developing opportunities to extend articulation skills as well as confidence in sharing one's own experiences within a safe space

Cultivating Cultural Capital

For many children from deprived backgrounds, they will have limited experiences beyond their immediate vicinity. This can mean little to no opportunities to visit libraries, museums, landmarks or places of interest; their cultural capital is ringfenced by their limited exposure to the wider world, and this becomes a significant barrier to learning in early years. Bryce-Clegg (2015) explains that children rely upon their personal experiences to build understanding and gradually develop their schema. This lack of diverse experiences can place a ceiling on their ability to relate to learning; they lack the basic schema to connect what they experience with pre-existing understanding. This makes it harder for them to engage with stories, discussions and activities that are designed to draw upon a wide range of cultural knowledge.

> **Definitions**
>
> **Cultural Capital** = the knowledge, skills and behaviours that are gained over time through a range of opportunities and lived experiences. Higher cultural capital has been shown to support a child's progress academically and socially.
>
> **Schema** = A network of previously gained knowledge that affects how new information is processed and stored in the long-term memory.

Children begin to accrue cultural capital from birth. The first few years of life are pivotal in exposing children to the world around them, helping them to make sense of what they see and build their schema for future connections. For our most vulnerable children, the exposure can be limited for a range of factors as previously outlined, from time poverty to lack of financial stability at home. The Social Mobility Commission (2024) highlights the things that can impact a child's cultural awareness, from parental education to occupation and even the lack of cultural assets at home. Their report stresses the gap in cultural enrichment, as many families are unable to spend the time or money necessary to share such cultural experiences with their children (Table 5.3).

Talking through Play

Play is crucial in fostering oracy development in young children. Through many forms of play, children can be immersed in imaginative scenarios that will help them to build empathy, social awareness and emotional resilience (Bryce-Clegg, 2015). By stepping into someone else's shoes, they have an opportunity to recognise the emotions of others, navigating tricky and unfamiliar social situations. Play also acts as a vehicle for children to practice their receptive and expressive language, rehearse conversations, solve problems and work collaboratively. In essence, play has the power to develop a child cognitively, emotionally, socially and linguistically.

Table 5.3 Strategies for building cultural capital

Plan for...	To impact oracy by...
Visits and visitors: Organise trips to libraries, museums, places of interest located beyond the immediate locality Invite people of interest, such as community figures (emergency services, artists), to speak with the children	Exposing children to new experiences, places and people Broaden their '*world*' beyond their familiar area, showing diversity and culture Encouraging curiosity about the people living in their community and the various aspects of daily life
Celebrating Festivals: Plan for festivals and cultural events to be part of the annual timetable of learning e.g. Diwali, Easter, Eid and other religious festivals Connect continuous provision and carpet time to these events, including arts, food, music, storytelling and guest speakers	Building new vocabulary related to a more diverse range of areas Encouraging discussion and asking questions to peers Promoting inclusivity and diversity which can help children's confidence in sharing about their personal experiences Putting learning into context through multi-sensory experiences (singing, dancing, creating, touching, tasting), helping make stronger connections to schema
Diverse Storybooks: Ensure there are a range of fiction and non-fiction books that represent different cultures, religions, geographic areas and families Build this diverse literature into the EYFS curriculum (Understanding the World), making it relevant to your specific cohort of children's own demographic make up	Generating a culture of sharing stories that relate to the children's home lives Developing tiers 2 and 3 vocabulary in context Support children in developing a sense of belonging and celebrating differences

Additionally, small world play and puppetry can be effectively used to provide children with a safe space in which to reenact social situations and rehearse language. Botrill (2018) recommends that adults can enhance and extend this oracy by playing alongside the children, asking open ended questions, narrating and modelling more complex language. This '*commentary play*' is an effective way to share key vocabulary in context, model how to build more complex sentences and start up dialogue within the play arena. This is supported by Siraj-Blatchford et al. (2004), whose research showed the value of high-quality adult interactions in boosting language acquisition (Table 5.4).

Get Them Outside to Talk

Continuous provision in Early Years settings across the country is a combination of inside and outside learning. Being outside is a fundamental part of early childhood development as it provides the opportunity for: strengthening gross motor skills (e.g. running, jumping,

Table 5.4 Strategies for developing play

Plan for…	To impact oracy by…
Thematic Role Play Areas: Set up role play spaces that mirror various familiar and unfamiliar settings i.e. Post office, supermarket, hospital etc Enhance these spaces with relevant props and costumes	Providing real world situations for children to rehearse language (seen from family or modelled by teaching staff) in context Building opportunities for conversational turn-taking
Puppet Play: Ensure puppets of all shapes and sizes are available (finger, hand or stick) at any time within continuous provision Consider puppets that link to the core themes, books or spaces in the setting	Allowing reluctant speakers to *'speak through'* the puppets, reducing anxiety and slowly building confidence with speaking aloud Giving opportunities for children to reenact social situations and rehearse stem sentences/key vocabulary used by the adults
Commentary play: As children play, commentate on what they are doing e.g. *'I see you are putting blocks on top – you're building a very tall tower'*	Introducing new vocabulary and sentence stems within the context of play Modelling descriptive and action language as the child acts out the physical action. This dual coding of hearing the words whilst performing the action helps the language to embed in memory

climbing), connecting to nature and continuation of learning from inside to outdoors. The benefits of being outside in the fresh air and sunlight have been well documented, and this is especially true for young children's healthy growth and development.

Outside provision can help children:

- Build resilience and self-esteem through different, more physical challenges
- Express themselves in bigger, more creative and messier ways
- Maintain good health and develop their balance, core strength, stamina and coordination
- Role play in different spaces with props and improvised settings

However, many disadvantaged children lack outdoor space at home, with many living in cramped conditions without any opportunities for outside play. This makes it even more essential for Early Years provisions to maximise their use of outside spaces. Whilst outside play appears to be more directed towards physical development, there is vast potential for oracy to flourish outside (Table 5.5).

Rowing against the Tide

Oracy is one of many root causes for social immobility, but it is also one of the levers we can pull to drive change for our more vulnerable children. What this chapter proves is that Early Years provisions can influence the trajectory of the children they serve – yet boosting oracy is not the sole solution. As the inequality gap widens across the country, and more

Table 5.5 Strategies for developing outside oracy

Plan for...	To impact oracy by...
Narrated nature walks: Take the class on a walk through a natural area (local woods, forest school area, park), narrating sensory experiences along the way E.g. What can you hear? Smell? See? Feel? Pause enroute to discuss observed features, posing open questions	Helping connect key vocabulary to the tangible, real world objects Building curiosity in the local area, as children see good modelling of asking questions of the world around them Facilitating conversations about the local environment and familiar places
Collaborative Building: Plan for and encourage group tasks for children to lead and adults to facilitate and support where required E.g. Building dens, obstacle courses and fictional settings Adults can pose open questions and model turn taking conversations	Encouraging problem solving and collaborative dialogue focused around a practical task Opening up conversations through adult questioning (and eventually child-led questioning) Helping scaffold opportunities for reflections ('What could we have done differently?')
Exploration stations: Set up resourced areas that have an array of open-ended tools and resources for enquiry and exploration. E.g. Bug hunting station with magnifying glasses, containers, species sheets. Or a bird watching area with binoculars, feathers, clipboards and bird books	Giving children the chance to use organisational language to structure their activities (solo or group) Collaboration between children, involving dialogue regarding assigning roles, planning next steps and other task-based language
Outside Stage: Find a suitable area, preferably raised from the ground, to create a semi-permanent stage that is large enough for several children to role play Resource the stage with props, costumes and masks that are accessible at all times	Enabling the children to act out familiar stories as well as innovate and create their own narratives Build confidence in performing, whether with or without an intended audience

children fall below the poverty line, it is the economic and social pressures that remain the largest barriers to social mobility for many families. Schools can help but are only part of the solution.

As educators, our sphere of influence is strongest within our local community and the families that we welcome through our doors. Oracy isn't the silver bullet to close the mobility gap but it is an under-utilised weapon that we need to harness and build our pedagogy around. In Early Years, it is imperative that oracy sits at the centre of the curriculum; if we can get our children to communicate better, we can narrow the gap before they enter formal education.

In the next chapter, specific interventions such as the Nuffield Early Language Intervention (NELI) will be examined to assess their nationwide impact.

Chapter Summary

- As per *'The Matthew Effect'*, the divide between the language-rich and language-poor starts to widen from birth and grows further apart as the children enter the education system
- Early identification of the main gaps in skills and knowledge of your children is essential. Using this gap analysis to inform your priorities and adaptations to your provision is important to focus on what the children need to strengthen
- Oracy is integral to meeting the early learning goals and should be considered across all areas of the curriculum and continuous provision. From displays to modelling, outside spaces to reading, settings should be seeking out opportunities to build a language-rich environment that encourages children to speak and listen with purpose.

Reflection Questions

- How do you currently use your EYFS baselines to inform your curriculum and provision mapping? Is this a structured process or is it informal and dependent upon the EYFS lead's approach?
- How prominent is oracy within your curriculum? Is it explicitly integrated into the planning process and are staff aware of how oracy fits within the wider curriculum in your setting?

Time to Take Action

Conduct a SWOT analysis of your current early years provision, including:

- The internal and external environments
- Curriculum maps
- Enrichment activities i.e. visits and visitors
- Staff CPD regarding early language

Use the template below to identify what is working well and what can be targeted as a priority (Figure 5.1).

- Strengths: What is effective in boosting oracy?
- Weaknesses: What areas do not foster/prevent oracy?
- Opportunities: What can be changed to improve oracy?
- Threats: What barriers need to be overcome to make the change?

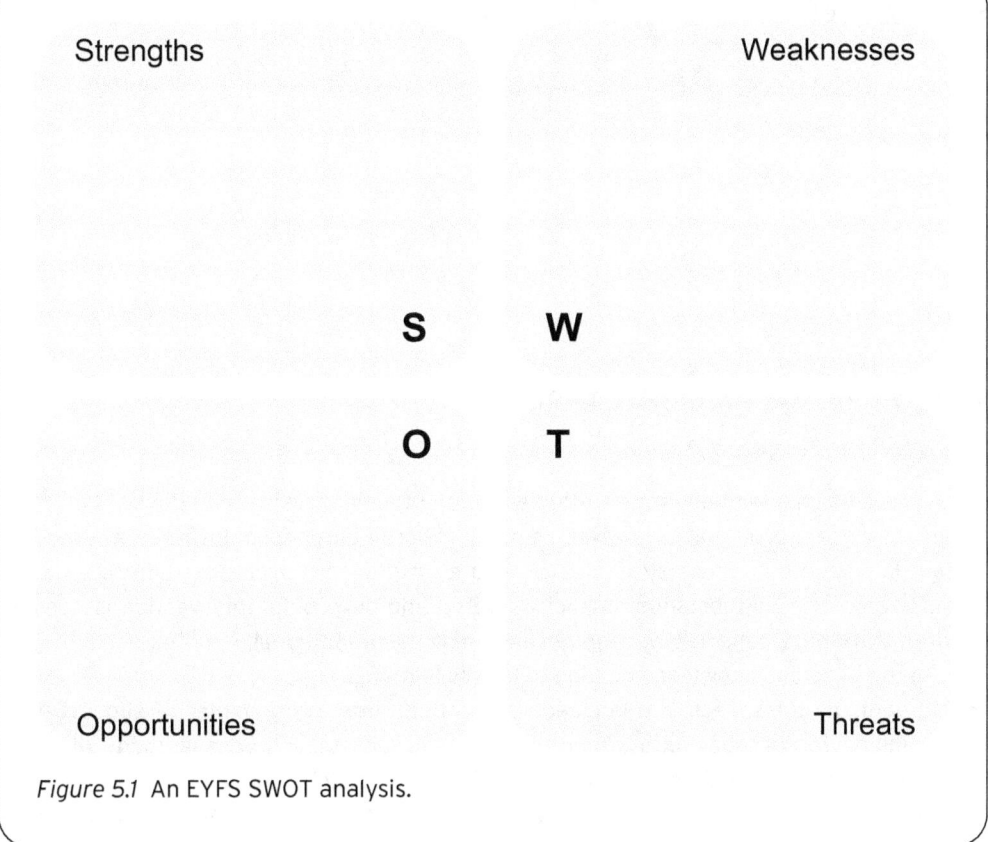

Figure 5.1 An EYFS SWOT analysis.

References

Alvarez, C. (2019) *The Natural Laws of Children: Why Children Thrive When We Understand How Their Brains Are Wired*. Boulder: Shambhala Publications.
Botrill, G. (2018) *Can I Go and Play Now?* London: SAGE Publications.
Bryce-Clegg, A. (2015) *Best Practice in the Early Years*. London: Bloomsbury.
Cameron-Faulkner, T. and Noble, C. (2013) 'A comparison of book text and Child Directed Speech', *First Language*, 33(3), pp. 268-279.
Dawson, N., Hsiao, Y., Ming Tan, A. W., Banerji, N. and Nation, K. (2021) 'Features of lexical richness in children's books: Comparisons with child-directed speech', *Language Development Research*, 1(1), pp. 9-53.
Norman, K. (1992) *Thinking Voices: The Work of the National Oracy Project*. London: Hodder & Stoughton.
Rigney, D. (2010) *The Matthew Effect: How Advantage Begets Further Advantage*. Columbia University Press.
Siraj-Blatchford, I., Sylva, K., Taggart, B., Sammons, P., Melhuish, E. and Elliot, K. (2004) *Technical Paper 10: The Effective Provision of Pre-School Education (EPPE) Project: Intensive Case Studies of Practice Across the Foundation Stage*. London: DfEE/Institute of Education.

6 Time to Intervene

Quality First Teaching Isn't Enough

The Need for Targeted Action

In the previous chapter, numerous strategies were outlined for increasing the level of oracy within early years provisions. However, as many children enter school with an already significant language gap, these strategies alone are insufficient for closing the oracy divide. To make any form of substantial impact, targeted and purposeful intervention is needed. Children with large gaps in language development need additional – and earlier – help to acquire the skills and knowledge needed to access learning.

Interventions for speech and language are nothing new; programmes of support have been running for decades with varying degrees of success. Historically, many of these interventions were focused on children with identified speech, language and communication needs (SLCN) which would be considered within the scope of special educational needs (SEND). However, in recent years, the number of children entering early years with poor language levels has significantly grown far beyond the historic numbers who would be considered for such interventions.

The impact of the COVID pandemic has further exacerbated this already growing area of need. This has seen the rise of larger scale programmes of oracy support across the country. One of the most prominent and well-evidenced programmes is the Nuffield Early Language Intervention (NELI); designed by a leading team from the University of Oxford, NELI has become the *'best-evidenced oral language intervention in the world'*.

NELI – Born from a Need for Change

A team of experts, led by Professor Charles Hulme and Professor Maggie Snowling, knew the importance of early identification of language need and giving targeted support for children entering early years with below-expected oracy development. By adapting best practices used by speech and language therapists, a programme of language support was developed that could be run by early years teams across the nation. This was the birth of NELI.

Working with the Education Endowment Foundation (EEF), initial trials showed positive impacts from NELI's implementation, including:

DOI: 10.4324/9781003607595-7

- NELI children making 3–5 months extra progress in a 6-month window
- Disadvantaged children made an average 7 months progress in language development
- Children with EAL made the same additional progress as peers who spoke English at home
- NELI children demonstrated sustained progress two years later in their reading levels
- Behaviour for learning was significantly improved in the NELI controlled group

From 2021, at the start of the pandemic and lockdowns, NELI was rolled out to over 10,000 schools (over a 2-year period). The programme was taken on by Reception classes in many schools and Early Years settings (for 4–5-year olds) and included a full suite of staff training, resourcing, language screening and ongoing support from the NELI organisation.

Whilst not explicitly designed to cater for just the disadvantaged children, the NELI programme has made a substantial contribution towards narrowing the oracy gap. As the oracy need grows in Early Years, so does the need for large-scale interventions such as NELI.

Case Study: The Impact of NELI

School: Nightingale Primary School, Woolwich, South East London
EYFS and Early Language Lead: Chloe Coady

SCHOOL DEMOGRAPHICS

Nightingale Primary School is a one form entry school based in a highly urbanised area of South East London. As Figure 6.1 shows, the school is centred within one of the most deprived areas of the capital (and country) and is a diverse melting pot of cultures, nationalities and communities.

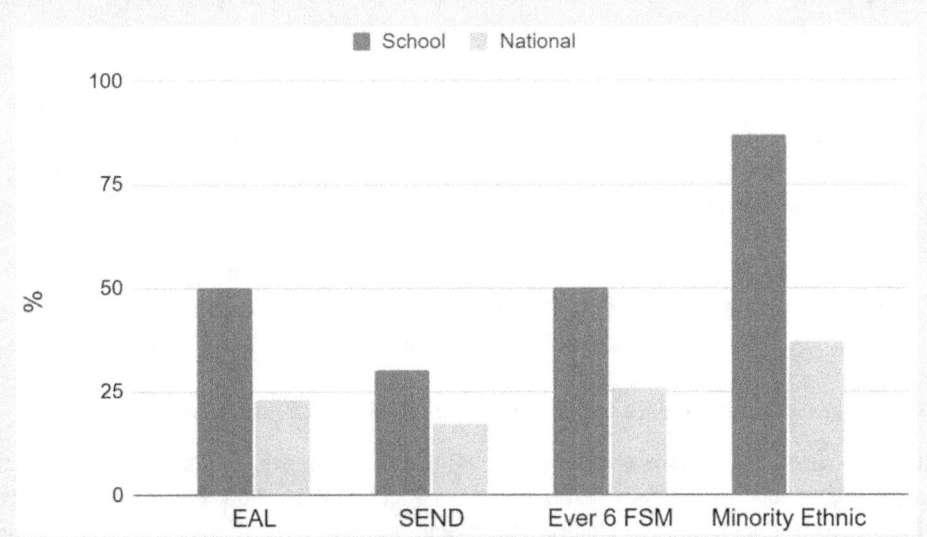

Figure 6.1 Nightingale Primary School demographics.

> Nightingale was selected as a case study due to their successful, albeit with many bumps along the way, implementation of NELI in their early years setting. Chloe Coady, the EYFS lead, reflects on the drivers for starting with NELI, the implementation and impact of the programme as well as the obstacles faced along the journey so far.

Interview with Chloe Coady: Reflections on NELI So Far
Q: What were the driving factors for implementing NELI at Nightingale?

A: Working in an area of high deprivation and high EAL, we always knew that many of our youngest learners entered EYFS with gaps in their language skills; this included early vocabulary acquisition, articulation and spoken fluency. We recognised that NELI was a suitable solution to support us in closing these oracy gaps.

Our baseline data showed that entire cohorts of Reception children were *'working towards'* age-related expectations upon entry into EYFS. The language need was growing year-on-year and we needed to find a different way to address this concern – NELI was our chosen route.

Q: How was NELI launched and embedded into the provision?

A: First introduced in 2020/21, we were early adopters of the EEF's early language recovery programme at the height of the COVID pandemic. During this initial trial phase, we had to be responsive and adapt to the needs of the cohort. Reflecting back on this period, we learnt:

- For children to access the materials assessed during the baseline screening, we needed to expose them to a wider range of unfamiliar vocabulary. Many children lacked the cultural capital and schema to recognise specific vocabulary, and we knew increasing this knowledge was a priority for our most deprived children.
- To address this vocabulary gap, more emphasis was placed upon where vocabulary integrated into the EYFS curriculum. This included reviewing our environments, resources and adult-led interventions to ensure vocabulary was front and centre.
- Staff were upskilled and continuously aware of the tiered vocabulary that needed to be fed into the provision, whether through modelled speech, shared discussion or through play.
- Listening skills were identified as being the weakest aspect of oracy in the baseline. Without listening comprehension, we knew the children would struggle to pick up reading and then writing capabilities as they moved into Key Stage One.

Q: Across the several cohorts trialled, what specific impact has been seen?

A: Through several iterations of NELI over the past 4 to 5 years, we have seen significant positive impact upon the oracy levels of each cohort in Reception. Many of our cohorts enter EYFS with the majority of children not at age-related expectations (ARE). Yet, through rigorous and targeted NELI interventions (alongside language-rich continuous provision), a large number of children graduated from the NELI cycle having met the ARE.

At Nightingale, self-reflection is a pillar of our pedagogy. As an EYFS team, we are constantly reflecting on the successes and challenges of NELI. As a result, we are always looking to refine our approach, and this has meant we have adapted NELI depending on the needs of each cohort. We have even introduced our own unofficial NELI for our Nursery cohort to close gaps prior to Reception – subsequently, NELI released the official Nursery NELI and we are engaging in their trial.

We have seen great gains in more qualitative measures. These include children being:

- More confident in expressing themselves
- Better at recalling narratives in stories
- More able to actively listen to instructions
- Stronger at inference
- More able to articulate their thoughts using tier 2 vocabulary

Q: What were the main challenges that confronted you? How were they overcome?

A: Whilst the outcomes tell a very positive success story, this roll out of NELI wasn't without it's challenges. Like every Early years setting across the country, we are constantly battling with the pressures of staffing, timetabling, data handling and other commonplace daily school challenges.

Some of our main barriers included:

- **Timetabling:** Delivering NELI is time consuming, especially if you want to implement it with fidelity. We run other interventions during the school day too, so balancing time for each within a very busy timetable is never easy. Our solution was to keep the timetable as compact as possible, ensuring all staff work in sync with each other so interventions can be done within their allotted timeframes.
- **Staffing:** Ensuring NELI-trained staff are within the reception class at the right times daily has always been tricky, especially when staff may work part time and varied days of the week. We eventually moved to a model where one member of staff, Julie, took ownership of delivering NELI, and the other staff led on the various interventions (i.e. fine motor skills, phonics, maths).
- **Parental Engagement:** In an area of very high EAL, many parents' own English language levels are limited. To support our families with practice at home, we share key resources via our online platform so they have accessible, bitesize chunks to digest and work on with their child.

Chapter Summary

- Nurturing a language-rich environment is not sufficient for closing the biggest oracy gaps for our most deprived children. Targeted, tangible interventions (such as NELI) are needed to support children in developing a range of oracy skills.

- Comprehensive baselining at the start of the intervention is critical to identifying the most significant needs that need addressing. Accurate baselining helps when measuring progress and impact at the end of the programme.
- With rising pressures upon schools, effectively implementing support such as NELI has become more challenging; finding consistent staffing, space in the timetable and opportunities for staff training are increasingly difficult to put in place

Reflection Questions

- What language specific early language interventions have you implemented in the past few years? What were your key drivers for selecting these interventions?
- How effective have the interventions been for oracy development? How can you measure progress and impact accurately?

7 The Key to Unlocking Learning

Building Solid Foundations

Language has always played a central role in early childhood development, from birth through early parenting and into our Early Years provisions. Parents can become easily fixated upon language milestones for their offspring; tracking when they say their first word, comparing their speech to the children around them, constantly checking for any speech concerns. The past four chapters have laid bare the importance of prioritising oracy development in these first 5 years of life, and this is mirrored in the increasing levels of research and campaigning for early language interventions.

However, children do not become fully fledged orators by the time they turn five. Language acquisition is a continuous process that never ceases and this is most certainly evident as children transition into Key Stage One. The shift from continuous provision into more formal learning, from free flow to set lessons and from carpet to desk can be challenging for many young learners. Possessing strong oracy skills can smooth this transition and unlock learning in many different ways.

Fundamentally, being able to absorb, comprehend and use language can open many learning doors.

Learning through Talk

Learning in Early Years is experiential as children absorb, observe, rehearse and refine their knowledge and skills through a combination of play and adult-led interactions. Transitioning into Year 1 is the first move towards more teacher-led learning models, where the pupil is the recipient of knowledge and teaching rather than the explorer of learning they used to be. This shift can be challenging for many children regardless of oracy, as the change is generally quite abrupt and unnatural for a five year old to understand. However, as will be shown, this transition is far more difficult for children with limited oracy skills.

Table 7.1 is a generalised view of how oracy can unlock learning or, conversely, set a child up for failure. This isn't to claim that a child with stronger language development will not experience any barriers to learning as individuals face a multitude of different challenges, whether it be emotional, cognitive or physical.

DOI: 10.4324/9781003607595-8

Table 7.1 Contrasting strong and weak oracy skills in the Key Stage One classroom

Strong oracy means they...	Weak oracy means they...
Understand the content of each subject being shared	Struggle to understand the content, making them disengaged and falling behind
More easily acquire new vocabulary (tier 2 and tier 3) and can connect it to their prior vocabulary to create new schema	Fail to understand content-specific vocabulary and therefore cannot fully grasp a curriculum topic
Can question and analyse new concepts, deepening their reasoning further and refining their ability to think critically	Develop a shallow understanding of a topic because they do not possess the critical thinking skills to unpick and question
Contribute confidently to class discussions, building self-efficacy and willingness to take risks	Feel reluctant to share within the class, leading to anxiety and poor self-efficacy
Can follow instructions and steps to complete tasks successfully	May misunderstand or just miss key steps in a method or set of instructions
Can actively listen to teacher modelling and thinking aloud, providing them with a rich scaffold to reinforce their understanding of what 'good looks like'	Struggle to listen and understand what the teacher says during modelling, resulting in recall being poor when starting on their independent tasks

In Early Years, the learner's voice is celebrated and encouraged at every possible opportunity. Adults are looking for language, motivating children to speak and tracking their oral development. Yet, as soon as they cross the threshold into the formalised classroom, the focus shifts onto knowledge transfer from teacher to pupil. In recent years, many educators have evolved their practice and pedagogy to move towards a more learner-led approach. However, this takes time, perseverance and leadership buy-in to migrate to a place where the learner is in charge of their own learning.

A good example of this is the proportion of *'teacher-talk'* in any given classroom. Whilst teachers may claim that they have an equal balance of teacher versus learner talk in class, the reality is more stark. John Hattie's (2012) meta-study of many research bases found that teachers dominate classroom discussion at a proportion of between 70 and 80% on average. In fact, his own research showed it to climb as high as 89%. If we want our learners to continue their oracy growth through the Key Stages, providing them with under 30% of talking time is never going to allow them the opportunity to refine their own language base.

Whilst teacher talk is clearly a valuable tool for scaffolding and modelling, those children with weaker oracy will be left behind if they do not possess the space and time to develop their language. Finding a better balance is a priority for every teacher from Reception to Sixth Form if we are to close this oracy divide.

In a similar vein, Wragg and Brown (1993) found that teachers ask a vast number of questions across the school day. Some may be closed, such as:

- Do you understand...?
- Is everyone following me as I model?
- Can you pick your coat off the floor?
- Who needs to sharpen their pencil?

 2 questions per minute

 400 questions per day

 70,000 questions per academic year

 2 to 3 million questions over a teaching career

Figure 7.1 Teacher questioning.

And some are more open-ended, such as:

- Why do you think the animals evolved to suit their habitats?
- How could I convert mixed numbers to improper fractions?
- In your opinion, why is King Henry VIII so well known?

Their research quantified the number of questions to show how even a few questions a minute can cumulate to a giant quantity over the academic year (Figure 7.1).

William (2011) builds on this quantitative study, arguing that, *'it would appear that how much students learn depends more on the quality than the quantity of teacher talk'*. Questioning is a skill that all teachers must learn how to master and use at the right times and right frequency to move learn on or check for understanding. For children who possess limited language skills, a bombardment of questions continuously throughout the school day can lead to extraneous cognitive overload, overwhelming them emotionally, physically and academically.

Understanding Is Everything!

As young babies and toddlers grow, they are constantly connecting new experiences they encounter to their rapidly expanding schema. The more experiences they are immersed in, the broader their network of connected memories and knowledge grows and strengthens.

A prime example is shown when 3- and 4-year olds pick up a book. Some children will be familiar with books, libraries and the concept of reading; they will know how to handle a book, what way round it is held, how to turn pages and follow the text alongside the pictures. On the other hand, a child with no schema of books – possibly due to no books at home, no library visits and/ or no shared reading with parents – finds books almost alien; they hold them upside down, turn pages randomly and do not follow the text as it is being read.

This is one small example of the impact of building cultural capital. Traditionally, cultural capital may be seen as:

- **Visits to museums and art galleries**: fosters curiosity and awareness of the world, history, geography and the arts
- **Outdoor exploration trips e.g. farms, nature reserves, beach:** connects child to the natural world
- **Theatre performances:** develop creativity and appreciation of story telling
- **Community events and festivals:** develops empathy and social understanding of different cultures, faiths and people
- **Library visits:** fosters a love of reading and interest in a wider range of genres

> **Definitions**
>
> - **Cultural Capital** = The accumulation of knowledge, skills, values and experiences that individuals draw upon to succeed, particularly in education, enabling access to opportunities, developing cultural awareness and understand the society they live in.

When children enter primary education, they bring their accumulated cultural capital with them. For our most disadvantaged children, their capital is far lower than their peers, bringing a whole new set of challenges to their learning experience.

Sonia Blandford (2019) argues that the National Curriculum was designed on the knowledge and learning dispositions of the middle classes. Many of the topics and content woven into the curriculum mirrors the cultural experiences of the middle rungs of the social ladder. Blandford states that many of the cultural references found within the SATs tests relate to middle class experiences, from safaris to museum trips; if testing gives these children an unfair advantage, they will find exams easier to grasp and will spend less working memory trying to understand the content. Children with limited cultural schema not only have to comprehend the questions being asked but simultaneously need to familiarise themselves with new concepts.

A core component of building cultural capital is the acquisition of new vocabulary, specifically language related to that experience. For children being exposed to a wide range of new experiences, they will develop a well-rounded, deeper set of vocabulary, such as:

- **Museums:** artifacts, curator, exhibit and conservation
- **Nature reserves:** species, fauna, preservation and fieldwork
- **Theatre:** interval, acts, curtain call and cast
- **Library:** genres, librarian, author and illustrator

But how does knowing these tier 2 and 3 words help with learning?

Imagine a teacher introducing a new topic on animals and their habitats. A child who had visited a wide range of places, from beaches to woodlands, mountain ranges to islands, would possess a firm grounding in how these habitats exist and how they vary from one another. Their lived experience, alongside parents acting as informative *'tour guides'*, will help them put introduced vocabulary into tangible contexts. For example, at the beach, a parent pointing out the rock pools and coastal erosion is helping develop their child's schema immensely.

Without such tangible opportunities to explore and put learning into long term memory, a child will struggle to embed unfamiliar, abstract concepts and tier 3 language into their schema. Just like an expat who is settling into a new country, a learner with narrow cultural capital will struggle to thrive, instead spending time and effort to grapple with new terminology, cultural norms and alien abstractions.

In the words of Sir Francis Bacon back in 1597, *'Knowledge is power'*. Children with cultural knowledge have the upper hand in accessing learning, thus widening the language gap even further.

Being Detectives

Rewind a century or more and the teaching model was a far more linear one, in which the teacher's main responsibility was to impart their wisdom to the listening pupils. Fast forward to the modern classroom and the teacher's role has evolved to become a facilitator of shared learning. Research shows that learners develop their knowledge and skills through a combination of observation, interaction, rehearsal and reflection. For learning to be fully understood and embedded into the long term memory, it needs to be practical, hands-on and active.

In terms of oracy, children need certain language capabilities to engage actively with this model of learning. It is not enough for a child to be able to listen, understand and respond. To truly engage with learning, pupils need to be skilled at analysing, evaluating, reasoning and questioning too.

Benjamin Bloom et al. (1956) led on the design of a taxonomy of learning (see Figure 7.2). This framework (revised in 2001) divides learning into six categories in an attempt to support educators better understand how their pupils learn. Starting at the bottom of the pyramid, each level moves through the learning process from basic recall to more complex knowledge analysis and creation.

For the pupils on the wrong side of the oracy chasm, moving up the tiers of the pyramid becomes increasingly harder. The top half of the pyramid requires a strong grasp of language, vocabulary and contextual knowledge. As Table 7.2 shows, language and learning are closely interwoven; as Professor Neil Mercer reinforces, one side of the oracy coin is *'learning through talk'*. Language is the enabler of learning and in its absence, children will fail to progress.

There is no quick fix to supporting our pupils to climb this pyramid of learning. The language-rich will scale the heights quicker and more confidently than their language-poor peers. The job of the teacher is to scaffold the climb for those stumbling in the foothills. Later

72 *Voices of Opportunity*

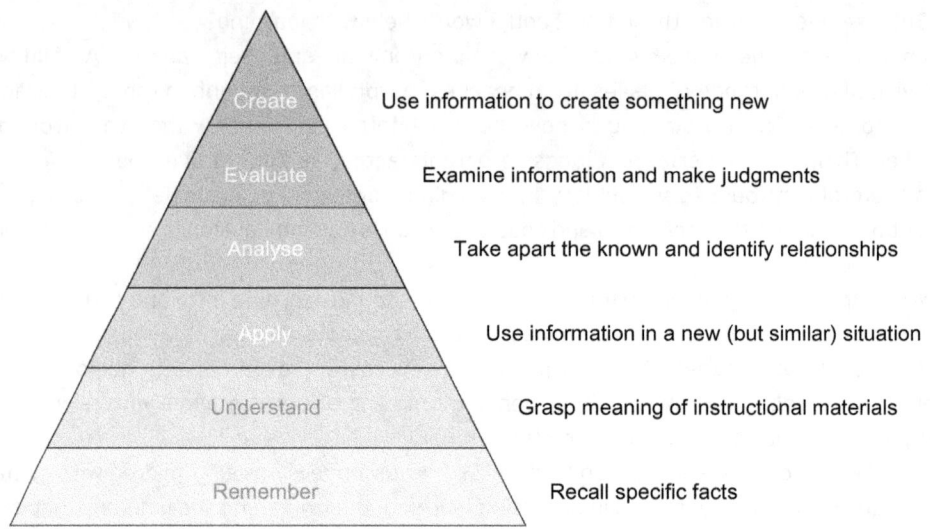

Figure 7.2 Bloom's taxonomy of learning.

Table 7.2 Oracy and Bloom's pyramid

Level	Without strong oracy, it leads to...
Remember	Poor recall due to a lack of active listening capacity
	Inability to accurately articulate what has been learnt
Understand	Difficulty in grasping new concepts, explanations or instructions
	Missed opportunities for clarifying any misconceptions due to lack of ability to articulate concerns
Apply	Challenges when explaining processes or steps to justify answers
	Disengagement when working within groups due to hesitancy contributing (having no 'voice')
Analyse	Inability in breaking new information down into manageable chunks
	Poor articulation of thought process and hence weaker analysis
Evaluate	Struggles when attempting to form coherent arguments or critiques
	Limited ability to compare and contrast differing viewpoints
Create	Challenges to express ideas and creative solutions
	Difficulty working with peers to generate ideas

in this chapter, strategies for boosting oracy along the learning journey will be delved into further.

Facing a Locked Door to Learning

The Impact of Poor Oracy in Class

> Tell me and I forget, teach me and I may remember, involve me and I learn.
>
> Benjamin Franklin

One of America's Founding Fathers recognised the importance of engaging the learner in the act of learning to realise the potential for growth and development. He understood the difference between simply *'talking at'* a pupil versus involving them in the practical application, rehearsal and unpicking of new concepts. Pedagogy has evolved in recent decades to enshrine this ideal of learner participation as a core principle for teachers everywhere. No longer is the teacher solely responsible for the transfer of curriculum content; now, the learner is expected to participate, enquire, challenge, reason and create with the learning. As referred to in Bloom's taxonomy, the learner cannot be an idle passenger but needs to be a co-pilot alongside the teacher.

Franklin's notion poses a problem for children entering the classroom with underdeveloped language capabilities. They lack the oracy to engage purposefully with the teacher's effort to include them in the class learning. This can be for many reasons, as previously stated, such as:

- Cognitive overload as a result of poor comprehension and understanding of key vocabulary
- Limited schema and cultural capital preventing them from grasping new concepts or curriculum content
- Low self-esteem and confidence leading to minimal participation or contributions

The Demographic Makeup Is Evolving

As a result of social, economic and geopolitical changes in the first quarter of the 21st century, the demographic profile of primary school classrooms across the country has been significantly changing. Whilst urban hubs, such as London, Birmingham and Manchester, have long been melting pots of diverse communities, deprivation and migration, there has been a substantial change in profile across the wider national population too.

Looking solely at the Key Stage Two results for 2024, the demographics of this Year 6 cohort showed:

- Over 31% of pupils were considered *'disadvantaged'*, defined by the DfE as, *'those who were registered as eligible for free school meals at any point in the last six years, children looked after by a local authority or have left local authority care in England and Wales through adoption, a special guardianship order, a residence order or a child arrangements order*
- 21% had a special educational need (SEN) – 16% were on SEN support and 5% had an Education, Health and Care Plan (EHCP)
- 23% had English as an Additional Language (EAL) and spoke another language at home

Whilst this book is focused specifically on the oracy gap for the most disadvantaged children, it is important to recognise the various other demographic groups of pupils that face the same challenges with language development. For children who either do not have the benefit of exposure to English language from birth or have a learning need that may prevent them from acquiring stronger oracy, they are also susceptible to falling on the wrong side of the oracy divide. Of course, many of these children may also fall into more than one category although this is not a causal relationship between such factors; for these children, their path to acquiring language is even more strenuous.

What does this mean for a teacher's practice?

This increasingly complex and diverse context of our primary school population only makes the case for more explicit oracy intervention even stronger. Teachers need to acknowledge the value of improving oracy levels, not only for the disadvantaged, but also for the other vulnerable groups who may be SEND and EAL.

Tracking the 3 Rs

This multitude of potential barriers to engagement have been shown to negatively impact the academic performance and progress of these pupils. In the UK, the main areas of academia that are tracked throughout primary education (ages 5 to 11 years old) are reading, writing and maths (nicknamed the '**3 Rs** of **R**eading, w**R**iting and a**R**ithmetic').

Historically, these were assessed as part of the Standardised Assessment Tests (SATs) at the end of Key Stage One (Year 2 for 6 to 7 year olds) and Key Stage Two (Year 6 for 10 to 11 year olds) although the Key Stage One SATs have recently ceased. These three core subjects form the backbone of the National Curriculum and this is often reflected in the substantial amount of time, effort and resource dedicated to these subject disciplines in schools up and down the country.

As will be revealed, the link between poor oracy and poor academic outcomes in the 3Rs is clear to see. The Education Endowment Foundation (2020), in their Key Stage One Literacy Guidance, outline the reciprocal relationship between oral language, reading and writing. They found a widening academic gap in Key Stage One for disadvantaged children as a result of under-developed language. Their report highlights the direct relationship between oracy and reading levels. As many teachers will acknowledge, the ability to read is the key to unlocking learning and poor readers will struggle to access the curriculum.

Poor oracy equals poor reading capability equals lost learning. This all equates to a growing gap as children move up the primary school ladder.

The Data Paints a Worrying Picture

Every primary school across the country not only measures the academic outcomes and progress of their whole Year 6 cohort, but they will be measuring the outcomes of certain vulnerable groups too. These will include measures for:

- Gender
- Children with English as an Additional Language (EAL)
- Children with SEND
- Specific minority groupings (relevant to the local demographics)
- Disadvantaged children

School leadership are held accountable for each group and any significant discrepancies between groups will be scrutinised by Governors, trustees and school improvement partners. This heightened scrutiny can be viewed as a positive way to identify vulnerable groups that require additional, targeted support. To support this benchmarking process, the Department for Education (DfE) provides data analysis for Key Stage Two SATs outcomes, split by pupil characteristic.

> **Definitions**
>
> **Disadvantaged:** defined by the DfE as those who were registered as eligible for FSM at any point in the last 6 years, and children looked after by a LA or who left LA care in England and Wales through adoption, a special guardianship order, a residence order or a child arrangements order.

For disadvantaged children, they have persistently been outperformed by their non-disadvantaged peers. In Figure 7.3, the *'disadvantage gap'* is clearly visible and remains consistently around the 21-22 percentage difference for many years (Social Mobility Commission, 2024). Whilst there was an upwards trend for both pupil groups pre-pandemic, since 2021, the percentage of pupils achieving expected standard (EXS) in reading, writing and maths combined has yet to reach the same heights.

In their 'State of the Nation 2024' report, the Social Mobility Commission calculated that around 114,000 disadvantaged children did not meet the expected standard in 2022/23, and this number has continued to grow since.

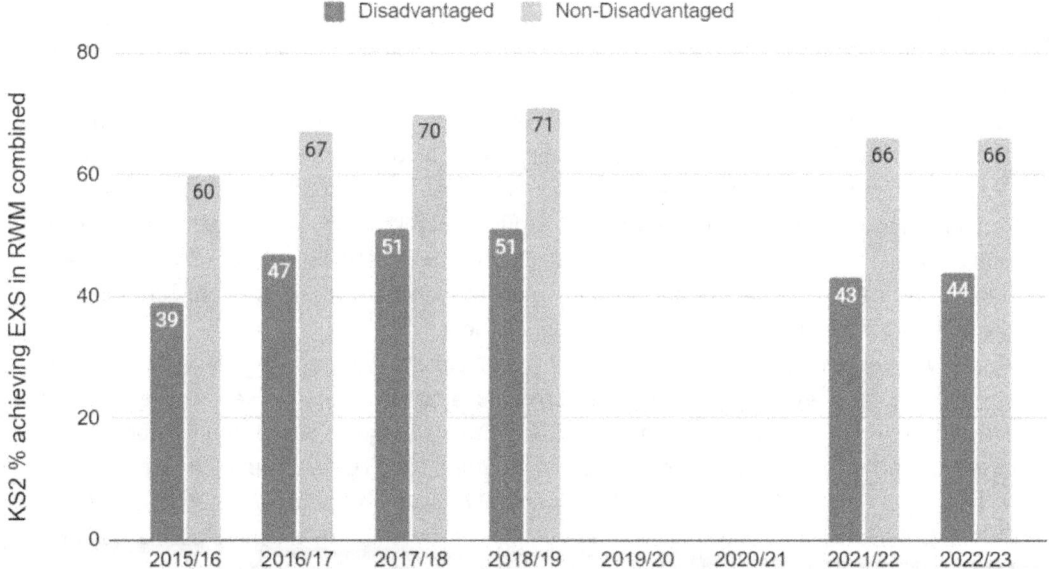

Figure 7.3 Key Stage Two pupils achieving expected standard (EXS) in reading, writing and maths combined.

In later chapters, the domino effect of leaving primary school with poor oracy (alongside poor SATs outcomes) will be examined for its implications for secondary school performance. If Early Years is the foundation for developing those initial learning skills, primary school is the training arena where children need to be strengthening and refining their oracy skills. If we can ensure children leave primary school as confident orators, they will have a far greater chance of future success. However, unlocking this door is no easy feat, especially for those children facing many barriers to learning.

Unlocking the Door

Whilst the oracy gap is clear and easily measurable, the solutions to narrowing this divide is less clear cut. However, even though there is no *'silver bullet'*, there are pedagogical strategies that can start the process of improvement across a school for the immediate. For more detailed, specific strategies, oracy-championing organisations are sharing high quality resources. These bodies include:

- Voice 21
- Oracy Cambridge
- The English Speaking Union (ESU)
- English Speaking Board
- Education Endowment Foundation (EEF)

What follows are some broader, more transferable pedagogical approaches to oracy that can be applied across classrooms, subjects and age phases.

Structured Talk Opportunities

Learning through talk is one side of the oracy *'coin'* that emphasises the importance of placing the learning in the hands (and mouths) of the learners. As an experienced teacher will tell a newcomer to the profession, the teacher should not be working harder than their pupils. Naturally, teachers dominate the conversational space in their classrooms; this can be due to a range of reasons, such as a fear of losing control, uncertainty about how well the knowledge has been absorbed and a lack of awareness around how long they speak for.

Shifting the balance of learning talk from adult to pupil can be far more attainable if some explicit talk strategies are deployed. By planning for purposeful talk to occur within a predefined structure, it is easier for the teacher to ensure learners are increasingly engaged and are able to contribute to the learning in front of them.

Every experienced teacher can tell tales of when class discussions have worked exceptionally well versus when they have been catastrophic; a commonality between these outcomes is how well organised, familiar and modelled the talk structures were. Upon reflection, it is easy to identify the *'weaker'* oracy outcomes resulting from rushed, muddled talk.

Ives and Rana (2018) studied the commonly used *'Initiation, Response, Feedback/ Evaluation'* (IRF or IRE) approach taken by many teachers; in IRF, teachers pose a question, select a single response then they provide their feedback. Their research demonstrated the limitations of IRF/E for equitable oracy, showing how this strategy can disengage many learners who are rarely asked to contribute. Talk structures are an alternative to IRF/E that aim to boost engagement, contributions and interaction.

> **Definitions**
>
> - **Structured talk strategies** = structured, interactive techniques designed to promote pupil engagement, equitable participation and collaborative dialogue to enhance understanding and communication skills in the classroom.
> - **Initiation, Response, Feedback/ Evaluation (IRF/ IRE)** = where the teacher initiates a question or prompt, the pupil responds and the teacher provides feedback to guide learning and extend understanding.

One of the forefathers of structured talk was Dr. Spencer Kagan. Over the past 40 years, Kagan has developed a wide range of talk structures that engage learners in cooperative learning. He categorises teachers into three stereotypes (Table 7.3).

Kagan has designed a multitude of talk structures over recent decades, too many to cover in detail within the parameters of this book. Yet, some of his core talk structures are effective across subjects, phases and settings. Here are some of his key structures that can be deployed to effectively organise oracy within the learning sequence:

Table 7.3 Kagan's three types of teacher for talk

Teacher	Approach to talk	Consequence
A	Poses a question, calls on a named pupil to respond, pupil responds	No interaction between pupils. Pupils seldom raise hands to contribute as the teacher chooses responder, leading to unequal participation and disengagement from many
B	Poses a question then asks pupils to 'talk it over' on their tables (without any specific guidance or structure to adhere to). This is referred to as 'group work'	Anyone in the group can talk as much or as little as they choose. Some pupils remain passive and avoid participation whilst the more confident dominate the discussions
C	Uses specified talk structures to carefully manage pupil interactions	Equalises participation of all pupils. This increases engagement, values all voices and develops healthy dialogue between pupils in a consistent and familiar structure

Source: Kagan (2003).

- **Rally Robin**
  - Just like a tennis rally, partners take turns orally sharing ideas and thoughts to construct a shared list i.e. In pairs, name as many adjectives to describe an elephant as you can in one minute.
  - A great starter to quickly engage the class and acts as a form of quick retrieval practice.
- **RoundRobin** (named differently to round robin)
  - An open-ended question is posed and the children are given time to think of a response. On tables (of ideally 4), pupils take turns to share their responses.
  - Effective way to practice active listening skills and equalise contributions.
- **Think Pair Share**
  - A question is posed and all pupils are given sufficient time to consider their response. Once the thinking time is over, pupils discuss their responses with their allocated partner (saving fuss and time) before pupils are invited to share within larger groups/ whole class.
  - Waiting time makes the question accessible to all pupils, including those with SEND and working memory needs.
  - All pupils have multiple opportunities to reflect, discuss and refine their ideas at the individual, partner and group level.
- **Talking Chips**
  - An open-ended question or discussion point is shared with the class. In groups/ tables, every pupil has one (or two) talking chips (these can be counters or anything to hand). To start the discussion, a child places their chip in the centre and has the chance to share first. Others then add in their chips, one at a time, to add their thoughts, attempting to build upon what they have already heard.
  - Effective way to build active listening, turn taking and the skill of deepening responses.

Whether you use Kagan-specific structures or other forms of talk strategies, the overarching principle is to place the ownership of learning in the hands of the pupils. By providing a framework for talk, it helps to elevate oracy within the learning sequence so that all talk is purposeful for every pupil.

Dialogic Teaching

Dialogic teaching makes use of rich classroom discussions to deepen pupil understanding and enhance critical thinking skills. By encouraging pupils to articulate their ideas, question and reason collaboratively, it supports the building of vocabulary, confidence and communication skills too. The aim is to mirror real-world dialogue and debate, through which all pupils have the safe space within which to rehearse and refine their dialogic skills.

Alexander (2008) outlines the five key principles of dialogic teaching as:

- **Collective** - discussion is inclusive for all to listen to and respond

- **Reciprocal** – pupils can respond to what they hear openly, considering alternative viewpoints to their own
- **Supportive** – dialogue is shared within a safe space, without fear of embarrassment or 'wrong' answers
- **Cumulative** – pupils can build upon responses to deepen learning further and lines of enquiry
- **Purposeful** – everyone is focused on a relevant topic or matter

Dialogic teaching is a cultural shift for teachers and pupils that moves the focus towards a classroom full of rich, purposeful conversation that helps deepen learning. Below are just a few examples of dialogic teaching strategies:

- **Socratic questioning**
    - A teaching method that involves asking questions that encourage learners to deepen their learning and develop critical thinking of a topic. By continued questioning, a teacher's aim is to challenge the pupil's accuracy and completeness of thinking.
    - There are six types of socratic questions (See Table 7.4) that a teacher can consider using throughout a class discussion to engage higher order thinking and deepen understanding as the lesson progresses.
- **Talking points**
    - A statement(s) or prompt is given to small groups for discussion. This can be related to the current (or prior) topic area or even be an unrelated topic if that aim is solely on oracy skills development.

Table 7.4 Socratic questioning

Question type	Example questions
Clarifying thinking and understanding	• Could you give me an example? • Can you explain further…? • What is the problem you are attempting to solve?
Challenging assumptions	• Are you assuming…? • How could you check or disprove this? • What would happen if…?
Examining evidence and rationale	• What makes you say that? • How do you know? • What evidence supports your case?
Considering alternative perspectives	• Are there any alternatives to consider? • Who would be impacted and how would they think? • What is the other side to the argument?
Considering implications and consequences	• How does this affect…? • What if you are incorrect? • What does prior experience tell us may happen?
Meta questions	• Why do you think I asked that question? • What else might I ask next?

- Pupils take turns to agree, disagree and/or build upon the statement, using their schema and justifications to support their point of view.
- Talking points is an effective strategy to practice turn taking, active listening and articulation of reasoning within smaller peer groups.
- The teacher can insert additional prompts during the discussion to reignite discussion and challenge perspectives with alternative evidence.

Thinking Aloud

Teacher modelling is a valuable opportunity for pupils to observe the *'expert in the room'* as they work through the learning. Thinking aloud is a deliberate approach to verbalising the thought processes during the demonstration of a task, making the invisible cognitive strategies far more explicit. If a teacher can show both *'how'* and *'why'* they make certain decisions as they work, pupils can address their own misconceptions or questions about the learning. The verbalised thinking acts as a scaffold for pupil understanding and demystifies more complex methods into smaller, more manageable chunks.

Here are some examples of thinking aloud across different subjects:

- **Reading comprehension**
  - 'Hmm, this word looks tricky. Let me break it into parts: "un" and "known." Oh, it means something I don't know.'
  - 'I wonder what will happen next. The author mentioned a storm earlier – maybe that's a clue.'

- **Maths problem solving**
  - 'I see the question asks for the total cost. I need to add these two numbers first, then subtract the discount.'
  - 'This number doesn't seem to work. Let me go back and check my steps to see where I went wrong.'

- **Writing**
  - 'I'm starting my sentence with "because," but I think it needs a main clause before it. Let me rewrite it.'
  - 'I want to describe the character's feelings here. What's a more vivid word than "happy"? Maybe "ecstatic" or "thrilled."'

- **Science**
  - 'If I add more weight to this side of the scale, I predict it will tip because it's already uneven.'
  - 'This experiment didn't go as planned. I think I might have added too much water. Let's try again with less.'

- **History**
  - 'This source says one thing, but another source contradicts it. I need to think about who wrote it and why.'
  - 'What if I lived during this time period? How would I feel about this way of life?'

Losing Control to Gain Control

As Hattie (2012) points out, many classrooms are filled with the voices of adults not children. To effectively embed oracy strategies such as dialogic teaching or structured talk, the learner needs to be empowered to find their voice. There are many reasons why a teacher may dominate the classroom talk, including

- **Fear of losing control:** letting pupils talk can cause many teachers anxiety about the potential for low level disruption and off-topic chatter. This can lead to the teacher dominating the conversation and disempowering the pupil's voice.
- **Lack of awareness:** some do not realise how much they are talking and may not have the understanding of finding a balance between teacher and pupil talk.
- **Time pressures:** With the squeeze of the modern timetable, teachers can often feel under pressure to *'move learning along'* at the expense of quality, deeper exploratory talk with pupils.
- **Perceived pupil readiness:** due to assumptions or poor formative assessment, teachers may think that pupils lack the readiness and knowledge to engage in meaningful discussion.

Dillon (1983, within Ives and Rana, 2018) identified the reticent nature of teachers to pass control over to their learners. They propose the need for teachers to become less authoritative and develop into the role of *'classroom facilitator'*. This change in role is a substantial cultural and personal shift for most classroom practitioners, as it requires them to step back, handing the reins over to the learners. However, for those who have transitioned successfully into the facilitator space, they will soon witness the benefits of increased learner empowerment, boosted oracy and classroom dialogue.

Interview: Addressing the Oracy Gap

Name: Julie Taylor

Role: Education Lead, Children's Literacy Charity (CLC)

Mini Bio:

Julie Taylor is Education Lead at The Children's Literacy Charity, with expertise as an EAL specialist teacher and literacy lead. She is passionate about storytelling and the link between oracy and reading in developing children's language. Julie created and leads *Story Lab*, an Early Years intervention programme enhancing storytelling, communication, and language. She is committed to inclusive, evidence-informed practice, and champions rich, language-driven learning environments where every child can thrive. Her work is grounded in a belief in the power of books to not only foster a love of reading, but to promote equity, amplify diverse voices, and support social justice from the earliest years. She is also the author of *Start With a Difference: Promoting Race Equality in the Early Years*.

Q: What are the main barriers to oracy for primary school children from disadvantaged backgrounds?
A: Many children are coming into primary school with a noticeable gap in their vocabulary. No longer is it mostly pupils with EAL but it is made up of disadvantaged children who lack the basics of grammar, sentence formation and restricted vocabulary. More concerns are being raised around attention and listening skills; without these, it is almost impossible to develop better oracy.

There are a whole range of reasons for this growing gap in oracy, including: increased screen time, effects of COVID on socialisation and the time poverty of many parents. Without early support, these gaps will only grow wider, making it much harder for these children to catch up.

Q: How are CLC trying to address these oracy gaps?
A: Communication and language is at the forefront of what we do. We've got some great initiatives in place to tackle the oracy gap. For example, we use the Story Lab, which incorporates tools like the Oxford Language Screen to benchmark where children are in their language development. In Key Stage 1, our Literacy Lab supports phonics, reading fluency, comprehension and writing, all of which are connected to building stronger communication skills.

We also emphasise thinking skills as a way to encourage oracy – it gives kids a structured chance to talk and develop ideas. Plus, we run small group sessions and one-to-one tutoring. These setups are great for building confidence and providing direct modelling, so children can see and hear language in action.

Q: What has the impact been so far? Can you share any success stories?
A: For 2023/24, we have supported many children from disadvantaged backgrounds (57% Free School Meals, 54% Pupil Premium) across our programmes. Through our Literacy Labs, 89% of children closed or significantly narrowed their literacy gaps; on average, a child made 4.6 months of progress in a one month period. This was as a result of over 8,000 sessions with nearly 250 children.

In our Reading Labs, children made on average 7 months progress across the duration of the 10 week programme. The children showed an increase in: confidence, self esteem and a love of reading – all of which helped improve in-class engagement too.

Q: How do you engage parents in this mission?
A: We actively involve parents, starting with introductory workshops, where we learn about their child's reading habits and share strategies to help them at home. We end with a celebration assembly where children talk about what they have learnt. This is also an opportunity to speak with parents about the changes they have seen at home in their child's oracy and literacy confidence.

Another key initiative is our Story Lab, where children take home a 'book in a bag' every fortnight. These books mirror the school interventions, so parents can reinforce the same skills at home, which really helps build a stronger partnership between school and home.

We need the school, our tutors and the parents linking together to make it work.

Q: What are the new challenges you are witnessing? How are you adapting to meet these new needs?

A: The COVID pandemic has certainly had an impact on children's oracy without a doubt. There's been a noticeable increase in SEND concerns, especially around communication and language needs, attention and listening skills.

At CLC, we believe early intervention can make a real difference. For some children, what might initially look like a SEND need can be addressed early, bringing them up to age-related expectations. The growing demand is clear – Speech and Language UK reports 1.9 million children with communication challenges. We're committed to tackling this head-on and developing programmes of support that help schools and families.

Chapter Summary

- Learning and oracy are intimately connected to each other; language is a core component of the learning process and without it, pupils will struggle to access new content and fall further behind in their academic development.
- Knowledge is power and developing cultural capital is a process that happens from birth. Disadvantaged children have limited exposure and opportunities to experience the wider world, thus restructuring their cultural capital and making new learning more unfamiliar and difficult to grasp.
- The Matthew Effect is tangible in our current education system – those with weaker oracy at the start will find learning more difficult as they advance through school, widening the disadvantage gap unless intervention is taken early.
- The disadvantage gap at Key Stage Two remains stubborn (at around 22%) and continues to grow as pupils enter secondary education. Early targeted intervention in Early Years is essential to narrow this divide as soon as possible.
- There are strategies to increase oracy and learner-led talk within the classroom. These strategies require a mindset shift for teachers as they transition into the role of facilitator of purposeful dialogue.

Reflection Questions

- Looking at your Key Stage Two outcomes for the last few years, how big is your disadvantage gap? What are you doing to narrow this gap at the different stages of learning (in Early Years, Key Stage One and Key Stage Two)?
- In your own teaching practice, how do you perceive your role in the classroom? What role (facilitator, dominant knowledge sharer, questioner etc) do you inhabit and at what stage of the learning sequence do you switch between roles?
- How do you explicitly plan for, and use, questioning to nurture dialogue and deeper thinking? Is this a school-wide strategy or a personal approach to questioning?

Time to Take Action

Reflect on your own teaching practice. With Bloom's taxonomy in mind, consider how often your teaching and learning incorporates each stage of the pyramid, from remember to create. Rate your practice on a scale from 1 to 10 in terms of the frequency with which each level of learning is actively happening within the classroom (Figure 7.4).

Once rated on each scale, reflect on the questions:

- Where does the majority of your teaching practice lie? Why is this the case?
- What barriers do you encounter that may prevent progression onto the higher stages of the taxonomy pyramid?
- How can improved and increased opportunities for oracy help pupils attain the full taxonomy?

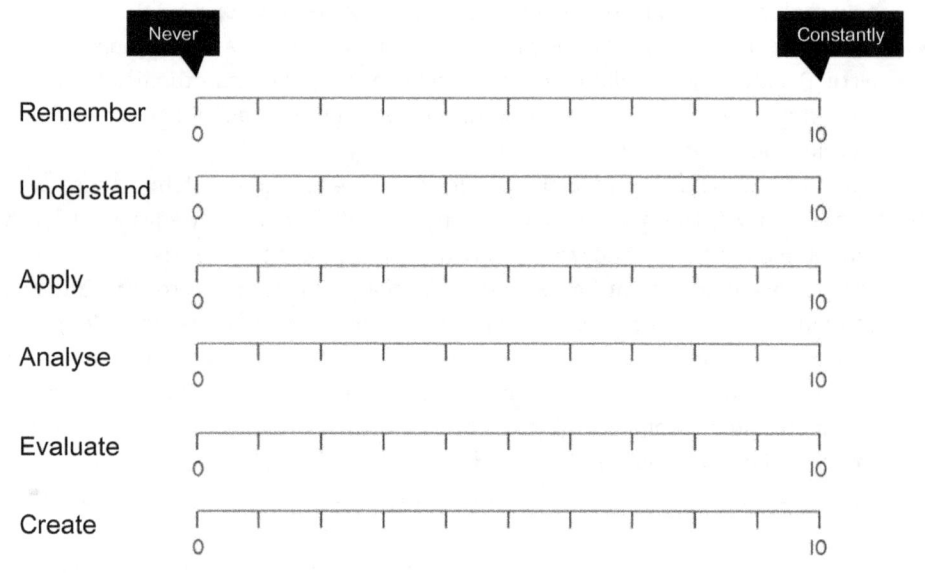

Figure 7.4 Rating practice against Bloom's Taxonomy of Learning.

References

Alexander, R. (2008) *Towards Dialogic Teaching: Rethinking Classroom Talk.* 4th ed. York: Dialogos.
Blandford, S. (2019) *Born to Fail? Social Mobility: A Working Class View.* Suffolk: John Catt Educational.
Bloom, B. S., Engelhart, M. D., Furst, E. J., Hill, W. H. and Krathwohl, D. R. (1956) *Taxonomy of Educational Objectives. Handbook I: Cognitive Domain.* New York: David MacKay Company.

Dillon, J. T. (1983) *Teaching and the Art of Questioning*. Bloomington: Phi Delta Kappa Educational Foundation.
Education Endowment Foundation (2020) *Improving Literacy in Key Stage One: Guidance Report*. Available at: https://educationendowmentfoundation.org.uk/education-evidence/guidance-reports/literacy-ks-1 (Accessed: 29 May 2025).
Hattie, J. (2012) *Visible Learning for Teachers: Maximizing Impact on Learning*. London: Routledge.
Ives, G. and Rana, R. (2018) *Language and Power*. Cambridge: Cambridge University Press.
Jones, K. (2018) *Love to Teach: Research and Resources for Every Classroom*. Woodbridge: John Catt Publications.
Kagan, S. (2003) *A Brief History of Kagan Structures*. San Clemente, CA: Kagan Publishing.
Social Mobility Commission (2024) *State of the Nation 2024: Local to National, Mapping Opportunities for All*. Available at: https://assets.publishing.service.gov.uk/media/66f68e33e84ae1fd8592ea6b/SOTN-2024.pdf (Accessed: 29 May 2025).
William, D. (2011) *Embedded Formative Assessment*. Bloomington, Indiana: Solution Tree.
Wragg, E. and Brown, G. (1993) *Questioning in the Primary Classroom*. London: Routledge.

8 The Vocabulary Gap

Why Vocabulary Matters!

The Enabler of Learning

In the last chapter, oracy was hailed as the key to unlocking learning. The link between academic success and language development is clear to see in practice. If oracy is the enabling factor, vocabulary should be considered the foundation for all learning to be built upon. By definition, vocabulary is all the words an individual can understand and use, whether they are listening, responding or thinking. The broader someone's vocabulary, the greater capacity they have to comprehend, communicate and reason as they learn.

As we will find out as this chapter unfolds, vocabulary acquisition can have a significant impact upon a child's ability to succeed academically; many elements of reading, writing and other subjects are dependent on the understanding and application of key vocabulary.

In the words of British linguist, David Crystal: *'Vocabulary is a matter of word-building as well as word-using'*.

Crystal is highlighting the two-pronged approach to vocabulary as something that can be acquired and stored as well as a word bank to be used in communication. Consequently, the greater the acquisition of new words means the broader the range of language that the individual can insert into their speaking and thinking.

For disadvantaged children, they face many barriers to vocabulary acquisition from birth; this has a compounding effect upon their application of language as they learn. A good metaphor to relate this to would be an artist's palette. An artist who has a wide spectrum of colours, different hues and tones, will be able to create a magnificently vivid and colourful painting. Whereas an artist with a very limited colour selection will be restricted in their creative endeavours. The oracy gap is directly (but not wholly) affected by the vocabulary gap.

> **Definitions**
>
> - **Vocabulary =** All the words known and used by a particular person OR all the words that exist in a particular language/subject

Poor Vocabulary Equals Poor Progress

Block and Mangieri (2006) wrote about the *'vocabulary-enriched classroom'* nearly twenty years ago in an attempt to analyse the importance of vocabulary for learning and strategies to develop vocabulary instruction. They argue that limited vocabulary knowledge can hinder comprehension and impede academic progress. Their claims are supported by numerous studies including:

- **Biemiller and Slonium (2001):** A lack of vocabulary is a key component underlying failure for many pupils, especially for those who are economically disadvantaged. Their study measured the vocabulary acquisition of pupils from different socio-economic backgrounds, finding how those from disadvantaged families fell behind in learning new words as they went through primary education.
- **Hirsch (2003):** Adequate reading comprehension depends on a person already knowing between 90 and 95% of the words in a text. If 90% of words can be understood, the learner can more easily grasp the meaning of the many of the unknown ten percent. Below 90%, and the learner not only struggles to comprehend but also misses the opportunity to discover the meaning of the unfamiliar words too.
- **Chall and Jacobs (2003):** if pupils do not adequately and steadily grow their vocabulary knowledge, reading comprehension will be affected. They found that, as learning becomes more challenging as children move up the age phases, the vocabulary becomes more advanced and harder to grasp. Children with limited initial vocabulary begin to fall behind when more technical words need to be grappled with.
- **National Institute for Literacy (2001):** Good oral vocabulary (words we use in speaking and listening) is linked directly to later success in reading, and pupils who have more vocabulary knowledge in kindergarten become better readers than those who have limited vocabulary.

Whilst most academic research on vocabulary connects it to literacy, this isn't to say that vocabulary does not impact other areas of the curriculum. Every subject domain requires the learner to use a varied set of skills, as laid out in Bloom's taxonomy, and oracy is an ever-present character in these learning journeys.

The Dimensions of Vocabulary

Receptive versus Expressive

Language is a two-way process of communication which has been separated into receptive and expressive language. Jones (2018) defines these two categories as, *'Receptive vocabulary is what we can know and understand. Expressive vocabulary is what we can confidently use in speech and writing.'* In essence, the word *'receptive'* means the ability to receive signals or stimuli which in this context refers to both verbal speech that is heard as well as non-verbal communication that is seen. Whereas *'expressive'* refers to the ability to effectively convey feelings or thoughts to others (Figure 8.1).

Receptive	Expressive
The ability to understand	The ability to communicate
Listening and Reading	Speaking and Writing
First language skill to be developed	Developed after receptive language
Relatively easier to develop	More difficult to develop

Figure 8.1 Receptive versus expressive language.

The Receptive Gap Appears Early On

Young children are linguistic sponges from the womb into early childhood. They absorb language audibly and visually through listening and observing the people and world around them. This is the early development of receptive language which we have covered in Chapter 3 and is such a fundamental influence upon a child's oracy development. The oracy gap first appears through the speed at which children are establishing their receptive language skills, widening considerably by the point at which they enter Early Years.

The ability to actively listen and comprehend are skills that are tested and assessed soon after a child enters the EYFS provision; recent data and teacher voice highlights the decline in attention spans and capacity to follow instructions as a growing concern across the country. As previously explored, a range of socio-economic factors are negatively impacting the receptive language development of our most vulnerable children and this is reflected in the barriers to learning these pupils face in school.

Expressive Language Needs a Secure Receptive Foundation

Whilst receptive language has a head start, it is not a long time before young children begin to develop their expressive language. From the early babbling of babies, through to the repetitive attempts at speech from toddlers, this is a natural process of language development through which children attempt to orally partake in the dialogue around them.

For the most socially disadvantaged families, the weaker foundations of receptive language provide an unstable base for a child's expressive language to bloom. Imagine being given the task of delivering a lecture on quantum physics. However, your basic understanding of the concepts, terminology and schema of this topic is shallow at best. This would significantly hinder your ability to articulate any coherent points, instead leading to extraneous cognitive overload. This is the same for children with underdeveloped receptive language, facing barriers to expression.

Anglin et al. (1993) measured the average receptive and expressive vocabularies of first graders (Year 2 - 6 to 7 years old), and their findings showed that receptive vocabulary exceeds expressive considerably. For a typical 6-7-year-old, they possess between 8,000 and 14,000 words in their receptive vocabulary against an approximate 2,600 words in their expressive vocabulary. This study does not differentiate between those children who are from professional, middle class backgrounds and those who are not, but wider research shows a clear gap in vocabulary between rungs of the social ladder.

> **Definitions**
>
> - **Receptive vocabulary =** The ability to understand language through sounds, words, gestures, movement, signs and symbols. For example, understanding that a green light means go or that a siren means a fire engine is coming.
> - **Expressive vocabulary =** The ability to use words to express thoughts, ideas and feelings.

Expressive Language Needs a Secure Receptive Foundation

Speech and Language UK, a leading charity on language development, sets out key milestones for children's oracy at different ages. For primary school (specifically ages five to seven), they outline the milestones as:

- **Receptive language skills (age 5-7)**
    - Focus on tasks and follow multi-step instructions.
    - Understand stories over several days and grasp synonyms and multiple meanings of words.
    - Comprehend descriptive and emotional words like '*carefully*' or '*surprised.*'
    - Recognise and respond appropriately to longer instructions or narratives.

- **Expressive language skills (age 5-7)**
    - Talk clearly for various purposes, including sharing ideas and solving problems.
    - Use longer, grammatically correct sentences with linking words like '*so*' and '*because.*'
    - Take turns in conversations with adults and peers in different settings.
    - Speak fluently, with clear pronunciation and minimal word errors.

In summary, it is far easier to identify expressive language strengths and gaps, whereas receptive language is a cognitive function that is less visible to observers. As educators, we need to be continuously assessing and considering the potential receptive language gaps in our classrooms. We cannot assume understanding as many children will mask their uncertainty through nods and smiles. Instead, it is important that learning is scaffolded so that vocabulary can form an integral part of the learning process.

The Three Tiers

Vocabulary by definition is a vast landscape of all the words encountered within a language and understood by an individual. Teaching vocabulary can appear daunting within this immense scope and this has led to the development of frameworks to categorise and organise words. Beck and McKeown (2013) first developed the *'tiered system of vocabulary'* (often referred to as the vocabulary pyramid), in which they sorted words into three distinct tiers (Figure 8.2).

Whilst the majority of children will pick up the tier one vocabulary through play and socialisation, there will be a visible gap in the levels of tier two and three vocabulary between pupils. This lack of tiers two and three language is as a result of various factors, some of which have been identified in prior chapters. These can include a lack of shared reading, exposure to fiction and non-fiction texts at home, limited cultural capital and poor verbal modelling between parents and child.

Teaching Tier two and three vocabulary should be an integral part of every lesson, as understanding and using subject-specific vocabulary is as critical in Mathematics as it is in English or History. To engage with the subject matter and connect with its key concepts, processes and systems, learners must first grasp the vocabulary relevant to the discipline they are studying.

The broader a learner's tier two vocabulary, the better equipped they will be to connect learning between subjects and apply their critical thinking skills flexibly. For example, by understanding how to use words such as 'examine', 'compare', 'contrast' and 'evaluate' properly, a learner will be able to understand what needs to be done and apply these words in the

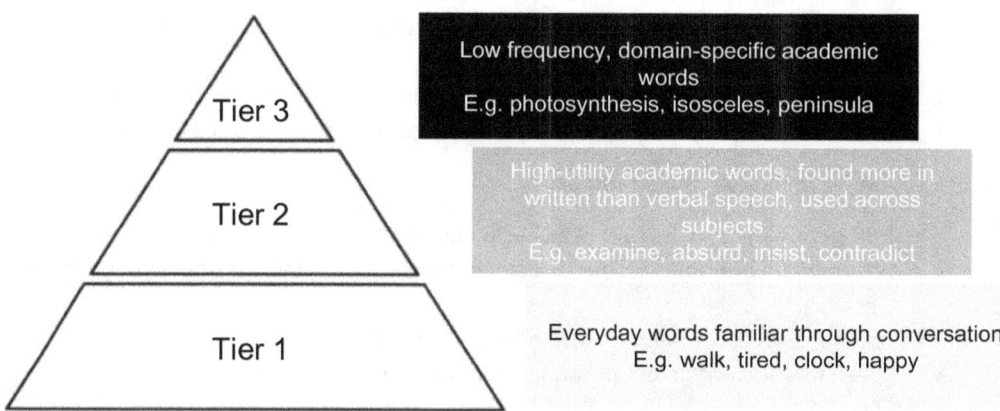

Figure 8.2 Tiers of vocabulary.

right context. Conversely, if a learner does not recognise or fully understand these terms, they will become confused or misled on what a task/ question is asking them to do.

The Lexical Bar

Corson (1985) defines a clear barrier between vocabulary used in *'everyday meaning systems'* (i.e. conversational language) and the vocabulary used in literature and by academics. This lexical bar sits between tier one and the other tiers. Corson claims that learners need to pass this linguistic bar in order to achieve academically. Being able to gain meaning from the written word – books, reports, news, websites, studies, letters and more – is vital for an individual to advance through education and into the working world.

It is the shared responsibility of parents, families and schools to support each child in crossing the threshold into the upper tiers of vocabulary. For the most disadvantaged, they require far more support to enrich their tier two and three language base to avoid hitting the lexical bar.

Bridging the Vocabulary Divide

Explicit Vocabulary Instruction

Vocabulary is not something that can be taught ad hoc and without thought. To narrow the oracy gap, vocabulary needs to be carefully planned for and explicitly taught in lessons. A targeted approach to teaching words directly is required to ensure pupils absorb, understand and can use subject-specific vocabulary effectively. This form of instruction helps bridge the divide between conversational language and academic language (Table 8.1).

Literature Is a Gateway

Tier two vocabulary mainly derives from the written word. This language tends not to be used in conversational dialogue (tier one) but lives within literature of all kinds. Hayes and Ahrens (1988) highlight the importance of reading with children as a gateway into the tier two and three realm; their study showed how books gave children access to more advanced vocabulary that they were unlikely to hear. This is supported by Dawson et al (2021) who argues that books provide a more contextually-diverse environment for words to be learnt in. This *'greater lexical diversity'* within the context of a broader range of known words helps the learner to connect the unfamiliar with their existing knowledge. Remember how many times a young reader is asked to *'read the word in the sentence for context'* to help them infer the meaning.

Hills et al. (2009) studied the way in which readers make semantic associations between new and known vocabulary. This emphasises the importance of exposing children to literature and reading as a means of introducing them to tier two and three vocabulary (Table 8.2).

Word-Learning Strategies

Equipping pupils with word-learning strategies enables them to independently examine and understand new vocabulary. By providing clear strategies for approaching an unfamiliar word, learners can decipher meaning and connect their growing vocabulary with their existing knowledge (Table 8.3).

Table 8.1 Explicit vocabulary instruction

Strategy	Approach	Oracy benefits
Pre-teaching key words	• Prior to a new topic, identify the essential vocabulary (tier 3 for content specific but also any tier 2 for skills application) • Share these words with pupils in advance; this could be as a whole word bank before the topic or on a weekly basis in smaller chunks • When sharing, include the definition, visuals (for dual coding and to support EAL children) and example use in sentences	Reduced cognitive load when learning begins Less unfamiliar words to face during learning Spark interest and curiosity in the topic Better comprehension of the topic matter
Active engagement	• Bring the words to life through interactive activities, such as: • Word maps • Matching games (words with definitions and visuals) • Connecting new words to known vocabulary (root words, synonyms)	Build engagement with topic Develop collaborative learning and exploratory talk around the new vocabulary Activate prior knowledge to make new connections
Repetition and application	• Reinforce vocabulary through repetition over time to mitigate 'the forgetting curve' • Provide multiple opportunities to apply the new vocabulary in different contexts e.g. 'Can you use it in a new sentence?' • Recap the vocabulary in a different topic or curriculum area to reinforce the idea that tier two vocabulary is transferable	Good retrieval practice will enable better recall of vocabulary in the future Many pupils require time and practice to embed vocabulary into long-term memory

Table 8.2 Literature for vocabulary

Strategy	Approach	Oracy benefits
Rich text selection	• Carefully choose the class texts (where relevant) that link to current learning topics • Ensure a range of fiction and non-fiction literature are accessible for free reading time and taking home (especially for those children with limited literature at home) • Review chosen texts to find the key vocabulary from tiers two and three • Select a range of diverse texts that encompass different cultures, faiths and beliefs	Non-fiction texts are a rich source of tier three vocabulary Accessibility to books demonstrates the connection with learning, encouraging curiosity and desire to read deeper More diverse literature helps children relate to their own lives

Table 8.2 (Continued)

Strategy	Approach	Oracy benefits
Contextual vocabulary discussion	• During reading, especially shared, find time to pause and explore the meaning of unfamiliar words • Consider the etymology of words, including roots, prefixes, suffixes, synonyms and antonyms • Model how to explore definitions through dictionaries, online sources and shared discussion • Implement talk structures to discuss potential meanings and draw out existing knowledge within the class • Consider dual coding and physical gestures linked to the new vocabulary	Opportunity to model the process of exploring word meaning Activate prior knowledge to connect new with known words Discovery via shared discussion is a more powerful learning mechanism than simply teacher-shared definition
Creative writing tasks	• Once learnt, provide opportunities for pupils to apply the new word in their own writing • This may take the form of simple sentence forming, creative story writing or persuasive writing	Through application, teachers can assess the pupil's understanding of the vocabulary Application helps to embed the knowledge of the word into long-term memory

Table 8.3
Word-learning strategies

Strategy	Approach	Oracy benefits
Contextual Clue Spotting	• When locating a new word, guide pupils through the process of using the context around the word to determine meaning • Model how to examine surrounding text in the nearby sentence(s) and paragraphs • Encourage pupils to search for other clues such as diagrams, glossaries, captions	Connect to prior knowledge Build awareness of the structural formats of different genres Develop inference skills when examining a page
Morphological awareness	• Model the process of breaking a word down into it's component parts (i.e. root word, prefixes and suffixes) • Focus on the grammatical features, such as prefixes, in class to build pupil understanding of how word meaning changes	Pupil schema can be drawn out to provide partial inference regarding word meaning
Using linguistic tools	• Model and support pupils in using dictionaries and thesauruses to find meaning and synonyms/antonyms of new words • Ensure repeated practice and accessibility of these tools (whether paper or digital) to build familiarity and confidence in using them	Develop independent learning Enriching vocabulary wider as well as linking known language with new, broader vocabulary

Vocabulary across the Wider Curriculum

In a similar vein to oracy, vocabulary should not be limited to English lessons but must be present across the whole curriculum. From maths to science, geography to art, vocabulary is crucial to the development of substantive and disciplinary knowledge. Every topic, concept or skill is underpinned by vocabulary, especially tiers two and three. To master learning, a pupil needs to understand the specific terminology and apply it in their reasoning, problem solving and thought processes.

Acquiring substantive knowledge clearly relies upon the embedding of subject terminology. For example, to describe the process of photosynthesis, a learner would need to know and use key words such as chlorophyll, glucose and aerobic. Similarly, for disciplinary knowledge, vocabulary is fundamental in understanding tasks e.g. to conduct a science experiment, knowing words such as hypothesis, observe and evaluate as necessary.

> ### Definitions
>
> - **Substantive Knowledge =** The content of a subject, or the *'what'* of learning. This is the knowledge of the products of a subject, such as concepts, theories, laws, and models. For example, in geography, substantive knowledge would include understanding tsunamis and rock formations.
> - **Disciplinary Knowledge =** The methods and practices of a subject, or the *'how'* of learning. This is the knowledge of how a subject's knowledge is established, revised and grows. For example, in science, disciplinary knowledge would include learning how scientists use experiments to test hypotheses (Table 8.4).

Table 8.4 Strategies for vocabulary development

Strategy	Approach	Oracy benefits
Subject-specific word banks	• Co-create visual glossaries that can be displayed in the room and in books • Apply dual coding wherever possible to support with recall, especially for pupils with EAL or SEND	Consistent and accessible scaffold that pupils can refer to as and when required Supports ongoing retrieval and embedding of new vocabulary
Contextualised vocabulary tasks	• Within the subject lesson, set up scenarios or problems to be solved collaboratively • Ensure tasks require application of new key vocabulary e.g. Ask the class to *'predict'* in science or to create their own *'hypotheses'* using the key word bank	Acts as a form of formative assessment, as the adults can observe how pupils apply vocabulary and address seen misconceptions
Cross-curricular links	• Highlight any connections between subjects • For example, the word *'environment'* can be seen in science and geography. The word *'medium'* appears in art and maths	Demonstrates the way words can appear in different contexts and how the meaning can vary Encourages pupils to spot overlaps and multiple meanings beyond subject boundaries

Interview: Narrowing the Vocabulary Divide

Name: Andy Sammons

Role: Experienced middle leader, author and Co-Founder of the Making EdTech Work Community

Mini Bio:

Andy Sammons is an experienced school leader with a specialism in English and literacy. As author of The Compassionate Teacher, he has been a prominent voice on teacher wellbeing, empathy and authenticity in education. He has extensive expertise in curriculum and assessment design, particularly within English and whole-school literacy, and has led on strategies that improve outcomes while keeping teaching purposeful and sustainable.

A regular speaker in schools and at conferences, Andy works with leaders and teachers on areas such as disciplinary literacy, the science of reading and the practicalities of embedding research-informed approaches into the classroom. He is also co-founder of the Making EdTech Work community, which helps schools harness technology in ways that genuinely enhance teaching and learning.

Q: What is the biggest challenge for disadvantaged children regarding vocabulary acquisition and application?
A: Without question, everything we are learning about vocabulary acquisition – and language acquisition more broadly – suggests that a confident, reflexive knowledge of words not only enhances children's positive experiences of language but it significantly enhances their opportunities for engaging successfully with new texts, opening them up to whole new worlds of ideas and thinking. Whether it be exposure to millions fewer words by the time they are a toddler, or accumulation of less diverse and enriching experiences, the cumulative impact of that is that disadvantaged children fundamentally have less tools in order to be successful in learning language. That doesn't mean that they can't; it just means that we need to be extremely clear in our planning, vigilant in our monitoring and precise in our interventions.

Q: How have you tried to address this vocabulary gap in your work with schools?
A: Closing vocabulary gaps in schools requires more than isolated interventions – it demands deliberate and purposeful curriculum design. At the heart of this is identifying and sequencing core knowledge concepts so that pupils encounter language within a carefully structured framework. Hirsch reminds us that knowledge and vocabulary are inseparable; if we don't deliberately ground children in the concepts that underpin complex texts, we leave them relying on chance encounters rather than structured learning. By isolating and exploring concepts thoroughly, we enable layered, deliberate learning where vocabulary is revisited and deepened over time.

Consistent reading, both within and beyond the classroom, is equally fundamental. When teachers and adults across the school act as visible reading role models, we create a culture in which vocabulary is not only taught but lived. Beck, McKeown and Kucan show us that explicit, robust vocabulary instruction, coupled with wide reading, accelerates word learning. But this requires healthy accountability – ensuring that reading is prioritised, visible, and embedded across the curriculum, not just an add-on.

Cognitive science strengthens this case. Sweller's work on cognitive load reminds us of the limits of working memory: to maximise retention, we must break down knowledge into component parts, scaffold carefully, and only gradually ease away support. Rosenshine frames this as part of effective instruction: modelling, guided practice, and eventual independence. Adaptive teaching is central here – necessary for some, but beneficial for all – allowing us to balance scaffolding with the gradual promotion of self-efficacy and independence.

Ultimately, closing the vocabulary gap is about purposeful curricular design, a culture of reading that runs through the whole school, and teaching that respects both the science of cognition and the human need for empowerment. When we commit to this, we give children not just words, but access to worlds.

Q: Why is tier 2 and 3 vocabulary so critical for learning? And for well-being?
A: If we don't have a robust, reflective vocabulary, it's impossible to navigate the challenges of the modern world successfully. More so than ever, with Artificial Intelligence becoming increasingly pervasive in our lives, we must remember that those with a strong linguistic foundation – will be in the best position to engage with these tools. Even more fundamentally than that, though, language is about literacy, and it is critical for understanding our own thoughts, feelings and emotions. Humans are fascinatingly complex beings, but we have a very archaic set of hardware in our brains regarding our own social and emotional well-being. Make no mistake: a thorough, robust emotional literacy places us in an immeasurably stronger position to enjoy longer, happier, healthier lives.

Chapter Summary

- Language needs to be understood (receptive) and then applied (expressive). Children from disadvantaged backgrounds have less exposure to rich language and this impacts their receptive, and therefore, expressive vocabulary ranges. As a result, these children will struggle to understand and grasp new learning without the prerequisite vocabulary.
- Vocabulary can be organised into three tiers. Whilst tier one is mainly acquired through conversation, tiers two and three vocabulary needs active engagement to be absorbed. These tiers are essential for better understanding of learning content. For a child with limited opportunities and poor cultural capital, their tiers two and three range of language is less developed than their peers.
- There are a range of vocabulary strategies that can be deployed, including: explicit instruction, prioritising literature in class and developing vocabulary exposure across the curriculum.

Reflection Questions

- How do you explicitly teach vocabulary in your class (or school) for each topic? Is it pre-planned? Does the vocabulary progress up through the key stages?
- Between staff, subject departments and age phases, have you coordinated your tier to and tier three vocabulary to ensure consistency in approach and full coverage?

Time to Take Action

Select one specific topic in your curriculum. Consider the vocabulary that relates to each tier of the vocabulary pyramid and list these words in Figure 8.3.

Consider:

- **Tier 1:** the conversational words they may use to discuss this content outside of academic learning. This is the starting point for identifying how much the class already knows.
- **Tier 2:** the vocabulary that they may use during this topic that they may find useful across other areas of the curriculum. Find words in any related literature for the topic (both fiction and non-fiction) that they may need to understand.
- **Tier 3:** Check for subject-specific terminology in the National Curriculum, any available resources as well as any example texts or reading comprehension passages to be used.

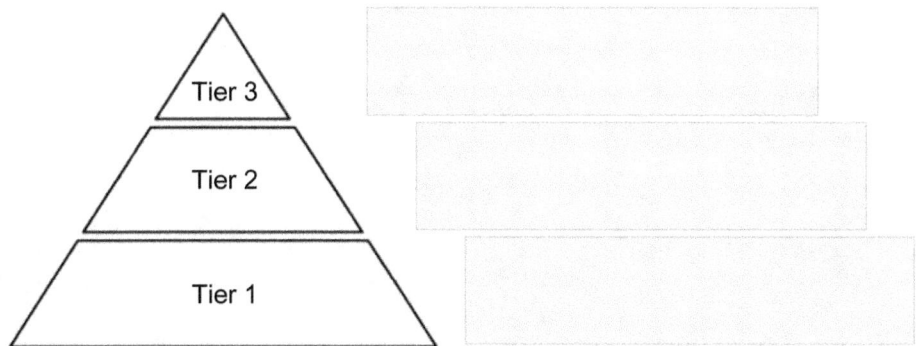

Figure 8.3 A subject-specific pyramid.

References

Anglin, J., Miller, G. and Wakefield, P. (1993) 'Vocabulary Development: A Morphological Analysis', *Monographs of the Society for Research in Child Development*, 58(10), p. 186.

Beck, I. and McKeown, M. (2013) *Bringing Words to Life: Robust Vocabulary Instruction*. Guildford: Guildford Publications.

Biemiller, A. and Slonium, C. (2001) 'Estimating root word vocabulary growth in normative and advantaged populations: Evidence for a common sequence of vocabulary acquisition', *Journal of Educational Psychology*, 93(3), pp. 498–520.

Block, C.C. and Mangieri, J.N. (2006) *The Vocabulary-Enriched Classroom: Practices for Improving the Reading Performance of All Students in Grades 3 and Up*. New York: Scholastic.

Chall, J. and Jacobs, V. (2003) 'Poor children's fourth-grade slump', *American Educator*, Spring.

Corson, D. (1985) 'The Lexical Bar', *Language in Society*, 17(1), pp. 143–146.

Dawson, N., Hsiao, Y., Ming Tan, A. W., Banerji, N. and Nation, K. (2021) 'Language Development Research', *Language Development Research*, 1(1), pp. 9–53.

Hayes, D. and Ahrens, M. (1988) 'Vocabulary simplification for children: A special case of "motherese"?', *Journal of Child Language*, 15, pp. 395–410.

Hills, T. T., Maouene, M., Maouene, J. Sheya, A. and Smith, L. (2009) 'Longitudinal analysis of early semantic networks: Preferential attachment or preferential acquisition?' *Psychological Science*, 20(6), pp. 729–739

Hirsch, E. (2003) 'Reading comprehension requires knowledge – of words and the world: Scientific insights into the fourth-grade slump and the nation's stagnant comprehension scores', *American Educator*, Spring.

Jones, K. (2018) *Love to Teach: Research and Resources for Every Classroom*. Woodbridge: John Catt Publications.

National Institute for Literacy (2001) *Put Reading First: The Research Building Blocks for Teaching Children to Read*. Jessup, MD: National Institute for Literacy.

Speech and Language UK (2024) *5-7 Years*. Available at: https://speechandlanguage.org.uk/educators-and-professionals/ages-and-stages/5-7-years/ (Accessed: 29 May 2025).

9 The Fourth R

The Pandemic Effect

The Absence of Oracy

Oracy was coined by Andrew Wilkinson 60 years ago and has been studied in academic circles over the past half century by theorists, academics and researchers. Historically, there has often been a wall between academics and classroom practitioners; research is conducted and published with limited input from educators and a large amount of this research fails to have impact in the classroom. However, with a range of social and economic factors driving the need for improved oracy, we have started to see the bridging between research and teaching.

Organisations such as the Education Endowment Foundation (EEF), Voice 21 and Oracy Cambridge have sought to bring their research into the modern classroom. As a result of their ongoing research pilots and case studies, they have helped raise the profile of oracy pedagogy in schools. Whilst this started before the COVID pandemic, it was the impact of multiple lockdowns that forced oracy into the spotlight of educators, families and national institutions.

In 2019, an All-Party Parliamentary Group (APPG) titled *'Speak for Change'* (2021) was established to explore the growing need for oracy to be prioritised in schools across the country. The Chair of this APPG, Emma Hardy MP, says:

> When my colleague and I launched this Inquiry in 2019, we said that spoken communication is as vital in the corridors and classrooms of our schools as it is in the committee rooms and chambers of Westminster. Part-way through the Inquiry the classrooms across the country closed and we discovered with even greater clarity what we lose when education is silenced.
>
> (Oracy All-Party Parliamentary Group Inquiry, 2021, p. 4)

Education was silenced.

For so many children from struggling backgrounds, the effects of the lockdowns compounded their already limited opportunities to develop their speaking and listening skills. As outlined in Chapter 2, disadvantaged children faced significant obstacles to oracy when at home, from time poverty to lack of books. Facing isolation from social interaction, with limited access to educational resources or in-person teaching, the *'Covid Impact'* on education has been well documented.

The Department for Education (DfE, 2021, p. 29) found that: 'The extent to which disadvantaged pupils lost learning by the summer term appears to be equivalent to undoing a third of the progress made in the last decade on closing the gap in primary schools'.

This widening divide was widely reported in light of the fallout from the pandemic and went on to drive the national call for change.

A National Call for Change

The APPG report *'Speak for Change'* (2021) finalised its inquiry during the pandemic, adjusting its findings to take into account the academic impact. In their summary, they argue that oracy is *'not fully recognised in our education system'* and we need a *'shift in emphasis with regards to the status of oracy'*. One of their key recommendations is for government and other organisations to play a more coordinated role in building momentum around oracy. Without a national effort, the disadvantage gap will widen further and at an exponential rate. As a result, the last four years has seen a significant shift in energy and dialogue around the importance of oracy.

Time to Walk the Talk

In the early Summer of 2024, the British General Election campaign was in full swing as the political parties shared their manifestos with the electorate. As with every General Election, education formed a core part of these manifestos, with promises for extra funding, solutions to the teacher staffing crisis and other pressing concerns for teachers, leaders and families.

In June 2023, the now Prime Minister, Sir Keir Starmer announced a pledge that he would commit a Labour government to make oracy a priority at all stages of education. He wanted every young person to leave school with the confidence and skills to use their voice to overcome barriers and be successful in adult life.

Labour had placed oracy at the centre of their education promise, acknowledging the need to narrow the language gaps that contribute to social immobility. As Labour entered Government in July 2024, so began the building of relationships between the new Education Minister, DfE and school leaders across the UK. As many voters will know from past experience, election promises are not necessarily guaranteed to turn into government priorities. However, since the arrival of the new Government at Westminster, oracy has received some much needed attention in the form of a new Oracy Education Commission and within the Curriculum and Assessment Review.

We Need to Talk

With the anticipation of a General Election later into 2024, alongside Labour's commitment to oracy, a new independent Commission on the Future of Oracy Education in England was established by Voice 21. The Commission's objective was to produce a set of recommendations

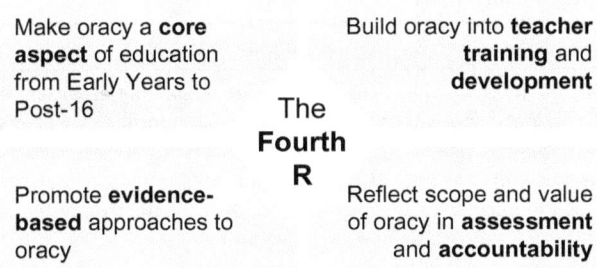

Figure 9.1 We need to talk – recommendations.

that would create a systemic shift in how oracy is valued and delivered across all classrooms nationwide.

The Commission's Chair, Geoff Barton, stresses the importance of placing oracy alongside reading, writing and arithmetic as the *'fourth R'* as it forms, *'an essential, foundational building block to support our young people on their journey towards living fulfilling adult lives'* (Oracy Education Commission, 2024, p. 5). The report goes on to say that there is a broad coalition of support for oracy to be prioritised, stating that *'parents want it, the economy demands it, democracy needs it, teachers welcome it and our children deserve it.'*

The report, published in October 2024, is an extensive review of oracy that covers a wide span of education from Early Years through to employment. Rather than try and paraphrase the substantial evidence base in this chapter, here are the key recommendations proposed by the Commission (see Figure 9.1).

The report's recommendations are far-reaching and cover all corners of education, from CPD through to assessment. As any experienced teacher will tell you, enacting sustainable change in education is never as straightforward as initially anticipated. Change on this scale requires a whole range of enablers, such as sufficient time, funding, staff buy-in, school leadership and effective guidance from Government.

However, there is cause for optimism about the future of oracy. The easily given label of *'fad'* has fallen away from oracy in recent years thanks to the high quality championing and research from multiple organisations, academics and educators. Oracy is now being taken seriously as both an enabler and a barrier to a child's development, and this is being reflected in the way national bodies are investing in oracy programmes. From Voice 21 to the NELI language programme, oracy is starting to receive recognition as a valuable area of learning development.

Curriculum and Assessment Review

With the incoming labour government came an opportunity to pause and reflect on the current state of the education landscape. A core prong in the new Education Minister's multi-faceted approach was a wide-sweeping Curriculum and Assessment Review. As outlined by the Department for Education (DfE) themselves, the main aim of this national review was to, *'ensure that the curriculum balances ambition, relevance, flexibility and inclusivity for all*

Table 9.1 Sutton trust recommendations

Recommendation	Action to Implement
Focus curriculum review on improving life skills like communication, resilience, motivation and confidence for disadvantaged students	Provide opportunities within the school curriculum for life skill development, especially for those with limited extracurricular access
Consult schools on the pros and cons of existing approaches, especially on oracy and speaking skills.	Use insights from both state and private sectors to identify effective methods and lessons learnt
Ensure state school students of all abilities can develop oracy skills, with advanced opportunities for highly able students	Encourage foundational oracy instruction for all and offer equitable access to stretch activities like debating for students from all socioeconomic backgrounds
Fund and evaluate activities improving life skills, including oracy	Support ongoing research and analysis to ensure interventions are effective before scaling nationwide

Source: As per 'Life Lessons' (2024).

children and young people.' Covering Key Stages 1 to 5, the review was seeking to gather a range of views from experts, teachers, education sector stakeholders, parents and young people over an 8-week window of consultation.

The DfE outline their areas of scope and oracy can be mapped closely to many of these identified educational foci. From the focus upon developing foundational skills to ensuring young adults have the attributes to succeed in the workplace, oracy has been recognised as an important factor to examine. So much so that The Sutton Trust (research led by Montacute et al., 2024) identified key recommendations on what aspects of oracy the DfE needed to cover in their review (Table 9.1).

This report underscores the urgent need for the DfE to integrate life skills, particularly oracy, into the review and whatever subsequent actions and initiatives follow in 2025. Its recommendations highlight practical, evidence-based strategies to ensure all pupils, especially those from disadvantaged backgrounds, can access opportunities to develop communication, resilience and confidence.

As with any government promise for change, there is always an air of realism and uncertainty within educational circles as to how promises and reviews translate into positive and sustainable action. It is vital that, after such an extensive and open review process, the recommendations and proposals are properly funded and prioritised during implementation. For oracy to be effectively adopted and embedded into classrooms nationwide, the change must have the support of all stakeholders; ministers, school leaders, classroom teachers, parents and young people all have a say as well as a responsibility to help deliver this change.

Aligning with the Teaching Profession

Undoubtedly, the Government review of the curriculum will produce a long list of desirable actions and initiatives to '*revolutionise*' the way teacher's practice. In terms of school-based oracy, the key stakeholders to bring onboard are the class-based teachers. Being '*at the coal face'* (a common expression used amongst teachers, especially when distinguishing themselves from those far-detached from actual daily teaching practice), teachers are in a prime position to improve the levels of oracy. Without support from the teaching profession, any significant changes to the way oracy integrates into the curriculum will fall at the first hurdle.

Through large-scale sampling, several organisations have been able to collate teacher feedback on the current status of oracy. The Sutton Trust and Teacher Tapp have conducted focus groups and surveys to find out what teachers believe is required for oracy to be effective.

Oracy Is Alive But Not Yet Kicking

Whilst the term *'oracy'* appears to have snuck into the contemporary education conversation in the last few years, the concept of high quality talk has been central to pedagogy and practice for far longer. It is no surprise then that teachers are already aware of, and implementing, a range of oracy strategies. This isn't to state that oracy is well embedded or that the strategies are rooted in a deeper understanding of the theory and cognitive science behind early language development. Yet, it does give a degree of hope and optimism that the teaching profession values oracy and has the desire to use it more effectively.

Figure 9.2 shows survey results from The Sutton Trust in which teachers were asked how frequently and widespread oracy is used in school. The results tell two stories. Firstly, that oracy is being implemented and staff are being trained to a certain extent across many schools. Secondly, however, the relatively low percentages indicate the potential for far more to be done in the oracy CPD and implementation space. As the next section will go on to examine, there are multiple barriers to effective and sustainable implementation.

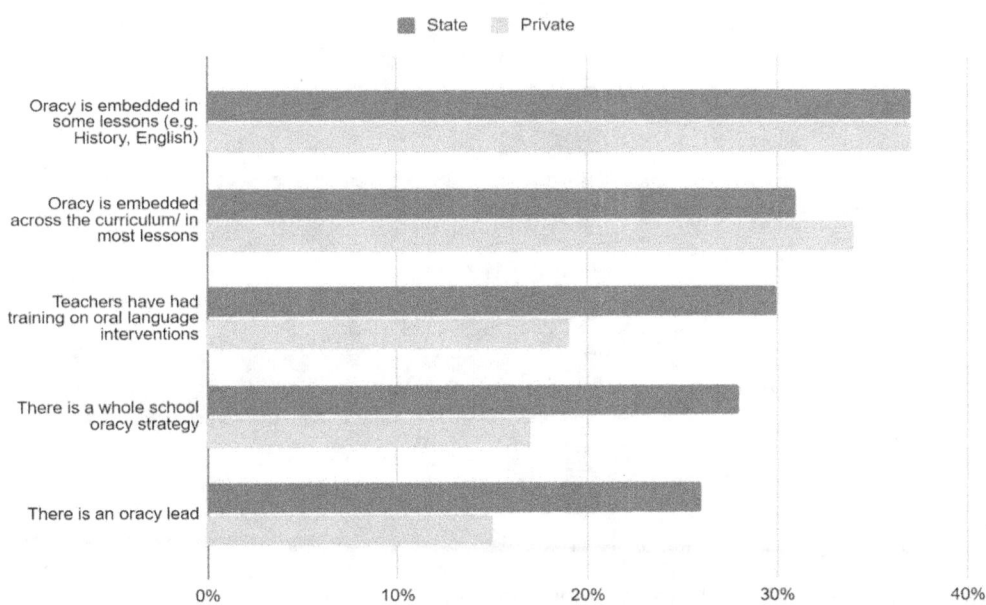

Figure 9.2 Pre-existing oracy within the classroom (Montacute et al., 2024).

This set of results does identify an interesting, and for many, a surprising comparison between state and private schools. Even though the levels of oracy seen across classrooms is relatively even between sectors, there is a significantly larger number of state schools that have already invested in the enabling structures surrounding oracy. It appears that state schools are spending more time and financial resources to implement oracy as a whole-school approach, with the necessary CPD and leadership structure to match.

Making Oracy a Priority

The case for oracy is strong. There is plentiful, high quality research from well respected organisations alongside impact effectiveness reports such as the EEF's. Many academics, educational experts and school leaders are championing the cause and all the evidence points to the fact that oracy and language development can be the key to unlocking wider areas of learning.

So, why do we not see oracy embedded and funded as a crucial part of every school's development plan? Teacher Tapp, a national teacher survey organisation, asked their 12,000 strong teacher audience what they would need to increase the importance of oracy within their schools. Figure 9.3 shows the responses; whilst the frontrunners were the need for professional development and high quality resources, many of the other factors are seemingly

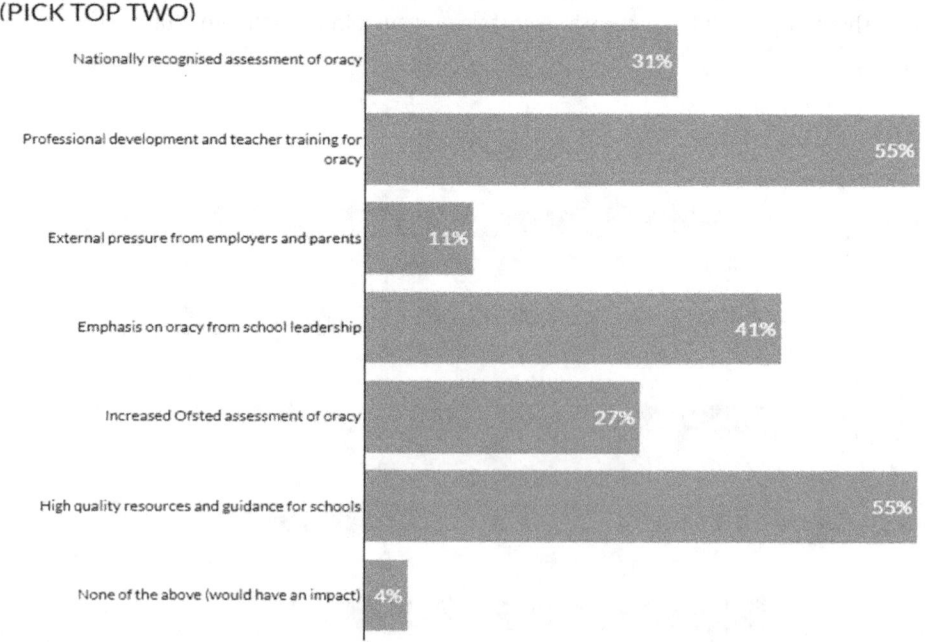

Figure 9.3 Teacher Tapp Survey on prioritising oracy.

just as vital for effective oracy implementation. This is especially true for the value that is placed upon oracy by national bodies (for accreditation and assessment) as well as by in-school leadership. Without leaders driving this forward, any initiatives or attempts at boosting oracy are unlikely to succeed in the longer term.

Finding Barriers to Overcome

In order to make oracy a feasible priority, there are obstacles to work around. Just like any change, especially one that requires a true cultural shift, a multitude of factors need to be addressed for it to be successful. The Sutton Trust's Life Lessons 2024 report identifies the most pressing barriers to oracy as:

- **Teaching time:** 48% said there was insufficient space in the timetable dedicated to oracy interventions and talk strategies
- **Teacher development:** 46% said more funding and capacity to send teachers on suitable oracy training was needed
- **Funding:** If government were to commit additional funding to oracy, 68% of state school senior leaders would like to see additional teacher training, 50% implementation of a whole school oracy strategy, and 30% one to one or small group oracy interventions outside of lessons

These barriers are not unfamiliar to anyone working in schools. With increasingly challenging budget constraints comes the difficulty of financing new initiatives, paying for cover to release staff for CPD and other oracy-related interventions. But if we want oracy to be taken seriously and implemented effectively, there has to be a national shift in our commitments to funding this change.

Chapter Summary

- Academic oracy research, despite its well established history, has often failed to have the desired impact in the classroom due to a disconnect between the academics and the educators. However, recent efforts, driven by organisations such as the EEF, Voice 21 and Oracy Cambridge, have begun to bridge this divide.
- The impact of the COVID lockdowns upon education has further exacerbated the inequities between social groups and this has resulted in growing language gaps. Reports such as the APPG's 'Speak for Change' have highlighted the widening oracy gap for our most disadvantaged children.
- There is a growing movement for change, both nationally and politically. Pledges from the new Government and commitments to oracy becoming a priority signal a shift in national focus. This is backed up by the Curriculum and Assessment Review and the Oracy Education Commission's work in raising the profile of oracy.
- With the drive for change comes, both a sense of optimism as well as trepidation from educators and school leaders. For any sustainable change to be effective, any new initiatives need the appropriate levels of funding and leadership buy-in.

Reflection Questions

- What steps could your school take to prioritise oracy as a key component of its development plan, and how can leadership drive this forward sustainably?
- Are you/your colleagues aware of the recommendations from key reports such as *'We Need to Talk'* and *'Speak for Change'*? If not, how will you share these findings with them in a way that encourages dialogue around oracy in your school?

Time to Take Action

Implementing change can be challenging for the multiple barriers that face schools. The Change Wheel allows you to plan for implementation of oracy-based interventions and initiatives, ensuring consideration for staff, resourcing, CPD and more (Figure 9.4).

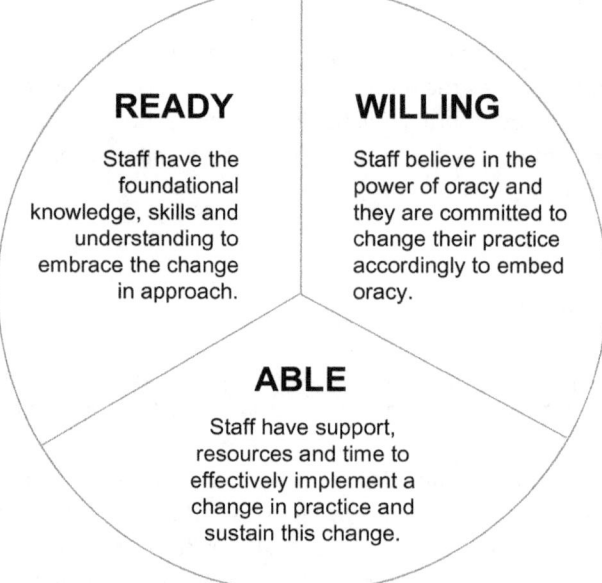

Figure 9.4 The Change Wheel 'Ready, Willing and Able'.

Using the Change Wheel, answer the following:

- **READY:** How can you get staff to better understand what oracy is and how to implement it in their own practice? What initial CPD and training is required for all staff/individuals?

- **WILLING:** How do you communicate the benefits of oracy to staff who may be resistant to change? How do you find champions to advocate for oracy and lead the change?
- **ABLE:** What structures need to be established in terms of staffing, resourcing and funding any initiatives or interventions? What ongoing checks and monitoring is needed to ensure staff are supported?

References

Department for Education (2021) *Understanding Progress in the 2020/21 Academic Year – Findings from the Summer Term and Summary of All Previous Findings*. Available at: https://assets.publishing.service.gov.uk/government/uploads/system/uploads/attachment_data/file/1062286/Understanding_progress_in_the_2020_to_2021_academic_year_Findings_from_the_summer_term_and_summary_of_all_previous_findings.pdf (Accessed: 29 May 2025).

Montacute, R., Holt-White, E. and Carter, G. (2024) *Life Lessons 2024 – The Development of Oracy and Other Life Skills in Schools*. London: The Sutton Trust.

Oracy All-Party Parliamentary Group Inquiry (2021) *Speak For Change – Final Report and Recommendations from the Oracy All-Party Parliamentary Group Inquiry*. Oracy All-Party Parliamentary Group. Available at: www.education-uk.org/documents/pdfs/2021-appg-oracy.pdf (Accessed: 29 May 2025).

Oracy Education Commission (2024) *We Need to Talk: The Report of the Commission on the Future of Oracy Education in England*. Oracy Education Commission.

10 Oracy for Well-being

Beyond Academic Impact

Well-being through Language

Over the past decade, there has been a surge in growth within the academic community on the power of oracy for learning. One side of the oracy coin is *'learning through talk'*, so it is no great surprise that research has heavily focused upon the benefits of oracy interventions for academic outcomes. However, with the definition and scope of oracy broadening and becoming more holistic, attention has been drawn to the impact better oracy can have upon a child's overall development.

Voice 21 and Oracy Cambridge's Oracy Framework (see Chapter One for reference) categorises oracy into four main areas: cognitive, linguistic, physical and social/emotional. This structure helps to show the wide-reaching nature of oral development beyond merely academic success. Ensuring all our children have the oral skills developed sufficiently to engage in social situations should be a priority for them to maintain a healthy sense of well-being, confidence and happiness. These are less quantifiable indicators than academic progress, but are nonetheless just as crucial for a child as they mature into adulthood (Table 10.1).

As this chapter will explore, the oracy gap that exists across social rungs of the *'ladder'* can also be viewed as a *'wellbeing gap'* too. For our most disadvantaged children, who already enter school with a linguistic and cognitive gap to peers, this has been proven to have a knock on effect on their general well-being and mental health in the longer term. If we are to address the disadvantage chasm that is continuing to widen, we need to be prioritising the well-being side to oracy just as much as the learning side.

Early Years: The Foundation of Well-being

The first few years of any child's life are some of the most important for building strong foundations for future growth. This is mirrored in the areas of Early Years that are closely baselined and assessed as children move through Nursery and Reception. Whereas Key Stage One and beyond are predominantly focused upon academic measures (Phonics, SATs, GCSEs, A-Levels and so on), the Early Years goals are far more holistic. There is consensus from

Table 10.1 Well-being in the oracy framework (Voice 21 and Oracy Cambridge)

Framework area	Well-being impact
Cognitive	• Ability to self-regulate independently • Being able to maintain focus and attention • Capable to express thinking and concerns in an articulate manner • Ability to ask questions in order to overcome confusion or frustration
Linguistic	• Ability to understand what is being said to them by others • Wider range of vocabulary with which to express themselves and their emotions
Physical	• Confidence with body language and engagement with others • Ability to speak clearly and project their voice within social situations • Capable of giving eye contact to others whilst in conversation
Social and emotional	• Understanding of social norms i.e. turn taking, conversational speech, which aids with socialising • Development of active listening and empathy towards others • Confidence and self-assurance that their voice is valued and therefore increased contribution within social situations • Ability to express emotions and anxieties to others

across the many stakeholders in this phase – the DfE, academics, Early Years specialists – that children need to develop across a range of different aspects of learning, not limited to the traditional academic measures of *'success'*.

This is demonstrated through the EYFS Areas of Learning that are tracked, with well-being appearing across many of these domains. The obvious area is within the *'Personal, social and emotional development'* (PSE) where it covers:

- Self-regulation
- Managing self
- Building relationships

To be measured as having a *'Good Level of Development'* as they exit Early Years, a child cannot simply demonstrate academic achievement. To be considered ready for Key Stage One, they also need to have developed their social and emotional skills.

Being orally able to express emotions, share thoughts, engage socially and develop healthy friendships within the class is an important aspect of growth that many professionals are raising concerns about at present. Whether as a result of the post-pandemic impacts of lockdowns or the increasingly stretched support for young families, there has been a clear increase in the levels of children being *'unready'* for school.

> **Definitions**
>
> **Well-being –** the state of experiencing good physical, mental and emotional health, enabling individuals to thrive and maintain a sense of balance and fulfillment in life.
> **Self-regulation –** the ability to manage one's emotions, thoughts and behaviours effectively in different situations to achieve goals and adapt to changing circumstances.

Yet there is a reason to be optimistic. Early Years is a period in which a child's brain is *'plastic'* i.e. flexible, and is able to adapt and reorganise to new experiences. If we can address the oracy gap at this stage, we can have a more substantial influence upon our children's well-being.

Earlier the Better

In 2012, a government report was published called, *'Seven Truths About Social Mobility'* in which they review the causes of social mobility (or lack of) and recommend policy changes to be made by policy-makers. Sonia Blandford (2019) delves into this reports findings on the importance of Early years for social mobility, in which it claims that:

- The 0 to 3 age phase is the point of greatest leverage, primarily within the home environment
- Key positive factors include: healthy pregnancy, early attachment, warm relationships, interest and engagement from parents at home

Blandford goes on to explain how emotional well-being, resilience and social skills are also critically developed in this early window of childhood. This emphasis upon early well-being is carried through into Early Years settings, where the Leuven scale (see prior chapter on the importance of Early Years) is used as a tool to measure and track every child's levels of well-being and engagement. If children lack the oracy skills, they will struggle to express their feelings, instead resorting to less mature responses of tantrums, physical reactions and non-verbal outbursts. Bryce-Clegg (2015) reinforces the need to develop oracy as a means to build self-assurance and confidence within our children.

As educators, we possess little to no control over a child's development in the years prior to them entering school. However, within our remit is the ability to structure our provisions to allow children the opportunity to feel happy, engaged and able to express themselves freely. In the following chapter, strategies to boost well-being will be shared but, before that point, it is important to identify how limited oracy can negatively affect a child's sense of well-being (Table 10.2).

Ask teachers across all age ranges, from Early Years to Secondary, and they will be able to recognise these behaviours in their pupils. Whilst every teacher has to contend with the challenges of pupil's confidence, resilience and emotional regulation, it is within the earliest stages that we can have the greatest influence upon a child's well-being and coping mechanisms.

The Importance of Play

To outsiders, any Early Years provision is seemingly a space full of chaos mixed with a healthy dose of children playing. To any practitioner within this critical phase, there is method to the apparent madness and the play is an essential, and planned for, aspect of the way the children interact within the provision. Play provides a safe space for young children to learn and explore different ways to manage their emotions, helping them to develop resilience as well as empathy towards others. The UN Convention on the Rights of a Child (UNCRC)

Table 10.2 The impact of oracy on well-being in Early Years

Well-being	Limited oracy impact	Strong oracy impact
Emotional Regulation	Limited ability to express emotions, leading to crying, physical outbursts and/or withdrawal Heightened emotional frustration due to low vocabulary, leading to unmet needs and therefore frustration and anger Difficulty with self-soothing as they are unable to talk to themselves about their emotions, relying instead upon external comfort or escalation of reactions	Ability to express emotions and articulate thoughts which can reduce frustration and ensure appropriate adult help is provided Improved self-calming techniques to help a child manage their emotions through talk
Social interaction	Struggle to form peer relationships as they misinterpret peer intentions, leading to conflict or confusion Isolation from social activities due to avoidance, reluctance or the inability to engage verbally within the activity Missed opportunities for empathy development as poor oracy limits ability to role play or use imagination in shared play	Stronger peer relationships as enhanced oracy helps to build bonds and solve conflicts Greater capacity for empathy through conversation, role play and shared interactions where the child can understand and respond to the feelings of others
Building Resilience	Inability to verbalise challenges, leading to stress being internalised and a lack of coping mechanisms Low confidence in problem solving as they are unable to request help or articulate solutions which raises dependence on others Increased risk of anxiety and withdrawal when problems are too challenging	Confident problem solving through discussion of challenges, seeking help when needed and building a sense of independence Increased perseverance through verbalising struggles and being able to understand encouragement and feedback

Article 31 even formally recognises the innate benefits that play can bring to a child's healthy development.

By facing challenging situations within a safe environment, children learn to adapt and learn from their setbacks. By engaging in different forms of plays, whether imaginative, energetic or collaborative, they are able to develop key life skills such as compassion, social interaction and effective communication. When coupled with stronger oracy, the benefits of play are amplified; children can use their language skills to engage meaningfully in play with peers. For those with limited oracy, they will not realise the potential benefits of play to the same extent. Together, play and oracy lay a strong foundation for emotional, social well-being.

Alistair Bryce-Clegg (2015) is a vocal advocate for creating opportunities for children to learn through play and he champions the impact play can have upon a child's well-being. He identifies role play as an effective strand of play that utilities oracy in a range of ways. Role play is far more than simply '*pretending*' and '*dressing up*'. With the capacity to communicate, role play enables children to:

- Rehearse social situations within a safe space. By role playing emotional reactions, including confrontation, disagreement, miscommunication and empathy, children can test out their own responses.
- Role play allows children to safely navigate challenging scenarios, building self-assurance and teaching them how to recover from setbacks.
- Through collaborative play, children practice turn-taking, active listening and effective communication, which are all critical for forming and maintaining healthy relationships.

For the most disadvantaged children, they need that extra support to ensure they have the right tools to engage in purposeful play. With limited oracy, low vocabulary and a lack of exposure to social situations, many children struggle to play well, and this has a clear impact upon their general well-being. The correlation between oracy, play and well-being is well documented but more needs to be done to address this inequity during the Early Years stage.

A Gap in Well-being

The Snowball Effect: Disadvantage and Well-being

The connection between oracy and well-being is clearly visible in Early Years settings. Poor oracy and limited social skills places a large barrier between the child and the rich benefits that play and social interaction brings. However, the link between advanced language skills and a child's holistic sense of well-being is not restricted to the foundation stage. In fact, there is a snowball effect of the early symptoms of poor oracy rolling into a larger, more entrenched '*boulder*' of well-being concerns as a child grows.

Across all Key Stages, from Year 1 to Year 13, there are pupils whose well-being is suffering; whilst oracy is not the only root cause for this, as educators we can certainly use oracy interventions to support these most vulnerable children.

When considering the domains of well-being (see Figure 10.1), we can start to identify areas where oracy influences an individual's ability to thrive and maintain a healthy body and mind. For children and young adults who struggle with these domains as a result of poor language development, it can lead to more deep-rooted mental health concerns as they mature into adulthood. Schools have a responsibility to nurture every pupil's sense of well-being so that they can enter society and the workplace as active, healthy participants.

Confidence and Self-efficacy

In an earlier chapter, Maslow's hierarchy of needs was examined in terms of a child's basic needs being met (or for many, unmet). However, the aspiration must be for every child to climb beyond the lower levels of this pyramid, towards self-fulfillment. The shift from survival to nurturing well-being is evident in the progression up Maslow's hierarchy. The pinnacle of '*self-actualisation*' i.e. meeting one's full potential in life requires an individual to possess a high degree of confidence and self-efficacy in their own abilities.

There is a clear link between levels of oracy and confidence to participate within school. Many private schools invest time and effort into building their pupils' confidence and self-efficacy levels; this can be seen through their participation in debating competitions, public-speaking events and other similar opportunities for children to hone their articulation skills.

Oracy for Well-being 113

Figure 10.1 Domains of well-being.

Geoff Barton, General Secretary of the ASCL and Chair of the Oracy Education Commission, recognised the overrepresentation of independent schools on the debating circuit. He said *that when he took students on the debating competitions, they were mostly surrounded by children from independent and private schools. This gave him the mission mission to make sure that children in his school (and similar) get equitable access to what is essentially the language of power* (Table 10.3).

Barton goes on to advocate for oracy to act as the bridge between confidence and social mobility. By equipping children, especially those from disadvantaged backgrounds, with the vocabulary and articulation skills to debate and verbalise their opinions aloud, we provide them with a better foundation on which to develop their confidence. And through this growing confidence, they will be able to reap the well-being benefits of healthier relationships, active contributions to society and ultimately fulfil their potential.

Definitions

- **Confidence** – belief and self-assurance in one's own abilities
- **Self efficacy** – beliefs about one's ability to effectively perform the tasks needed to attain a valued goal
- **Sense of belonging** – feeling accepted, included and connected to a group of people, a community, or a place, where you feel like you are a valued part of something larger than yourself
- **Social connectedness** – the experience of feeling close and connected to others. It involves feeling loved, cared for, and valued.

Table 10.3 Impact of oracy on confidence and self-efficacy

Impact of poor oracy	Impact of strong oracy
Fear of speaking up: avoids responding, hides from discussions, becomes disengaged	**Willingness to engage:** Actively contributes, shared ideas, knows their opinions are valued
Limited self-expression: struggles to articulate thoughts, leading to frustration, withdrawal or physical reactions	**Improved emotional regulation:** able to express emotions and thoughts, leading to reduced anxiety or stress
Negative peer perceptions: socially excluded due to difficulty communicating with peers, leading to potential teasing, bullying and isolation	**Stronger social connections:** able to build better relationships and friend networks, developing a stronger sense of belonging
Reduced risk-taking: more hesitant to try new challenges due to social anxiety, leading to further withdrawal	**More confident in new opportunities:** develop a wider range of skills and experiences through taking chances
Lower aspirations: struggles with communication in interviews, networking and persuasive language, limiting higher education and career opportunities	**Increased future prospects:** stronger communication coupled with self-efficacy leading to more opportunities in education and career

Social Connectedness

Alongside the aim for our children to be confident orators is the need to ensure they have the social skills required to build and maintain healthy relationships. '*Social connectedness*' refers to the feeling of belonging and a sense of connection to those around you. Developing these healthy, sustainable relationships is only possible through the development of a wide range of social interactions and the ability for an individual to use language to communicate with others. This need for oracy harks back to the theoretical standpoints of Bruner and others who highlighted the importance of language as a vehicle for social interaction.

The Oracy All Party Parliamentary Group (APPG) inquiry (2021) points to an '*urgent and pressing need, post-lockdown, to prioritise oracy in schools*'. Within this landmark report, a teacher is quoted as saying, '*Oracy heightens a community's ability to belong to each other, whilst valuing individuality. It makes every voice matter; these processes are built on the principles of a democratic society.*' Fostering a sense of belonging is crucial to address the growing concerns around social isolation and detachment in children and young adults; the collective nature of talk can help counter these negative feelings by supporting vulnerable children in building and sustaining relationships (Oracy Education Commission, 2024).

This need for social connectedness links to multiple domains of well-being, from social to societal, and schools need to have this identified as a priority for their most disadvantaged and vulnerable learners. The National Literacy Trust (2024, p. 15) reinforces the importance of spoken language for, 'successfully navigating social interactions and different cultural contexts. Strong oracy skills enable children and young people to express their feelings, advocate for their beliefs and build and maintain healthy relationships' (Figure 10.2).

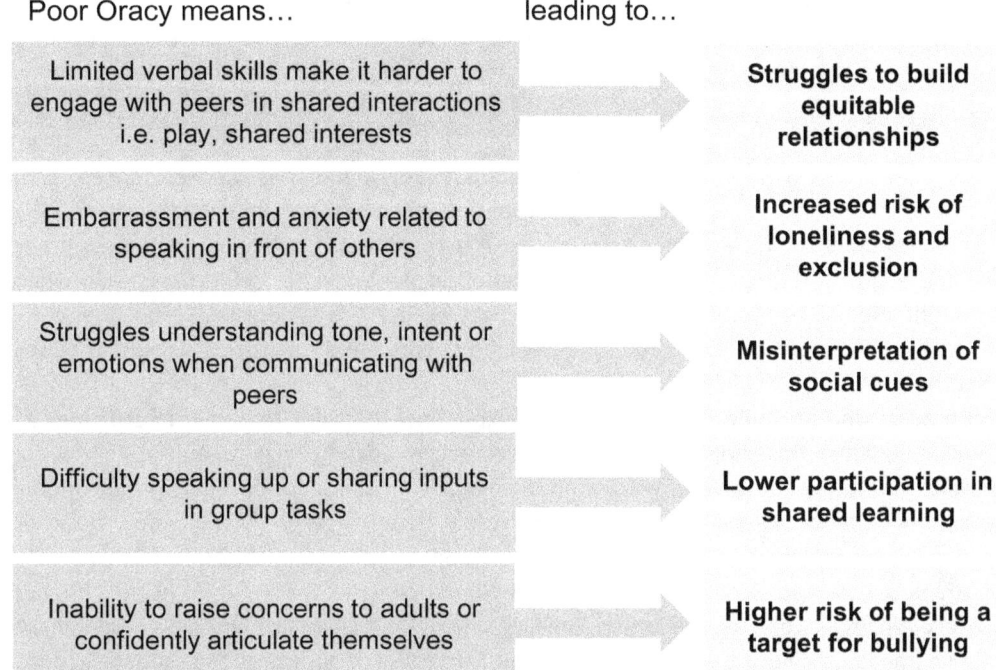

Figure 10.2 Oracy and social connectedness.

What may appear as minor social *'awkwardness'* or shyness in a young child, if not addressed early on, can grow into a more substantial and harmful mental health crisis in adolescence. Equipping the most vulnerable children with the language tools they need to become socially active and connected to others must be a priority for all educational institutions, from Early Years to Primary and into Secondary. Otherwise, the already growing mental health crisis seen across our Secondary school system will continue to swell beyond control.

Mental Health: A Growing Crisis for Children

In recent years, mental health concerns have worsened significantly amongst children and young people, with rising levels of anxiety, depression and self-harm. The NHS (2023) reports that 20% of children and young people now experience a probable mental disorder; this is a sharp increase from previous years. Schools, who play a crucial role in supporting the well-being of pupils, are struggling to meet the increasing demands for mental health support, with many young people feeling their needs are unmet.

A study the mental health charity Mind (2023) found that:

- 78% of young people felt school had made their mental health worse
- 96% reported that their mental health had impacted their academic work
- 25% of school staff reported concerns of pupils being excluded as a direct result of mental health struggles

These statistics paint a worrying picture of mental health within the education system. Without appropriate levels of support in place, these challenges can negatively impact a young person in the long term, in terms of academic achievement, employment and overall well-being.

So how does this relate to oracy?

The link between mental health and language development is well evidenced, with poor communication skills significantly increasing the risk of mental health crisis. The Communications Trust (Gascoigne and Gross, 2017) found that young people with poor oracy are one and a half times more likely to experience mental health difficulties, even when accounting for other factors influencing their way of life. This is because verbal communication is vital for articulating emotions, seeking support and navigating social situations effectively.

Children who struggle with oracy often experience barriers to social interaction, as detailed earlier in this chapter. From embarrassment to anxiety, physical outbursts to withdrawal, poor oracy can severely affect an individual's mental state of mind. In educational settings, these behaviours can be misunderstood as defiance or disengagement, rather than being recognised as symptoms of underdeveloped oracy. Mind (2023) found that 48% of young people had been punished for behaviours linked to their mental health, further exacerbating the problem. In addition, 56% of school staff claimed that pupils who did not receive adequate support would engage in self harm; this underscores the urgent need for oracy to be prioritised as a crucial component in the mental health space.

As discussed throughout this book so far, poor oracy has a strong correlation to deprivation and disadvantage. This is seen in higher levels of mental health concerns appearing amongst lower-income pupils. Research by Gutman et al. (2015) found that the most disadvantaged children were 4.5 times more likely to suffer severe mental health problems compared to better off peers. Many of these young people come from language-poor home environments and lack the oral skills of expression and emotional regulation.

Social inequalities further contribute to this crisis, with 70% of young people who experienced racism in school reporting a negative impact on their well-being (Mind, 2023). Without strong communication skills, these children may struggle to advocate for themselves, seek emotional support, or develop resilience in the face of adversity. Addressing the oracy gap is therefore not just an academic concern, but a vital step in ensuring that all children – particularly those from disadvantaged backgrounds – have the tools they need to maintain positive mental health and emotional well-being.

Chapter Summary

- Early oracy development is foundational in ensuring our youngest children are able to emotionally regulate and express a wide range of feelings verbally. This can be supported through a multitude of approaches, including role play, small world simulation and social interactions within a safe space.

- As children grow and develop into young adults, their levels of oracy can directly affect their confidence and social connectedness. For those with weaker language skills, they may become withdrawn, isolated and anxious at school, leading to a decline in well-being.
- There is a growing mental health crisis within our younger population and oracy is not only a cause but a possible solution. For the most disadvantaged children, their oracy gap can often act as a catalyst for worsening mental health and this has been well reported amongst this social demographic in recent years.

Reflection Questions

- How do your Early Years teams consider the relationship between low oracy and non-verbal reactions i.e. physical outbursts, emotional disregulation?
- Can you identify an individual(s) whose behaviours in class are symptoms of weaker oracy levels?
- As a school, what strategies do you have in place to support children with anxieties, low self-efficacy and reduced confidence? How do you focus on developing their oracy to address these mental health concerns?

Time to Take Action

Consider two pupils in your class/school, one with strong oracy skills and one with poorer oracy. Reflecting on both, spend some time looking at the link between their oracy and well-being (Table 10.4).

For Pupil B, what can you do to support their well-being through oracy intervention?

Table 10.4 Comparing pupil oracy skills for emotional regulation

How does their oracy support/hinder their	Pupil A (strong oracy)	Pupil B (weak oracy)
Confidence and self-efficacy?		
Social connectedness and ability to build and sustain healthy relationships?		
Ability to express emotion and self regulate?		

References

Blandford, S. (2019) *Born to Fail? Social Mobility: A Working Class View*. Suffolk: John Catt Educational.

Bryce-Clegg, A. (2015) *Best Practice in the Early Years*. London: Bloomsbury.

Gascoigne, M. and Gross, J. (2017) *Talking About a Generation*. The Communications Trust. Available at: www.bettercommunication.org.uk/tct_talkingaboutageneration_report_online_update.pdf (Accessed: 29 May 2025).

Gutman, L., Joshi, H., Parsonage, M and Schoon, I. (2015) *Children of the New Century: Mental Health Findings from the Millennium Cohort Study*. London: Centre for Mental Health.

Mind (2023) *Not Making the Grade: Why Our Approach to Mental Health at Secondary School is Failing Young People*. London: Mind.

National Literacy Trust (2024) *Creating confident communicators: How the government can help every child find their voice*. London: National Literacy Trust. Available at: https://nlt.cdn.ngo/media/documents/Creating_confident_communicators_-_How_the_government_can_help_every_child_fin_4zRs95n.pdf (Accessed: 15 August 2025])

NHS (2023) *Mental Health of Children and Young People in England, 2023 – Wave 4 Follow Up to the 2017 Survey*. London: NHS Digital Publications.

Oracy All-Party Parliamentary Group Inquiry (2021) *Speak For Change – Final Report and Recommendations from the Oracy All-Party Parliamentary Group Inquiry*. Oracy All-Party Parliamentary Group. Available at: www.education-uk.org/documents/pdfs/2021-appg-oracy.pdf (Accessed: 29 May 2025).

Oracy Education Commission (2024) *We Need to Talk: The Report of the Commission on the Future of Oracy Education in England*. Oracy Education Commission.

11 Leveraging Oracy for Well-being

A Safe Place to Talk

Safe to Speak

Maslow's hierarchy of needs reminds us that for a child to reach the higher tiers – self-esteem, belonging and self-actualisation – their foundational needs must first be met. Beyond essential physiological needs such as food, shelter and warmth, a sense of safety is paramount. In schools, this extends beyond physical security to emotional and psychological safety. If children feel anxious, unheard or fearful of judgment, their ability to engage, learn and develop a sense of self-efficacy is significantly hindered. Schools must be proactive in creating environments where pupils feel secure enough to express themselves openly.

A classroom should be a sanctuary where every pupil feels able to share their thoughts, opinions and questions without fear of embarrassment or dismissal. When children trust that their voice will be heard and valued, they are far more likely to contribute. This helps deepen both their academic understanding and their overall well-being. This creates a *virtuous cycle of oracy and well-being* (see Figure 11.1), where increased confidence in speaking leads to greater classroom engagement, which in turn fosters a stronger sense of self-esteem and belonging.

However, cultivating this kind of safe space is no small task – particularly in classrooms filled with young people at vastly different stages of oracy development, emotional maturity and lived experiences. Whether they are three or fifteen, children need to believe they can speak freely and be met with respect, both from peers and adults. This is a challenge faced by teachers worldwide, but it is also a non-negotiable. If we want our young people to thrive, we must ensure that classrooms become environments where purposeful talk is not only encouraged but embedded into everyday learning and interaction.

Nurturing a School Where Talk Can Flourish

Every school will have a set of values that it promotes and celebrates. They often range from academic values (such as excellence and aspiration) to personality (such as determination and resilience) to social (such as respect and empathy). If we want oracy and well-being to

DOI: 10.4324/9781003607595-12

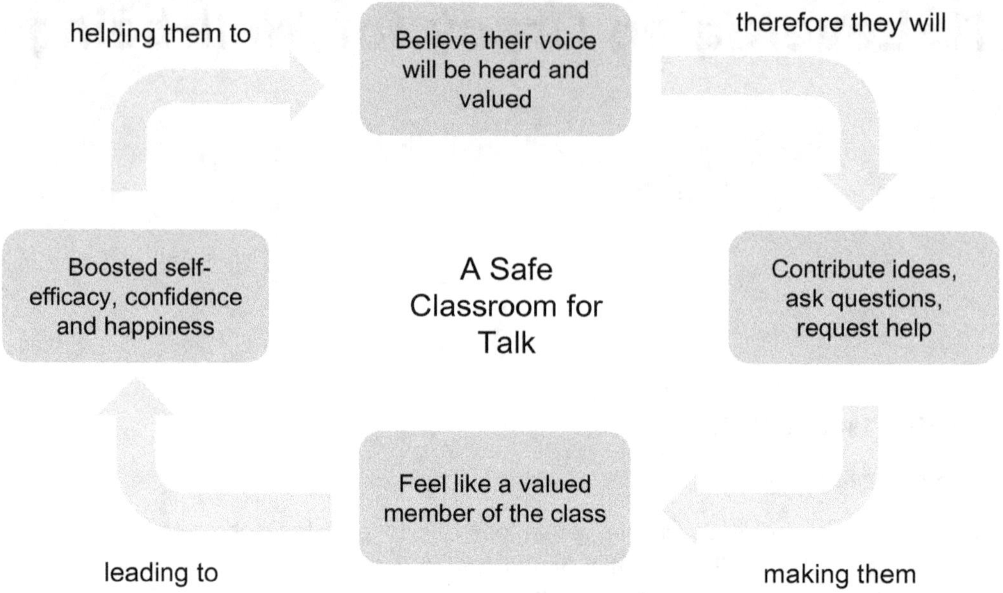

120 Voices of Opportunity

```
helping them to  →  Believe their voice will be heard and valued  →  therefore they will

Boosted self-efficacy, confidence and happiness        A Safe Classroom for Talk        Contribute ideas, ask questions, request help

leading to  ←  Feel like a valued member of the class  ←  making them
```

Figure 11.1 A virtuous cycle of oracy and well-being.

both sit within our values, it is important to make them more explicit, considering if our values:

- Celebrate and actively encourage participation in learning?
- Aspire towards school being a safe haven for children to express themselves?
- Prioritise every pupil having a voice that is listened to and equally valued?
- Foster a culture of risk-taking in learning and development?

Putting oracy and well-being within a school's values may not have an immediate impact upon but it is a crucial starting point for building our oracy principles upon. If a school fails to recognise the connection between language and well-being, they are likely to be also failing to prioritise oracy in the classroom. Ironically, the clue is in the word '*value*' itself.

Whilst you could argue that every school shares the same core values as all others – especially when they all share the same educational goals – some may question the impact these values have on our children. A value that stays dusty above the school entrance is not being actively delivered upon in the daily life of the school. It is imperative that school leaders examine how they thread oracy through the wider curriculum, beyond the content of the core subjects, into areas that enhance well-being. Leaders need to ask themselves if pupils feel safe to express themselves orally in the various spaces and events of a school day.

As a school, do you:

- Think about promoting and encouraging oracy in assemblies? Are pupils sharing their opinions and thoughts aloud? Do children have the opportunities to present to their peers? Do assemblies provide a forum for shared discussion, whether talk partners, think, pair, share or other talk structures?

- Have clear expectations of how everyone (adults and children) are to speak to each other with respect, manners and grammatically correct sentences? Do staff know how to subtly model social language? For example, when a child asks, *'Can I get one of them?'* the adult responds, *'Yes, of course you may take one of these pencils for your work. Thank you for asking'*.
- Is there a culture of greetings and goodbyes? Do staff model how to welcome each other upon arrival into the classroom with a *'Good morning, and how are you on this sunny morning?'* or a similar greeting that sets expectations for all to follow.
- Is there consistent modelling of language for behaviour to demonstrate effective ways to express emotions and concerns without resorting to physical reactions? Are adults modelling how to express their feelings so that children of all ages can see different ways to self-regulate?
- Are the school values, whether they are empathy, respect, kindness or similar well-being-related ones, being explicitly referred to and celebrated as part of everyday school life? Are these behaviours recognised and commended by adults to reinforce these values further as part of 'how we are and what we do'?

Creating a Risk-Taking Culture

If you listen to classrooms across the country, you will undoubtedly hear teachers saying that *'mistakes are all part of the learning experience'* and *'failure is the First Attempt In Learning'*. Educators know the importance of failure in the learning process and are constantly trying to convince pupils of this point. However, it is a far trickier task to establish a culture in which mistakes are consistently valued and the pupils understand why failure is a positive step forward.

For a child to actively contribute within the four walls of the classroom, they need to feel psychologically safe and believe that their voice will be heard. They need to know that they can share an idea, answer or opinion without fear of embarrassment or judgement from adults or peers. A child who feels safe to share will inevitably be happier and more active within the class. This can positively impact well-being and help individuals to enjoy coming into class.

So, how do we nurture risk-taking in lessons?

First, we need the teachers (and support staff) to be explicitly modelling mistakes (deliberately planned into their scaffolding process) for all pupils to see. Thinking aloud when modelling is an effective way for teachers to openly show their learning thought process as they work. As they describe their cognitive processes, there is an opportunity to make planned mistakes; examples could be spelling errors in writing, missing the placeholder in column method or forgetting to capitalise a letter. The teacher can then identify their own error, describing how they may resolve this through a range of desirable strategies. Maybe they refer back to a working wall, or check their steps to success or simply sense check by rereading their own writing.

A key element of this correctional process is for the teacher to acknowledge their mistake, logically consider how to fix it and then show what they have learnt from the mistake.

By visibly modelling mistakes, the class is able to think about the importance of failure in their own metacognitive reflections.

This will help normalise, even celebrate, mistakes as a vital ingredient in learning. For more anxious children who possess lower levels of oracy, they are more likely to avoid sharing openly due to a fear of being *'wrong'*. This participation avoidance can further increase anxiety. Therefore, for our less confident pupils, we need to carefully but openly praise efforts and help our learners to learn from their mistakes.

Some considerations when embedding a *'risk-taking'* approach in class include:

- Ensuring listening pupils do not respond in a way that may negatively affect the one responding i.e. no calling out, no impulsive responses of *'No'* and *'You're wrong'*.
- Avoiding using generic verbal feedback, such as *'Great answer!'*, *'That's correct'*, *'Sorry, you are wrong'* or *'Good try!'*. Instead, feedback needs to be specific, balanced and acknowledging any good attempts. For example, *'I can see how you tried to connect your knowledge of... with this...'* or *'You have clearly considered how to follow the method but be careful to check.... when completing the following step'*.
- Developing peer feedback so that individuals become used to giving and receiving constructive feedback on where they can improve. As with any cognitively mature task, adult modelling of what this looks like is essential.

The ABC Approach

One way to remove the fear of failure is to provide structures for all pupils to respond to each other. Having a clearly defined approach to responding helps manage the feedback process and encourage responses that are less reactive and more constructive. One such approach is the ABC – Agree Build Challenge (see Figure 11.2).

Figure 11.2 The ABC approach to feedback.

Table 11.1 Benefits of the ABC approach

Element of ABC	Oracy benefits	Well-being benefits
Using hand gestures	Allows all pupils to participate without forcing them to verbalise Supports active listening skills as pupils need to respond to what has been said without speaking themselves	Pupil sharing can see the feedback quickly and easily from peers without the noise of 'calling out' More balanced view across ALL peers rather than asking for hands up to respond
Use of stem sentence starters to feedback	Provide a scaffold for less confident pupils to articulate their feedback Stem encourages pupils to give specific feedback supported by reasoning	Feedback may feel less personal and more focused upon the task/learning All pupils know what to expect from the feedback, reducing uncertainty
Teacher modelling how to respond in ABC approach	Sets the expectations for pupils to follow in their feeding back	Shows the value placed upon this approach to feedback by staff Pupils know that teacher is going to support and facilitate this process in a way that fosters psychological safety

During class discussions, pupils can use non-verbal hand gestures to indicate whether they agree, disagree or want to build upon someone's point. The teacher can then ask a pupil(s) to articulate their feedback using given stem sentence starters. These stems should be clearly displayed in class alongside dual coded visuals of the hand gestures.

Using this approach has multiple benefits for both those with weaker oracy as well as those pupils who fear participation (Table 11.1).

Enabling Emotional Expression

Opportunities to Express

As children transition from toddlers into young children (age 3 to 4), they begin to learn how to emotionally regulate themselves. In pre-verbal toddlers, they often lack the vocabulary or articulation to express their emotions. This can result in tantrums and emotional outbursts, where they are out of control for a period of time. As they grow, they begin to learn how to better regulate their emotions through the use of language. This is typically developing by the age of four as they enter Early Years settings. However, for a multitude of reasons, more children are entering schools *'unready'* to interact with peers. Part of this *'unreadiness'* is the absence of emotional regulation that develops alongside expressive language.

As these children move through into Key Stage One and up, many continue to struggle with emotional regulation and this can disrupt theirs, as well as peers, experiences inside the classroom. However, there are ways that schools and teachers can support emotional regulation.

Emotional Vocabulary

In order to effectively express emotions, an individual must first possess a range of emotional vocabulary. It is not enough just to be able to speak and communicate – the knowledge and understanding of emotive language is important for conveying an emotive state of mind.

Emotions can be categorised into different levels: primary, secondary and tertiary (Ekman, 1992). As children begin to recognise emotions, they focus on the primary emotions, such as happy, sad and angry. As they mature, understanding of the more nuanced secondary emotions helps individuals to be more specific in their expression. For example, a child who may initially say they are '*angry*' may actually be feeling more humiliated, frustrated or let down. Whilst these all fall within the realms of anger, the support and care needed to support a child experiencing frustration is very different to the support for a child who has been let down. When a child cannot distinguish between the secondary emotions, they grasp at the most suitable primary emotion to express their current state of mind. For the listening adults, it can become more of a guessing game to identify the secondary emotion and root cause of their emotions. This uncertainty means the support they offer is not always meeting the needs of the child.

Similarly, for a child saying they are '*happy*', they may be feeling calm, playful or excited. A content child may be happy enough taking time alone whilst a playful-feeling child may require active engagement from peers and adults to match their energy levels (Figure 11.3).

How can we build this emotional vocabulary within our pupils?

Firstly, Early Years teams need to integrate the primary emotions within their continuous provision and interactions with their children. We cannot assume that all children recognise or understand the six basic emotions, especially considering those with SEND needs or EAL too. As with any new learning, it is not enough to simply say these words to the young learners. New learning needs to be experienced and absorbed in a range of ways, including:

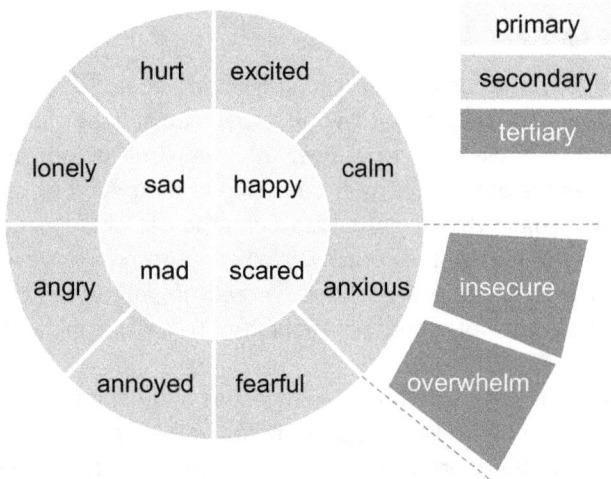

Figure 11.3 The emotion wheel.

- **Verbally** – are you introducing the new emotion and saying it to/ with the children
- **Dual coding** – whilst they hear and read (or at least see the word) the emotion, can they see this emotion in real life? This can be a mix of imagery and adult-modelled expression (facial, body language)
- **Role played** – are there opportunities within the provision for children to role play the emotions? They can use small world figures, puppets, cuddly toys or even costume dress-up to re-enact social situations where characters experience a range of emotions
- **Modelled** – the staff should be modelling their emotional expression openly and clearly within the provision so children can observe. For example, a staff member can say, *'Oh no my tower has tumbled. Now I feel sad and need some help to rebuild it'*. Consistent, explicit modelling by all (not just teachers) adults can reinforce new emotional vocabulary.

Definitions

Emotional vocabulary – words and phrases used to describe how you feel. This includes words that label emotions as well as words laden with emotion.

Primary emotions – The six basic emotions (as defined by Ekman, 1992) include sadness, happiness, fear, anger, surprise and disgust. These are a pure reaction to an experience.

Secondary emotions – The emotions felt immediately after the initial primary emotional response. These can be categorised under the primary emotions. For instance, under anger, the secondary emotions include frustration, betrayal and outrage.

Tertiary emotions – Emotions experienced as a consequence of experiencing a secondary emotion. For example, within the secondary emotion of being vulnerable, this may be a tertiary emotion of feeling victimised or fragile.

These strategies are not only confined to Early Years but should be adapted for every year group. Children are not emotionally-mature by Year One so our support should continue to match their development. Using daily opportunities to model emotional language, whether during learning or other non-academic moments, is essential (Table 11.2).

Resolving Conflicts through Dialogue

One direct effect of poor emotional literacy is the potential conflicts a child or young person may face on a frequent basis. For children with weak oracy, they may find it more difficult to navigate disagreements and misunderstandings with peers (and even adults) because they do not have the communication skills required for conflict resolution.

Table 11.2 Emotional vocabulary strategies for primary (and secondary)

Strategy	How	Wellbeing benefits
Thinking Aloud	Teachers explicitly describe their thought process when modelling a new element of learning e.g. maths procedure. As they model, they describe their emotive state and how they may support themselves E.g. '*I am getting quite frustrated with this step. Maybe I need to reread the instructions on the screen to help myself*'	Pupils can see firsthand the strategies and potential emotional responses being modelled during the learning process. This helps build understanding of situations where emotions may be affected and remove anxieties related to challenges in class
Emotions Charts	A range of emotions are prominently displayed in a range of places where pupils will see them throughout the school day. This is not limited to class but also corridors, halls and playgrounds. The signs should be dual coded with related symbols/imagery	Children absorb the emotional language, and it helps scaffold their verbal responses in different situations Having the signs visible also reinforces the importance of emotional regulation as well as the need to empathise with peers
Writing Emotionally	As part of writing outcomes in Key Stages One and Two, ensure emotive writing is integrated into the genres covered. Whether poetry, narrative or persuasive letters, check for opportunities for teacher-modelled emotional vocabulary that can be woven into the learning sequence	Writing can be a safe place for pupils to role play emotional situations that they may experience in the real world. By viewing these emotional responses through the lens of the narrator or author, they can take an outside perspective on their own emotional needs

Three key ways oracy can support pupils in this challenge include:

- **Clearer expression of emotions and needs:** Pupils with strong oracy skills can articulate their feelings and perspectives clearly, reducing frustration and misunderstandings.
- **Active listening and empathy:** Better oracy encourages pupils to listen attentively, acknowledge different viewpoints and respond thoughtfully, fostering mutual understanding.
- **Constructive problem solving through dialogue:** With strong communication skills, pupils can negotiate solutions calmly, using reasoning and restorative language instead of reacting impulsively.

Teaching pupils how to cope better in these situations is no easy task. A general push for stronger oracy will have a positive impact in the long term, but for the immediate, other approaches are needed to support pupils in the here and now. Staff need to be trained in structured dialogue techniques that enable restorative conversations to take place. Teachers and other adults known to the pupils need to understand and rehearse the approaches so they feel confident to manage these with their classes.

Restorative conversations are a way to address and resolve conflicts in a healthy and managed structure. We will not delve too deep into the mechanisms of this approach here as it is a whole topic in it's own right. However, related to other oracy strategies, one tool for restorative dialogue is the introduction of stem sentences to scaffold questions and responses. Scaffolds help ease extraneous cognitive load and allow the individual involved to focus brain power on what they want to reflect and say.

Examples of such stems include:

- **'I' statements:** *'I feel _____ when _____ because_____'*
- **Empathetic listening:** *'Thank you for sharing that with me.'* and *'I want to ensure I have understood you correctly. Did you mean _____?'*
- **Reflective questions:** *'Who was impacted by your actions and how?'* and *'How were you feeling at the time this happened?'*
- **Affective questions:** *'How were you affected by their behaviour?'* and *'How are you currently affected?'*

Strengthening Social Connectedness

Collaboration Builds Belonging

A sense of belonging is crucial to a child's well-being, self-efficacy and participation in school. Children have an intrinsic desire, as do all humans, to be accepted, valued and feel safe within a group. Yet, for many disadvantaged children with poor oracy and lacking social skills, they can often feel like outsiders who are isolated and separate from peers. Due to a gap in language, these children are vulnerable to disengaging actively or passively from social interactions and their well-being can be severely affected. Oracy can equip children with the tools to express themselves and connect with others, acting as a powerful force for inclusion and engendering a sense of belonging.

Oracy as a Protective Factor

The Oracy All Party Parliamentary Group (APPG) Inquiry highlighted the importance of oracy for belonging, with one teacher quoted as saying, *'Oracy heightens a community's ability to belong to each other, whilst valuing individuality. It makes every voice matter; these processes are built on the principles of a democratic society'* (2021). In the English-Speaking Union (2016, p. 23) report titled *'Speaking Frankly – The case for oracy in the curriculum'*, Dr Fiona Pienaar of Place2Be states,

> The connection between oracy and well-being is crucial and while there are many other risk factors that can impact on a child and young person's well-being, oracy is one that we can turn into a protective factor. Society literally cannot afford to ignore the potential impact of young people facing a lifetime of challenges to their mental health and emotional well-being.

Instead of simply viewing oracy as the barrier to belonging, we can flip the focus onto positioning it as a protective factor for well-being. Nolan and Smyth (2021) studied the importance of language for social connection in younger individuals and shone a spotlight on the benefits of oracy for promoting inclusion:

- **Oracy builds social connections** - strong communication skills support young children and teenagers in forming healthy relationships, which decreases feelings of isolation and internalising of anxieties.
- **Oracy supports positive peer relationships** - Through clearer expression of emotion and thoughts, relationships can be more empathetic and supportive. This can strengthen closer friendships as well as minimise the chance of bullying.
- **Oracy-centred activities enhance well-being** - Extra-curricular activities, such as drama, debating clubs, board games, choir and team sports, build collaborative dialogue, resilience and confidence in social situations.
- **Oracy boosts teacher-pupil relationships** - A child who is able to communicate effectively with adults will have more positive interactions with adults, which supports a sense of belonging within school.

As this chapter will continue to unpick, oracy can be a force for good and act as a shield to defend well-being. Our role as educators is to arm our pupils with the oracy skills through varied and frequent opportunities as outlined by Nolan and Smyth.

> **Definitions**
>
> **Social connectedness =** the sense of belonging and meaningful relationships individuals have with others, fostering emotional support, shared identity and a feeling of being valued within a community.
>
> **Belonging =** the deep sense of acceptance, inclusion and connection to a group or community, where individuals feel valued, understood and safe to express themselves openly.

Oracy Buddies

Many primary schools operate some form of *'reading buddy'* system through which older children visit their younger peers on a regular basis to share reading experiences together. In a similar vein, *'oracy buddies'* is an approach to pair up pupils so they have the opportunity to develop their language skills in a safe, supportive environment. These pairings can be within a year group or cross-age depending on what works best for the school and the cohort needs.

Structuring the Oracy Buddy System

A system such as oracy buddies must be well structured and have a clear purpose in order to have impact in the long term. It isn't sufficient enough to simply start by pairing children between year groups and then running a few infrequent sessions in the hope that it supports the less oral pupils. Table 11.3 lays out some key considerations when designing a buddy system that fits your school context, as there is no *'one size fits all'* approach to any system such as this.

Table 11.3 Oracy Buddy setup considerations

Area	Consideration
Frequency	**How often will you run the sessions?**
	Too often and it becomes unfeasible within a busy teaching timetable
	Too spaced out and relationships between paired pupils will not become established
	How long will each session run for?
	It needs to be long enough to include transition times from classrooms to meet as well as sufficient for purposeful talk to occur.
	However, with increasing pressures on the curriculum coverage, it needs to slot into a part of the week that will not impact other subjects.
	When should it happen?
	If it is in the morning, consider how this affects the delivery of core subjects such as phonics, maths and English.
	If in the afternoon, find a slot where the children are not missing out on wider curriculum areas such as PE and art.
Pairings	**Should it be cross age?**
	Pairing older with younger pupils can help both ways in terms of building confidence and having an older child as the initiator of dialogue. For example, Year 6 buddy with Year 1, Year 5 with Year 2 and so on.
	However, keeping buddies within a class or between neighbouring year groups (i.e. a Year 1 with a Year 2 child) as they are on a similar level of understanding and there is a better balance to the dialogue (less dominated opposed to when an older child may initiate then guide the talk).
	Does it matter who I pair together?
	It is helpful to pair children who come from different ends of the oracy level together so there is one buddy who is more able to support and share more confidently as a role model. Pairing two weaker pupils together would not have as large an impact as they lack the language and confidence to converse.
Activities	**What would the buddies do in this time?**
	There are a range of activities that can be rotated and repeated, such as:
	• Role playing scenarios – getting into character, empathising, acting in different voices and varied emotions
	• Guided discussions – centred on a given question(s) that both children can comprehend. Try to keep these fun and not too dependent on knowledge that they may be lacking
	• Decision making tasks – ask the pairs to solve a problem or decision together that requires dialogue, debate and consensus. For example, asking them to order a set of animals from the slowest to the fastest
	Do these sessions need a lot of preparation?
	Ideally, the focus is predominantly geared towards talk so resourcing and preparations should be light at best. Where props and visuals may help stimulate conversation, what would be more beneficial is providing stem sentences and scaffolds for children to use when thinking of what to say

Benefits of a Buddy

The benefits of running an oracy buddy programme extend beyond language development – it plays a vital role in fostering social connectedness and well-being. When children feel heard and valued by peers (not necessarily just adults), their sense of belonging and self-esteem grow. Through consistent, familiar interactions, children can feel less isolated. For our most disadvantaged children, this may be one of the most valuable opportunities for verbal exchange which may not be possible at home.

Furthermore, by discussing emotions, ideas and opinions within a low-pressure environment, pupils can develop their emotional literacy and conflict resolution skills. This can equip them to better socially navigate interactions as they grow up and enter adolescence and then adulthood.

The Opportunity of the Playground

When adults think about school they naturally gravitate towards lessons, curriculum, learning, assemblies and classrooms. However, ask a child about school and they will start to tell you about what happened at play time, lunch, forest school, after school clubs and other activities that do not fit within the National Curriculum. As school leaders, we need to start thinking about oracy opportunities that exist within this substantial part of school life, especially in regards to the well-being benefits they can bring.

Integrating Talk into Play

The playground can be a daunting place for many children, especially those lacking the language to confidently communicate with peers in the absence of classroom routines and boundaries. Ask any teacher and they will tell you how children come in from play full of emotions, tears, bumps and bruises – often these can be attributed to incidents and interactions that have occurred during break time. Playtime can be an opportunity for children to explore their emotions and rehearse social situations with their peers. However, without adult modelling and structured activities, children may often encounter situations where they need to rely upon their verbal communication.

Examples of such situations include:

- **Misunderstandings**: children may misread a peer's intentions during a game or free play, leading to conflict and escalation of responses. For example, a child accidentally bumps into another child during an active game and the other individual perceives this as deliberate.
- **Isolation**: children naturally gravitate towards their familiar friendship groups at playtime. For those children who struggle with words, they can easily find themselves excluded from shared play. This may be as a result of self-withdrawal from participation or because they lack the ability to engage with those involved in the game.
- **Lack of structure**: Class-based activities are planned and led by experienced adults who have carefully considered routines, roles and expectations. These structures mostly disappear when children exit the classroom onto the playground leading to confusion, uncertainty and a lack of direction in play. For less oral pupils, this can increase anxiety and stress levels, causing them to avoid unorganised play.

Whilst these situations can be a great opportunity for children to freely express themselves and develop independence away from adults, there is a chance to integrate talk into

Conversation stations

Zones displaying prompt questions for discussion, such as "What is your favourite _____ and why?" or "If you had a time machine, where would you go?"

These can be made adaptable so new, topical questions can be updated on a regular basis.

Talking trails

Mapped out routes shown on the ground with conversation starters, stem sentences and questions. The aim of the trail is for children to travel along together and have a shared dialogue as they walk.

Empathy areas

Quiet spaces where children can come to reflect and self-regulate supported by dual-coding of emotions and stem sentences on display to express feelings to a friend.

Figure 11.4 Playground talk.

the playground too. The best place to look at outside talk opportunities is within our Early Years provisions, where purposeful talk across the environment is planned for, encouraged and nurtured. This is not to imply that all playgrounds should mirror Early Years but there are lessons to be learnt from the lowest end of the school.

Figure 11.4 showcases just a handful of potential oracy approaches that can be deployed to boost well-being in the outside spaces. As long as schools are considering the following key principles, pupils will feel better supported and able to use language for their own well-being:

- Are there **scaffolds** to help them articulate their emotions to others?
- Are there opportunities for **shared dialogue** through imaginative play and debate?
- Are there different spaces where children can **self-regulate** and reflect on how they are feeling at that moment?
- Are games and activities deliberately planned to **encourage communication** and active listening skills?

Ensuring the playground can act as an independent space for language development cannot happen without effective adult support. Pupils of different ages still require help to engage with peers, structure activities and develop shared dialogue and the adults on duty are key to making this happen.

The Role of the Adult Outside

Play duty can often be seen by school staff as something you *'have to do'* on your designated slot in the rota. Teachers and support staff across the country will have countless memories of being stood in all weathers, thinking about the next lesson, what they may eat for lunch or how many minutes they have left standing in the freezing cold. However, if we want to create language-rich outdoor spaces, in which all children feel happy and able to express themselves freely, the adults need to actively support oracy (Table 11.4).

For some adults, these sorts of positive interactions may seem second nature, but for the majority of staff, training is required to equip them with the knowledge and skills to support oracy in the playground.

Boosting Confidence

Fostering a sense of self-worth and confidence in our most disadvantaged children poses a significant challenge to both their well-being as well as academic success. A child who lacks confidence to verbally engage not only struggles in class but also finds it difficult to develop and maintain a healthy sense of self-efficacy. Supporting a child in building confidence is a slow and gradual journey that cannot be rushed or forced upon them. Yet, schools can provide a range of opportunities beyond the classroom that nurture oracy and confidence in more holistic and creative ways.

Extra-Curricular Oracy

As discussed in the earlier chapter on social mobility, the ability to effectively and confidently communicate and nurture relationships is a fundamental skill for upward mobility. The correlation between stronger persuasive oracy skills and success in education, university

Table 11.4 Adult-led interactions in the playground

Area	Oracy approach	Well-being impact
Model positive communication	Demonstrate active listening, open-ended questioning and respectful responses	Set high expectation for what healthy dialogue looks like
Facilitate conversations	Initiate group discussions, support quieter children to participate and encourage turn-taking	Increased engagement by all pupils, especially more socially-anxious individuals
Support conflict resolution	Guide children through restorative dialogue, provide prompts for expressing feelings and concerns	Children feel a sense of justice and are able to resolve disputes effectively
Encourage inclusive play	Help integrate more isolated children into shared activities, explaining rules and ensuring all children play together	Promoted sense of belonging and less children excluded from group activities
Create spaces for expression	Actively listen to children's concerns, modelling empathetic responses	Children feel valued, listened to and respected.
Praise verbal sharing by pupils	Provide specific praise for pupils who contribute using effective oracy	Boosted confidence and self-efficacy of less verbal pupils

and the workplace has been recognised and addressed within private schools for a long time. These private institutions acknowledge the importance of confident public speaking and the power of language for their pupils to navigate the *'upper rungs of the social ladder'*. This is reflected in their broad offer of extra-curricular activities and clubs. From debating societies to journalism clubs for the school newsletter, they place oracy, especially public speaking, at the centre of their wider curriculum.

Schools serving our most deprived communities across the country need to reflect on the extra-curricular offers. They have and how oracy can become integral to them. Clearly, the financial disparity between state and private education acts as a barrier to the breadth and quality of extra-curricular activities that can be offered. Yet, through initiative and resourceful creativity, schools are finding ways to enrich such oracy opportunities.

Assemblies and School Events: An Opportunity to Speak

Throughout the school year, there are numerous opportunities for children to take the lead and rehearse their speech and language skills within a safe and familiar environment. Class assemblies are a standard reoccurrence across schools nationwide and should be viewed as a forum for pupil voice. Ensuring all children have the chance to speak to an audience is tricky, especially with 30 individuals and a tight timetable, but even a short window of opportunity can act as a stepping stone for more anxious speakers. Providing more reluctant children with stem sentences and time to rehearse in advance can help ease anxiety.

Opportunities in assembly can include:

- Narrating from a script and/or reading set lines – this is helpful for children who struggle with pronunciation and articulation as they can practise beforehand
- Performing a poem, either from a published poet or one of their own – sharing their own work gives purpose and a boost for self-efficacy
- Acting out scenes with more confident peers – allows for free expression and ability to develop the physical aspects of oracy

Aside from assemblies, there are multiple other ongoings in a typical school through which oracy can be developed. End of year productions, recitals and other community events pose the opportunity for targeted individuals to take a supporting (or even leading) role in. When choosing children to participate, it is useful to consider which individuals would benefit from the chance to come slightly out of their comfort zone, with support, and find their voice.

One effective role that schools should be considering is that of *'school ambassador'*. Selected children (not necessarily the most articulate or confident) are trained to act as ambassadors of the school community, and they can then lead on:

- Welcoming guests to the school, from Ofsted to councillors, school governors to visiting staff – builds confidence with social norms of greeting others
- Leading learning walks with guests to see learning within the classrooms – allows them the chance to showcase their oral abilities with unfamiliar guests whilst talking about very familiar aspects of their own school

- Attending community events as a representative of the school – a great chance to develop social interaction skills with adults and children alike

Clubs and Societies

School clubs are often focused on sports, games, choirs, drama and the arts. For these more traditional clubs, there are many spaces in which oracy can flourish and children can develop confidence amongst peers. Regardless of the type of club, school staff should be thinking explicitly about where oracy can integrate, such as:

- **Collaborative dialogue** – for example, in team sports for discussing strategies and using verbal communication during a game to engage with team mates.
- **Performances** – for choir or drama clubs, finding purposeful occasions for pupils to perform to an audience, whether a handful of familiar faces or a large hall of unknown ones.
- **Debating –** running debate clubs/societies can provide meaningful structures for individuals to practise their debating skills in a safe format, developing resilience, articulation and reasoning skills.

Just as oracy is expected to be integrated across the curriculum – not be ring fenced into specific language-heavy subjects – it should appear pervasively across extra-curricular enrichment too. Otherwise, schools are missing a valuable opportunity to boost well-being through language during the non-class based periods of the day.

Chapter Summary

- Schools need to place oracy at the heart of their culture and ethos to ensure all children feel safe to freely express themselves. The importance of oracy should be reflected in the school values and the ways in which it exists alongside well-being priorities.
- For pupils to feel able to openly express their emotions and thoughts, schools should be focusing on developing and supporting emotional literacy (including vocabulary) as well as scaffolding conflict resolution dialogue.
- Well-being is directly linked to social connectedness and sense of belonging. School leaders should reflect upon the systems and structures that exist, and could start, to promote oracy between children. From oracy buddy programmes to clear playground talk initiatives, oracy can act as a scaffold for individuals who need help engaging with their peers.
- Confidence and self-efficacy are inextricably linked to the ability to orally express opinions and emotions whilst knowing your voice will be heard. State schools can learn from private schools to find new ways to boost oracy through extra-curricular activities and existing opportunities within the academic calendar, such as assemblies, shows and ambassadors.

Reflection Questions

- Considering your current school values, how does oracy align to them? Is oracy for well-being explicitly shown in the values so all school members know it is a valued priority within the culture and ethos?
- Looking at EYFS and Key Stage One, how is emotional vocabulary scaffolded, displayed and modelled by practitioners, teachers and support staff? Does it form part of the continuous provision as well as the classroom environment?
- Within the play time set up, what systems are in place to support children with articulating their needs and emotions with their peers? Are there areas and activities organised to allow for free expression, self-regulation and restorative practices?
- How does oracy feed into the extra-curricular programme of clubs, societies and events? Are club leaders aware of, and proactively supporting, the use of language by children?

Time to Take Action

Examining your current extra-curricular activities and clubs being run at school, consider where oracy is already integrated and where there are opportunities for oracy to be incorporated (Table 11.5).

Table 11.5 Extra-curricular club – Oracy analysis

Club/activity	Current oracy opportunities	Potential areas for oracy

Table 11.5 (Continued)

Club/activity	Current oracy opportunities	Potential areas for oracy

Before attempting to implement changes to these clubs/activities, consider:

- Do the leading staff have the necessary understanding and skills to integrate oracy purposefully?
- Are there any common language principles that all these clubs should be adhering to i.e. use of visuals, stem sentences, body language, emotional vocabulary?
- What direct (or even indirect) impact will these oracy strategies have upon pupil well-being? Is there a way this can be monitored for effectiveness and impact?

References

Ekman, P. (1992) 'An argument for basic emotions', *Cognition and Emotion*, 6(3-4), pp. 169-200.

English-Speaking Union (2016) *Speaking Frankly - The Case for Oracy in the Curriculum*. London: English-Speaking Union. Available at: www.esu.org/wp-content/uploads/2019/01/ESU-Speaking-Frankly.pdf (Accessed: 29 May 2025).

Nolan, A. and Smyth, E. (2021) *Risk and Protective Factors for Mental Health and Wellbeing in Childhood and Adolescence*. Economic and Social Research Institute.

Oracy All-Party Parliamentary Group Inquiry (2021) *Speak For Change - Final Report and Recommendations from the Oracy All-Party Parliamentary Group Inquiry*. Oracy All-Party Parliamentary Group. Available at: www.education-uk.org/documents/pdfs/2021-appg-oracy.pdf (Accessed: 29 May 2025).

12 Barriers to the Workplace

A Foot (Not) in the Door!

The correlation between oracy, academic success and well-being is clearly evidenced and studied. The key objective of all educational institutions is primarily to prepare young adults to enter the adult world and successfully fulfill their potential in their chosen careers, social endeavours and family lives. For the most disadvantaged young people, they will have faced many hurdles along the way that will have hindered their progress at the same time as limiting their language development. At the point of leaving education, this weakened oracy proves to be just as significant a barrier to their job prospects.

Siraj et al. (2024) highlights the association between poor language skills and diminished career opportunities, worsened health, higher risks of unemployment and offending. Whilst there are a wide range of socio-economic factors, a lack of oracy is certainly a crucial one in relation to career trajectory.

Being able to use language effectively can be a huge advantage in successfully getting a job and then thriving within the social cliches and networks of the modern work environment. Like the old adage says. *'It's not what you know, but who you know'*, which outlines the importance of relationships and rapport building to progress up the career ladder.

Impressing at Interview

Anyone who has ever attended a job interview will be able to identify the key factors that a potential employer is looking for in a candidate. A study by Yale found that *'60% of interviewers know within the first 15 minutes'* about a candidate's suitability for a role (Frieder et al., 2019) and other research narrows this down to under 5 minutes for nearly a third of interviewers. This only goes to reinforce the saying *'First impressions matter!'* and these impressions are heavily reliant upon soft, human capital rather than skills and competencies for the role.

Making a positive impression is a skill that is learnt from a young age. Through observing parents, family members and even teachers, children learn to mirror and adopt seen behaviours related to social interactions; these learnt behaviours can be moulded and influenced as a child grows into a young adult but this requires consistent modelling by those around them as well as repeated opportunities for rehearsal.

DOI: 10.4324/9781003607595-13

Confident greeting
Clear, well paced introduction along with a firm handshake and a friendly smile

Eye contact
Able to maintain natural eye contact to show engagement and confidence

Body language
Good posture, open gestures and avoiding fidgeting shows self assurance and professionalism

Tone and clarity
Speaking at a steady and clear pace, removal of filler words (e.g. the 'ums and ahs')

Active listening
Use of affirmations, both visual (nodding) and verbal (repeating the question then answering)

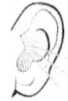

Mirroring the interviewer
Able to subtly match energy and communication style helps build rapport

Figure 12.1 Oracy at interview.

For a young person who has limited exposure to positive adult interactions in their daily life, they will struggle to develop their own social interaction skills. Conversely, for children coming from a home life full of positive and frequent interactions between adults, including involving them in the greetings and conversations, they will nurture their own social competencies to a far greater extent than peers. These social norms and cues translate into the interview scenario and have a substantial impact upon the impressions they make from the moment they enter the room (seen Figure 12.1).

Being able to effectively use these communication tools can make or break a candidate's chances of being hired. Effective communication during an interview is far broader than a mere handshake; it requires a full range of language skills that include receptive and expressive language.

Private schools have historically invested a substantial amount of time and effort into training their pupils in these social skills. This advantage is compounded further by the reality that many of these children already have well developed social capabilities as a result of language-rich home lives. This relates again to the Matthew Effect, where already linguistically advanced young people are further boosted within private school whilst less language-developed peers lack much needed support to close the gap.

Confidence Is Crucial to Selling One's Self

Confidence and self-belief are key ingredients for making a positive and lasting impression upon others, especially in the job hunting process. Since the covid pandemic, Corfe and Bhattacharya (2021) found that young people from more disadvantaged backgrounds possessed less belief in their own ability to achieve their desired goals than their more affluent peers. 43% of disadvantaged young people expected to end up in *'dead-end jobs'* (compared to only 29% of peers from middle class rungs of the social ladder). Their study found that these young people stated they were ill-equipped to compete in the job market and this worsened the *'outlook inequality'* for them today.

Earlier in the chapter on wellbeing, confidence and self-efficacy were identified as being closely tied to levels of language development. For young people to feel confident, they need to believe their voices are valued and heard; this begins far earlier in childhood as they are supported and encouraged to use their voice to strengthen their confidence speaking aloud and interacting with both peers and adults.

Walking into an interview room is a daunting prospect for most individuals, nevermind young adults who struggle with social interaction outside their usual comfort zone. Schools and parents have a responsibility to provide structured opportunities for our young people to observe, rehearse and receive feedback on their approach to interviewing.

Schools can:

- **Hold mock interviews** – Reduce levels of anxiety and boost familiarity with the intricacies and formats of interview processes. This can be led by familiar school staff but also with external colleagues who can add an element of outside perspective.
- **Run interview-technique sessions** – these sessions can focus upon the non-verbal cues i.e. handshakes, eye contact, gestures and facial expressions. Pupils can have the chance to ask questions, see demonstrated behaviours and rehearse.
- **Invite employers in to share insights** – host careers talks and fairs, workplace visits and other platforms for young people to interact with prospective employers in a low-stakes environment.
- **Conduct interviews for school positions** – Mirror real-world interview processes for in-school roles, such as head pupil(s), prefects and school council. This can include application forms, screening, telephone interviews and in person interviews.

Parents and families can:

- **Encourage topical conversations and 'small talk'** – through relevant discussion at home, families can model positive social interactions and conversational skills.
- **Role-playing interviews** – in a safe, familiar setting, families can act out interview scenarios to support their young person with articulating responses and engaging with the non-verbal behaviours to learn how to build rapport (e.g. handshakes, eye contact).
- **Exposure to professional workplaces** – bring young people into the workplace to interact with colleagues and observe workplace communication and etiquette.
- **Build self-efficacy through positive reinforcement** – providing constructive feedback on any displays of communication and interaction. This should include positive praise of progress and attempts at social engagement with others.

Fitting in Matters

It is primitive human nature to want to belong to a group and share common interests, traits and ways of life with others. Over time, these groups form their own communication styles, lexicons and ways of conversing with each other that is clearly known by the members but may appear unfamiliar to *'outsiders'*. Examine the social interactions of any school playground and it is clear to see the various cliques as well as those individuals who find it difficult to integrate for whatever reason.

Look closer at any adult workplace and these social groupings are just as evident to see. As mentioned throughout the early chapters of this book, language is a vehicle for social mobility but it can also act as a wall to enforce boundaries against social *'climbers'*. By the time at which young adults are entering (or attempting to enter) the modern workplace, they will have acquired varying levels of oracy which will influence their trajectory in their early careers and beyond.

The Language of the Modern Workplace

Persuading an interview panel to offer a job is a major hurdle for prospective employees to overcome. For those individuals whose oracy is lacking depth, this can become a significant obstacle to receiving a direct offer. Ives and Rana (2018) found that many top companies are not employing qualified, talented candidates from working class backgrounds as they cannot *'put them in front of a client'*. This prejudice can be as a result of conscious or unconscious opinions about how a person speaks, including accent, use of grammar, clarity as well as limited vocabulary.

Accent Bias

The Social Mobility Commission (2023) masterclass on accent bias in the workplace stated:

> Accent bias can have many repercussions in the workplace, with the potential to affect hiring decisions or promotion opportunities. Research shows that it has a devastating impact on individuals too, producing anxiety or worries about their accent affecting their ability to succeed in the future.

Their research highlights the importance of raising awareness of this bias with employers. They state that we all rely upon shortcuts to process information quickly, and this can lead to the use of social stereotypes, whether negative or positive. For our children hailing from the most disadvantaged upbringings, they are already swimming against a tide of financial, economic and social challenges and accent bias is compounding these problems even further.

A research study by Fleishman Hillard (2023) centred on social mobility and equal opportunities within the creative industries. They explored the impact accent bias can have upon someone's initial chances of getting a job as well as the obstacles facing them in regards to progression and opportunities with clients. Their study found that:

- Between 60% and 77% of respondents were directed to be self-conscious about the way in which they spoke by their parents growing up

- 35% of adults believed you need to *'speak better'* to receive a job offer
- 35% had been told to change their accent when talking to clients or customers
- Having a *'posh'* accent functioned as a way to *'slot in'* with clients. They even define them as *'plug-and-play'* candidates, whose accent allows them access regardless of talent or merit.

> **Definitions**
>
> **Accent bias** = the prejudice or discrimination against an individual based upon their accent
>
> **Code switching** = the process of shifting from one linguistic code (a language or dialect) to another, depending on the social context or conversational setting

Switching Codes

For young professionals who enter the working world from a diverse range of backgrounds, whether geographic, social and/or economic, they often need to find ways to fit in linguistically. Mirroring and matching the language of others within the professional environment is a social process that new members to a group will follow in order to feel like they belong.

For many individuals from lower socioeconomic backgrounds, they are entering workplaces dominated and led by people from higher social classes. Their accents, idioms, vocabulary and rhythm of speech do not match their managers so, in order to fit in, they code switch. Code switching has become a far more high profile aspect of workplace social integration in recent years as research studies shine the spotlight on social mobility.

The study by Fleishman Hillard reveals the factors driving people (within the creative industries in this case) to code switch as:

- 67%: to be taken more seriously by colleagues and leadership
- 53%: to be seen as being smarter
- 32%: to be seen as originating from a higher social class

Code switching is a difficult but essential strategy to raise with our young people whilst they are within the education system and before they enter the realities of work. It is clearly a well-used approach by many people to fit into a workplace culture in order to progress. However, as educators we are dedicated towards building our pupils' self-efficacy and belief in themselves as individuals; this conflicts with advising them to switch their ways of speaking in order to mask their linguistic origins.

Ultimately, the ideal aim is for workplaces to increase diversity in all its forms so that cultural, social and racial barriers can be broken down; more diverse representation across the social spectrum leads to increased acceptance of people's origins including the way they speak. This is an enormous challenge across society and comes with no easy *'fixes'* but requires coordinated alignment across political, educational and industrial bodies.

Insiders and Outsiders: A Social Mobility Divide

Adapting the way you speak, whether it is code switching the tone or formality, is only one aspect to fitting into the modern workplace. It is not only how words are spoken that makes a difference – it is the actual types of words that are spoken that can help or hinder an individual's career progression.

Language is a social construct that evolves in different ways amongst cultural, ethnic, geographic and social groupings. Looking at the United Kingdom, we all share English as the national language. Yet, anyone who has travelled to the four corners of this country will have experienced very diverse linguistic variations to the vocabulary, idioms, grammar and pronunciation of the English language. In terms of social mobility, there is language variation between social classes that go beyond merely the accent.

Jargon

Every industry has its own specific language related to both the content they specialise in and the way colleagues communicate with each other. In teaching, for example, there are a plethora of terms that would be fully understandable to educators but would appear almost alien to anyone who has no experience in schools. Terms such as formative assessment, digraphs, pedagogy, metacognition and Bloom's taxonomy are just a few examples. These words and expressions are referred to as '*Jargon*'.

Jargon is a highly useful form of vocabulary that can:

- Act as a shorthand way to communicate within the workplace, making communication efficient and direct
- Foster a sense of shared understanding and community between members of an organisation or social group
- Demonstrates expertise amongst a learning community of like-minded individuals

However, there are negative connotations associated with jargon, such as:

- Alienation of those who do not fully understand the terminology
- Lack of clarity around important messaging, in which key points are misinterpreted or confused
- Overuse of specific language rather than more direct language use, leading to a lack of trust from those who are not '*in the know*'

Definitions

Jargon = special words/expressions that are used by a group or a profession that are more difficult for others to understand

Lexicon = the language used by a person, language or branch of knowledge

---

Lexicon

Similarly to jargon, a person's lexicon – their full range of receptive and expressive vocabulary – can impact their ability to integrate and progress in their career. From birth, an individual is absorbing and understanding the words spoken to them and around them. As per Hart and Risley's *'30 million word gap'*, children from opposing ends of the social spectrum are exposed to a wide range of new vocabulary as they grow. This trend continues into secondary school and by the time a young adult is ready to move into the work the vocabulary gap is immense. This disparity of language acquisition plays a significant role in the career trajectory of individuals as they begin to build relationships and networks in the workplace.

There are various categories of lexicon that may be used within the workplace. Table 12.1 outlines these groupings and highlights the wide range of potential words someone needs to comprehend and use in order to socially integrate at work.

Differences in lexicon between middle-class individuals and those from socially-disadvantaged upbringings often reflect access to education, cultural capital and exposure to language-rich settings. These lexical differences can range from the breadth of vocabulary to the use of abstract language (see Figure 12.2).

But What Does This Mean for Social Mobility in the Modern Workplace?

Ives and Rana (2018) highlight the importance of lexicon and jargon for individuals to access various situations in the adult world. Without a secure understanding of language nuances and terminology, it becomes more challenging for *'outsiders'* to integrate with social cliques. This is supported by the works of Bernard Spolsky (1998), a sociolinguist who examined the social impact of language variations such as accent, dialect, lexicon and jargon. Spolsky says, *'If you cannot understand my jargon, you don't belong to my group'*.

Spolsky expands upon the field of sociolinguistics, stating how the principal use of language is to establish and maintain social bonds. The way in which this language is conveyed is influenced by social, geographical and cultural factors and sends both subtle and explicit signals about someone's background. Thus, lexicon and jargon act as both a bonding tool as well as an enforcement of boundaries to *'outsiders'*.

Table 12.1 Lexicon in the workplace

Lexicon	Definition	Examples
Professional	Industry-specific terminology (jargon) used in a particular field of practise	Diagnosis (in healthcare) Stakeholders (in business)
Formal	Polite, structured language seen in meetings, presentations, emails etc	'I'd like to propose a solution' 'I appreciate your time and effort'
Colloquial	Everyday, conversational language that is more relaxed yet still suitable for work environments	'Let's touch base soon' 'We need to think outside of the box'
Informal (slang)	Casual sayings/phrases used socially between colleagues	'We'll have to wing it!' 'That's a no-brainer!'
Buzzwords	Trendy phrases or words used in work environments that convey shared values	'Deep dive' 'Blue sky thinking'

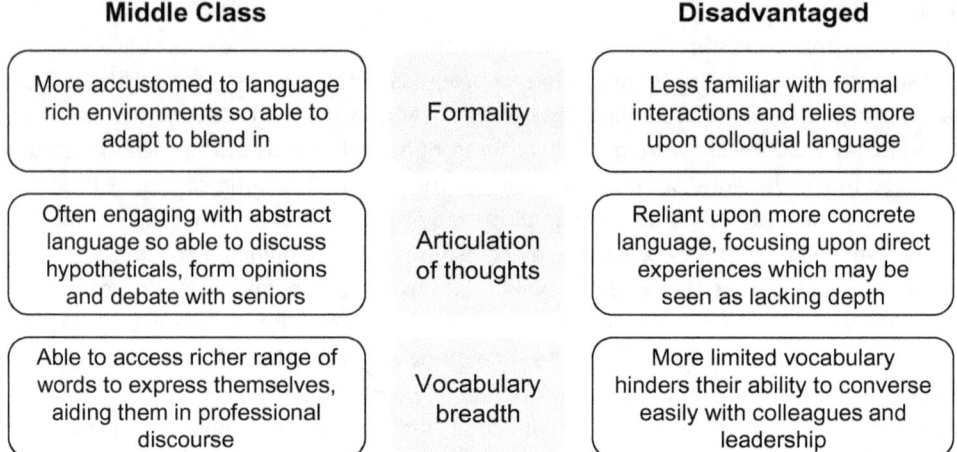

Figure 12.2 Lexicon social class differences.

At the beginning of this book, we defined the concept of social mobility and the '*stickiness*' that persists at both ends of the social ladder. Throughout the education system, from Early Years through to Sixth Form, professionals and academics have examined and measured the disadvantage gap. However, aside from merely academic progress and attainment, the language divide has stubbornly refused to narrow before our young people exit formal education. Entering the adult workplace, this gap between the language haves and have-nots plays a significant role in the career opportunities available to different social classes.

No Easy Fixes

Whilst Government initiatives and reports have identified the need to address this language discrimination, policies and regulations alone will not bridge the gap. Instead, we need a collective effort between families, schools, universities, employers, unions and Government bodies to positively affect the way language is perceived in the workplace.

A whole separate book could be authored on the specific strategies, both immediate and long term, that are needed to address the work language gap and improve upwards social mobility. However, in summary, we need:

- **Government must embed oracy into education policy by:**
    - Ensuring oracy forms a central component of the National Curriculum (even to be seen as the 'Fourth R')
    - Ensure workplace communication skills are woven into the secondary wider curriculum to prepare our young people as they approach the transition into work
    - Fund initiatives and programmes that support the most disadvantaged pupils, such as mentorships and public speaking platforms
- **Schools/universities should provide opportunities for rehearsal by:**
    - Organising structured opportunities for practise with job interviews, workplace scenarios and coaching

- Running employer-led workshops, where pupils can observe different communication styles and receive direct feedback from experienced professionals
    - Teach the nuances and raise awareness of code switching, professional language and body language
- **Employers must improve their inclusive hiring practices by:**
    - Offering accessible workplace mentoring and communication training for new-entry employees from disadvantaged backgrounds
    - Recognise and challenge unconscious accent bias by reflecting upon recruitment strategies and awareness of interviewing participants
- **Families need to foster communication at home by:**
    - Encouraging positive social interactions and opportunities for conversation between children and adults. This includes modelling eye contact, posture, tone of voice and other non-verbal communication styles.
    - Motivate children to develop their self-confidence through participation in school and/or community activities that require speaking and social interaction e.g. school productions, debates and presentations

Interview: Challenges Facing the Next Generation

Name: Mira Magecha

Role: Founder and Trust Leadership Coach

Mini Bio:

Mira has led teams of 5 to 1,000s in listed giants and chaotic scale-ups. She has also led organisations as a former Chief People Officer. Today she work with leaders, navigating change, tough decisions and teams that look fantastic on paper but aren't delivering. She has developed the frameworks using research, curiosity and real life experiences in leadership both the successes and failures.

Mira asks the questions no one else dares, the ones internal teams won't. With a sense of honesty and impact, she is always driving forward change. She helps leaders build the kind of trust that speeds things up, sharpens performance, and actually gets things moving.

Mira believes that when you unlock trust, everything shifts.

Q: What kinds of skills do you think the next generation needs as they enter the workforce?
We keep talking about 'soft skills' like they're optional extras. Adam Grant calls them Character Skills and that's much closer to the truth. They're not soft, they're the hard edge of leadership. The next generation needs one thing above all: trust. Trust in themselves to take

risks, to speak before they're polished, to learn and fail in real time. And they need leaders who trust them enough to back potential over perfection.

Technical skills will expire every five years. What doesn't? The ability to make decisions, be curious, influence and build relationships. That's what earns you trust and trust is the currency that moves people forward. If organisations don't start hiring for that, they'll keep filtering out brilliant people who don't 'look the part' but could have been game-changers.

Leaders need to stop judging candidates on polish, their accents, confidence, networks and start valuing character and humanness. These qualities are harder to teach, but in my experience, far more predictive of success.

Q: Are there particular challenges that young people face when entering today's workforce?

Absolutely. Organisations don't get potential. They trust the old playbook: the right schools, the right accent, the right network.

The irony is that the very barriers young people face are what make them great candidates. If you've hustled just to get a foot in the door, you're already resilient, adaptable and a problem-solver. But instead of valuing that, too many organisations filter it out because it doesn't 'look right on paper' or it doesn't look familiar.

I've been mistaken for the *'tea lady'* in rooms I was leading. If that happens at the exec level, imagine what it's like for someone just starting out. If organisations want the next generation to thrive, they need to stop gatekeeping and start trusting difference. Otherwise, we'll keep hiring the same voices, and wondering why nothing changes.

The question is not whether the next generation is ready for work. It's whether organisations are ready to trust the next generation.

Q: How can organisations better support young employees, especially those from diverse or disadvantaged backgrounds?

Support isn't glossy initiatives. It's where leaders are willing to place their trust.

Recruitment is the first test. If you only trust the top schools or familiar journeys on CVs, you've already decided who belongs. Widening the gate means that talent can arrive raw, and the question is whether organisations are courageous enough to back raw talent.

Mentoring is another form of trust. A mentor isn't just giving advice; they're lending their credibility until someone builds their own. When it works, it's a transfer of trust across diverse and disadvantaged candidates. It really can be the difference between someone just surviving or thriving.

Networks and employee groups are too often underfunded or treated as side of desk projects. If leaders don't resource them properly, what they're really saying is: we'll support you, but only if it costs us nothing. Young employees especially notice that gap instantly. And when support is for image and has no depth, trust erodes.

This isn't complicated. Supporting young employees isn't about policies on paper. It's about leaders proving, in visible and tangible ways, that they trust difference enough to invest in it. Anything less is just window dressing.

Q: What role does oracy - or communication skills - play in all this?
Oracy isn't just about speaking well. The ability to communicate shapes every career milestone.

Whether you get through the interview, whether your ideas land, whether you're seen as leadership material. But fundamentally people only speak up when they trust it's safe. If someone believes their accent will be mocked, their grammar picked apart or their ideas dismissed, no amount of training will fix that silence.

Debate, discussion, storytelling these aren't extras, they're the foundations of voice. Yet too often schools and parents treat communication as a by-product not a skill in its own right. Without it young people are under-prepared for workplaces that still reward confidence as much as competence. And let's be clear confidence is not the starting place. Trust is.

Remote and hybrid work has widened the gap. You no longer overhear how a senior colleague handled a tough client call or watch body language in a heated meeting. Those invisible lessons are stripped away. Organisations must now create deliberate spaces for employees entering the workplace to practise, stumble and grow in public. Otherwise, we risk a generation with ideas worth hearing, but no platform of trust to speak them on.

I'll always be an advocate for those who fought their way in. They bring a resilience you can't teach. The missing ingredient isn't talent, it's trust. Give them that, and they don't just join the table, they'll help reshape it.

Chapter Summary

- First impressions matter and can make or break an individual's success at the interview stage. The manner in which someone communicates, verbally and non-verbally, during the course of the interview can help (or hinder) the building of rapport with potential employers. For those who lack the necessary language 'know-how', they can struggle to positively engage with employers at this stage; as a result, many young people stumble at this first hurdle of the career ladder.
- Research shows that accent bias is prevalent within society, and this is reflected in the recruitment process across many organisations. This language discrimination can limit opportunities to individuals new to the workplace. Code switching is one commonly seen strategy that many people feel is necessary to integrate into the social cliques and expectations of their own workplaces.
- Alongside the bias placed upon how words are spoken (i.e. accent and dialect), the content and structure of the words themselves are social signals about a person's background. The modern workplace is full of specific lexicon and jargon that are harnessed for social integration but can also act as a boundary against social 'outsiders' too.
- There are no quick fixes, no low-hanging fruit here. A coordinated, long term approach is required between Government, education, employers and the public to implement meaningful change in the way language can become more inclusive and accepted.

Reflection Questions

- How are you explicitly and implicitly modelling positive body language (eye contact, posture, mirroring) within your school to support your pupils?
- Considering your local community and context of your school population, how do you celebrate differences in accent, dialect and language?

Time to Take Action

Reflecting on the three tiers of vocabulary, the third tier consists of words that are subject-specific and used by experts and professionals in that designated field of work. Within school, we need to be exposing our pupils to third tier vocabulary throughout the curriculum. By increasing the breadth and depth of their vocabulary in this way, our young adults will be better equipped to communicate within whatever field of work they choose.

Consider one year group and one subject. In Table 12.2, list as many third tier terms related to the subject as possible.

Table 12.2 Third tier vocabulary

Year Group	
Subject	
Third Tier Vocabulary	

References

Corfe, S. and Bhattacharya, A. (2021) *A Matter of Perspective? Outlook Inequality and Its Impact on Young People*. Social Market Foundation. Available at: www.smf.co.uk/publications/a-matter-of-perspective/#:~:text=Drawing%20on%20new%20survey%20data,further%20deepened%20by%20COVID%2D19 (Accessed: 29 May 2025).

Fleishman Hillard (2023) *The Language of Discrimination*. Available at: https://fleishmanhillard.co.uk/wp-content/uploads/sites/27/2023/02/FleishmanHillard-and-Creative-Access-Language-Bias-Report-2023-DEI-1.pdf (Accessed: 29 May 2025).

Frieder, R., Van Iddekinge, C. and Raymark, P. (2019) 'How quickly do interviewers reach decisions? An examination of interviewers' decision-making time across applicants', *Journal of Occupational and Organizational Psychology*, 89(2), pp. 223-248.

Ives, G. and Rana, R. (2018) *Language and Power*. Cambridge: Cambridge University Press.

Siraj, J., Maths, S., Gross, J. and Buchanan, C. (2024) *The Role of Early Language Development & Social Mobility*. BERA: Presidential Roundtable.

Social Mobility Commission (2023) *Recap: Accents in the Workplace*. Available at: https://socialmobility.independent-commission.uk/resources/recap-accents-in-the-workplace/#:~:text=Accent%20bias%20can%20have%20many,to%20succeed%20in%20the%20future (Accessed: 29 May 2025).

Spolsky, B. (1998) *Sociolinguistics*. Oxford: Oxford University Press.

13 Workplace of the Future

Preparing the Next Generation

In the last decade, technology (especially AI-driven), has radically changed the way we live, learn and work. Whilst we do not have hoverboards (as promised by Back to the Future), modern society has witnessed huge steps forward in terms of the way we interact with technology.

It is difficult to predict how technology and AI will evolve over the coming years, as it is on an exponential upwards curve. As a result, educators need to think more openly and critically about the skills required to thrive in the workplace of the near future. As we will go on to explore, oracy skills are going to be even more central to future industries and sectors, and it is our job to ready our children for this unknown landscape.

Soft Skills as a Priority

Over the past decade or so, there has been a notable shift by employers towards soft skills. Where previously technical expertise was highly sought after, more employers are now prioritising soft skills and attributes in their recruitment. In an increasing automated and technology-driven job market, where many routine tasks are no longer human-led, these human-centric skills are becoming important differentiators for those looking to climb the career ladder. Skills such as communication, resilience and collaborative problem-solving are valued and rewarded within many organisations; employers are recognising employees who are more able to communicate ideas, articulate solutions and influence others (Figure 13.1).

According to Major and Machin (2018), fundamental aspects of oracy – such as articulacy, confidence and teamwork – are now critical components of employability and not only impact recruitment but also how individuals shape their career progression. Their research focuses on the impact of oracy upon social mobility, and they identify how this shift towards soft skills will disproportionately benefit young adults from higher socio-economic upbringings.

They specifically acknowledge the role played by private schools in nurturing these human-centric skills as part of their wider curriculum. In contrast, state schools tend to be more focused upon academic attainment and have less capacity to invest time and resources

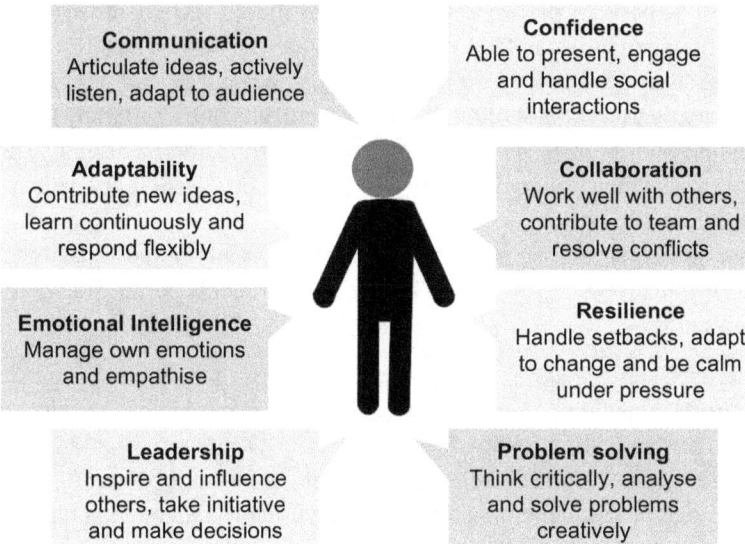

Figure 13.1 Soft skills.

into oracy skills development. This deliberate effort upon nurturing emotional intelligence within the private education system provides a significant advantage for these young adults as they approach the job market. This further entrenches the social mobility gap beyond education and into the workspace.

> **Definitions**
>
> **Soft skills =** the personal attributes that enable an individual to effectively interact and collaborate with others. Examples include: time management, empathy, teamworking, leadership, work ethic, creative thinking and conflict resolution
> **Articulacy =** the ability to speak with clarity, coherence and meaningfulness

Changing Expectations

Schools have traditionally focused upon academic achievement, whether it is Phonics screening, Key Stage Two SATs, GCSEs or A-Levels. The main duty of schools was to prepare pupils for college, university, apprenticeships and eventually work by means of qualifications. In 1997, Tony Blair entered 10 Downing Street and declared *'Education, education, education!'* as his number one priority to improve the life chances of young people nationwide. This translated into a continuous rise of university applications and an even greater focus upon grades. However, with this increased push for academic excellence came a decline in the efforts placed upon non-academic development of our young adults.

Anyone who has been in the workplace for more than a few years will know that academic qualifications are a partial foot in the door; once established in a work setting, other less academic skills and traits help an individual build a reputation and progress upwards. Whilst a university degree or a set of A-Levels is a useful starting point, they take a back seat to experience and on-the-job skills in the long term. As educators, we need to find a better balance between academic outcomes and softer, human traits whilst the young people are within our sphere of influence.

Over recent years, large-scale workforce surveys have attempted to better understand the priorities of employers in this fast-changing environment. Some examples include as follows:

- Recent surveys surveyed employers to discover the skills they value the most amongst their workforce population. 49% of employers ranked communication skills – presenting, negotiating and delivering feedback – as a top priority for staff to possess.
- Reports also reported that 26% of employers valued the importance of people management skills, including supporting and motivating others, leadership and teamwork.
- The National Foundation for Educational Research (NFER) identifies communication, collaboration, problem solving and creative thinking as key employability skills.

These reports are not arguing for a full-scale shift away from academic measures but for a rebalancing of the curriculum to allow more space and opportunities for human capital to be better taught and developed. These characteristics of oracy can be integrated without drastic change in several ways, including:

- Examining how oracy skills are embedded into the teaching and learning pedagogy across all subjects and curriculum areas. Whether it is maths or PE, building in chances for pupils to observe and then rehearse language skills within the subject is a less disruptive way of developing oracy. Not only will this directly strengthen academic learning through purposeful talk, it allows our young people to practice the employability skills of collaboration, critical thinking, negotiating and presenting in a safe environment.
- Oracy skills can be taught and practised through deliberate, explicit teaching opportunities. Opportunities can range from: presenting, problem solving on real-world tasks, articulating solutions. In a similar way that pupils are openly taught how to be metacognitive, there is a chance to model oracy skills to them and not just subtly incorporating it into lessons.

Aligning Oracy with the Rise of Technology

For those who remember the 1990s, it was a decade of technological change; the internet was taking off slowly, mobile phones were getting a foothold in society and it ended with the fear of the Y2K bug (a.k.a. The Millennium bug). Yet, the end of the last Millennium was merely the foothills of a steep upwards climb into the 2000s. Since the start of the new millennium, the rate of technological change has been faster than most would have anticipated. From the dominance of the internet to the more recent evolution of AI-driven technologies,

Table 13.1 AI-driven technological change in the workplace

How is AI-driven technology changing work?	Relevant Oracy Skill	How will oracy support the employees involved?
Routine and repetitive tasks are being automated, reducing the demands on manual labour	Creative expression	With a decline in manual labour comes an increase in need for people to focus on more complex challenges. Staff need to **innovate and add value beyond automation** through creative ideas sharing
Data insights and analysis generated by AI	Critical thinking and reasoning	With increased layers of data insights, employees need to be able to **interpret, question and make considered decisions** regarding information AI is sharing
With more AI tools/platforms in use, more people will require upskilling on the new technology	Clear articulation skills	Employees need to be able to clearly and **simply explain the new technology** to others
Changes to ways of working as a result of technology leads to ethical dilemmas and the need for human judgements	Empathy Emotional intelligence Critical thinking	There is a growing need for a **human perspective** to decision making that AI cannot replicate. This is especially seen in real-world situations where technology is not able to navigate with the same emotional intelligence

every aspect of modern life has changed, including the way in which we work. This digital revolution of industries and services will continue and educators need to prepare the next generation to thrive in the future.

The English-Speaking Union (2023) states that AI is reshaping whole industries, making uniquely human skills – such as creativity, critical thinking and verbal reasoning – more crucial. Employers are increasingly searching for employees who can creatively problem solve in the spaces where AI cannot help. In addition, possessing stronger capabilities to articulate and reason can be useful in collaboratively working with AI. A YouGov poll found that 68% of business leaders believe the rise of AI will increase the critical nature of spoken language and active listening skills. This is encapsulated in the Labour Government's mission to prioritise oracy as a core skill for work readiness (Table 13.1).

As the demands and requirements of the working world evolve, our education system needs to adapt just as quickly to prepare young adults accordingly.

Equipping Pupils for an AI-Driven Future

As AI continues to take over many routine and technical aspects of work, schools must prepare pupils with language skills that technology cannot replicate. Verbal reasoning and critical thinking need to be embedded throughout classroom dialogue to encourage pupils to examine, challenge and question. With the rise of AI comes with it the challenges of *'fake news'*, misinformation and a breakdown of trust with knowledge shared online. Our young people need to strengthen their capacity to form their own informed opinions, able to reason and debate different points of view.

Similarly, using structured talk routines such as *'I think... because...'* empowers pupils to make valuable, evidenced contributions to collaborative teamwork. Equally, empathy, emotional intelligence and team working skills must be nurtured through purposeful group discussions, role play tasks and group problem solving.

Critics of AI claim that technology will eventually take over the decision making and strategic aspects of organisations. On the other hand, AI advocates claim it is a tool to be harnessed, and those individuals who understand AI and can articulate the challenges and solutions facing them will be best placed to deploy AI effectively. Schools need to find a balance between embracing AI versus blocking it's spread as ultimately the future will be dominated by AI and our pupils need to feel confident to utilise it with familiarity and without fear.

Bridging the 'Work Readiness' Gap

In the earlier chapter exploring oracy in Early Years, the concerns around *'school readiness'* were outlined. At every stage of education, schools are measuring just how *'ready'* their pupils are to progress on to the next key stage (whether it is the Early Years Profile, Key Stage 2 and 3 SATs, GCSEs or A-levels). This worrying trend has translated into the transition from education to the working world with *'work readiness'* sitting high on the priorities and concerns of employers at present.

Even as far back as 2014, employer surveys have shown concerns around the levels of readiness seen amongst new entrants to the adult workforce. Findings for work unreadiness include the following from the *'Future of Skills and Lifelong Learning'* (Government Office for Science, 2017):

- The UK Commission for Employment and Skills (2014) found that 36% of employers claimed school leavers were *'poorly'* prepared for work due to weak communication skills.
- The Federation of Small Businesses (2016) reported that young people struggled with: presenting themselves, time-keeping and professional communication skills.
- The McKinsey survey found that new hires are generally weakest in problem solving, written communication, basic maths and leadership, with the first two seen as more important in recruitment.

As the nature of work continues to evolve due to AI and technological advancement, the demand for human-centric skills – such as articulacy, collaboration, critical thinking, and empathy – is rising quickly. These are the very skills that machines struggle to mimic, and they're becoming the distinguishing factor for employability in future-facing roles. Oracy lies at the heart of these soft skills, supporting young people to interpret information, express complex ideas, collaborate in diverse teams, and navigate ethical dilemmas in an AI-augmented world. The ability to speak with clarity, listen actively and reason effectively is no longer a *'nice-to-have'* – it's fundamental to thriving in the workplace of tomorrow.

However, this poses a significant challenge for young people from disadvantaged backgrounds who may lack access to language-rich environments and opportunities to develop oracy. Without intervention, these pupils risk being further marginalised by a workforce increasingly driven by soft skills and professional communication.

To break this cycle, schools and employers must work together to embed oracy as a core pillar of education and workplace readiness – ensuring every young person, regardless of background, is equipped to succeed in a future shaped by both technology and human connection.

Chapter Summary

- The recent rise of AI-driven technologies has increased employer demands for those uniquely human traits, such as critical thinking and collaborative problem solving. Individuals with these skills sets are primed to flourish in the workplace of the near future and this hands a significant advantage to those young adults who have grown up in language-rich surroundings.
- Young people from lower socioeconomic upbringings often face a widening language gap to peers, hindering their success in the job market and career progression. This is reflected in the decreased levels of *'work readiness'* noted by employers
- Schools and universities must embed oracy across the curriculum to provide ample opportunities for pupils to observe and rehearse their key soft skills within a safe environment.

Reflection Questions

- How effectively does your current curriculum prepare pupils with the soft skills needed for a future workforce shaped by AI and automation?
- Are there meaningful opportunities across subjects for pupils to develop verbal reasoning, collaboration and critical thinking through talk?

Time to Take Action

Getting pupils to understand the importance of oracy and soft skills when considering their own futures is crucial. Conduct a **pupil survey** with a sample, using the questions below. Remember to include pupils from disadvantaged backgrounds as they are especially vulnerable to workplace barriers as a result of weaker language skills.

Section A: Values of Communication

1 Why do you think speaking clearly and confidently is important for adults in their work?
2 How will poor speaking and listening affect someone's chances of getting a better job?

Section B: Preparing for Your Future

1 Think about a job you would love to do when you leave school. How would strong communication skills help you in this career?
2 For these communication skills, do you get the chance to practise them in school? Can you think of any examples?
3 The future workplace will be heavily connected to AI and technology. What communication skills will help you to succeed?

Section C: Your Strengths and Development

1 What are your best strengths when considering your ability to speak to others? How confident are you speaking in front of classmates, adults or strangers?
2 What speaking and/or listening skill do you want more support to improve?
3 For the areas you want help with, what type of support would you find most useful?

References

English-Speaking Union (2023) *Oracy and Employability*. Available at: www.esu.org/news-and-views/oracy-and-employability/ (Accessed: 29 May 2025).
Government Office for Science (2017) *Future of Skills and Lifelong Learning*. Available at: https://assets.publishing.service.gov.uk/media/5b51fbdae5274a3fd124c916/Foresight-future-of-skills-lifelong-learning_V8.pdf (Accessed: 29 May 2025).
Major, L.E. and Machin, S. (2018) *Social Mobility and its Enemies*. London: Pelican Books.

14 Fostering an Oracy Culture

Leadership Matters

As in any organisation, implementing change in a school starts at the top. School leaders – and this is not limited to Heads and their deputies, but all staff who lead – are the ones who must effectively plan for change and set the structures, systems and people up for success. If we want to put oracy at the centre of education, school leaders must ensure it lives and blossoms across their values, priorities, ethos and culture. Leaders need an understanding of why oracy is needed for their setting and then set a clear vision for the future. Only then can the school work together to change the way they use talk.

Strategic Vision for Change

Every school updates their School Development Plan (SDP)/School Improvement Plan (SIP) annually to reflect the priorities for the year ahead. Commonly, SDPs will focus a range of areas including:

- Core subject foci (In primary, reading writing, maths, phonics)
- Behaviour management strategies
- Approach to assessment (summative and formative)
- Professional development
- Family and community engagement
- SEND and inclusion
- Technology for learning (AI, blended models etc)
- And other related areas

Whilst speech and language may feature in some aspects of many SDPs, oracy has been too often neglected in this space. With the wider exposure of oracy as a result of the UK Government's priorities, as well as the *'We Need to Talk'* report, schools and trusts are beginning to incorporate oracy into their SDPs/SIPs as an explicit and separate priority area.

Table 14.1 outlines the key considerations for any school leader hoping to incorporate oracy in a manner that is not *'tokenistic'* but valuable and measurable.

Table 14.1 Considerations for oracy in the SDP

Consideration	How to add into an SDP/SIP
Clear **intent and rationale** i.e. why do we need oracy within our SDP	• Link oracy into your existing school values • Use strong evidence base and research to support rationale (e.g. referring to social mobility, academic impact and wellbeing effect) • Ensure oracy is explicitly named in the SDP, not subtly embedded under the umbrella terms of literacy, communication or *'speech and language'*
How will we **measure** oracy outcomes and milestones?	• Include specific, time-bound targets (which can be measured via learning walks, observations, pupil voice) such as: increased pupil voice in lessons, observed evidence of talk structures in use • Consider measures that can assess the oracy progress of disadvantaged pupils
How will we **phase implementation** across the school?	• Identify a pilot phase/year group that can roll out any new initiatives first • Plan for a phased approach to staff training, initial introduction of oracy approach, refreshing of curriculum (and associated resources) • Align any oracy milestones with other aspects of the CPD calendar to avoid overlap or clashes and to find areas of synergy (e.g. looking to integrate aspects of oracy PD into other CPD such as inclusion, behaviour management or subject-specific sessions)
Assigning **clear roles and responsibilities** for leading and delivering the change	• Assign one member of the Leadership Team to lead on the oracy strategy and coordinate any initiatives and training across departments/phases • Clearly identify oracy leads within each area of the school (whether within phases, subjects or year groups) to act as *'oracy champions'* – do not forget members from the SEND and Inclusion teams too • Establish a structure for selecting pupils as *'oracy ambassadors'* or *'pupil voice leaders'*
Building in opportunities for **reflection** and feedback loops	• Build in regular review points at which feedback can be gathered from all stakeholders (staff, pupils, parents) in the form of learning walks, voice surveys • Incorporate oracy into the teacher pupil progress meetings and parent meetings to gather feedback and identify next steps for individual pupils as well as groups • Plan for sustainable implementation of oracy initiatives that goes beyond the first year of this iteration of the SDP

Oracy Is All Around: Or It Should Be

Changing a culture can be challenging; it requires sustained resource, leadership and effort by all stakeholders over a long period of time. To embed oracy into a school's culture, leaders cannot expect an immediate shift; they need to use the tools at hand to influence the way staff, pupils and parents use language effectively – those tools are the policies, procedures and daily routines.

The CIPD (2025) explores the need to focus efforts on organisational climate not culture. They state: 'Rather than culture, focusing on organisational climate – the meaning and behaviour attached to policies, practices and procedures employees experience – is a much more specific, tangible way to positively influence the workplace.'

Whilst they are predominantly focused upon the business world, this concept of organisational climate translates into education. By examining the policies and procedures we adhere to, there is an opportunity to place oracy into practice within our schools. This is reinforced by the Oracy Education Commission's seminal report, *We Need to Talk* (2024, p. 37), which claims, 'Oracy should be a whole school consideration embraced and embedded in the school's pastoral, personal development, creative and extracurricular provision and imbuing its routines, ethos and culture' (Table 14.2).

Table 14.2 Oracy integration into school policies and systems

Area	Oracy integration by...	Impact
Teaching and learning policy	Oracy stated as a *'non-negotiable'* aspect of the teaching sequence Outline the expected core talk structures to be used across all classrooms Signal importance of spoken language across all subjects (not solely restricted to English)	All staff (teaching and support) aligned on what oracy is and how it is to be used Greater consistency of strategies, leading to familiarity and more effective and sustained use
Behaviour Policy	Define the positive speaking and listening behaviours to be expected and modelled as part of school values (e.g. We listen respectfully to the speaker by....) Explain the importance of pupil contributions in class, whether at whole class discussion or small group level Outline strategies for self-regulation and supporting pupils through clearly defined talk routines	Clearly defined expectations help set boundaries Importance of oracy for all is clearly outlined for staff and pupils Staff follow consistent approach to supporting children who struggle to self-regulate
Parent/family engagement	Build in opportunities to inform and upskill families in the importance of oracy at home Share talk strategies to enrich home learning tasks for parent-child interactions e.g. question of the week	Parents become better informed on their role in supporting their child's oral development Oracy is valued by families as an important skill alongside reading, writing and maths
Pupil voice systems	Opportunities for pupils to engage with oracy through councils, pupil parliaments, guest visits and more to be formally recognised as part of 'what we do' Ensure inclusive selection for speaking opportunities so pupils needing confidence boosting can also participate	Pupil empowerment and ownership over their own language development
CPD and induction	Staff induction to include walk through of core oracy pedagogy, vision and practical strategies CPD sessions should include links to oracy as a core learning principle e.g. How can we ensure pupils are purposefully speaking to each other in this new initiative?	All staff join the school with the same understanding of oracy and related strategies Rather than being a separate domain, oracy spans all aspects of the curriculum and CPD

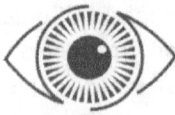
Learning walks/ observations
Proforma for observation notes and feedback to staff to include oracy prompts e.g. Were talk structures used to deepen class reasoning? Was tier 2 and 3 vocabulary explicitly taught and visible in the room?

Pupil Voice
Conduct frequent pupil voice focus groups to gauge levels of oracy in class and its impact upon pupil confidence and access to learning. Ensure disadvantaged and more anxious pupils are represented well.

Staff self-audit
Ask teaching staff and support staff to reflect on their own current practice, identifying strengths and areas to develop oracy further. Tie this into professional development and coaching between staff.

Evidence in learning
Incorporate oracy practice into classroom formative assessment strategies (e.g. rubrics and success criteria), through which pupils and staff assess the use of effective talk structures.

Figure 14.1 Monitoring oracy.

Look and You Will Find

If a school wants to see change become embedded as a natural part of *'what we do'*, leaders need to be looking for the specific strategies, attributes and adaptation that are laid out in the initial designs set out for all staff to buy into. As an analogy, consider the Key Stage 2 SATs in Year 6. The KS2 results are a leading measure of a school's performance by the Department for Education (DfE), parents and other stakeholders from inside and outside the school. As a result, the majority of schools dedicate added time, effort and resources towards the KS2 outcomes. In essence, SATs-related strategies and initiatives are widespread and engrained across schools nationwide because the final outcome is so well scrutinised and judged.

If school leaders are hoping to see oracy become a central component of their pedagogy and practice, they need to value it and seek it out in many different ways. Building oracy into the monitoring cycle can be an effective way to naturally integrate it into the daily classroom practice of the school whilst ensuring it is kept alive – not allowing it to lose steam and cease (Figure 14.1).

A Curriculum for Talk

The great minds of learning theory, from Vygotsky to Bruner, knew of the importance of language for learning. Oracy is learning through talk therefore surely all learning requires talk to be at it's core. Yet, in recent times, the UK National Curriculum has steered schools towards the transfer (and recall) of knowledge from teacher to pupil. Our education system is heavily geared towards the learning of facts and less so towards the practice and refinement of key learning skills, such as curiosity, critical thinking and problem solving. As laid bare in

Fostering an Oracy Culture

the previous chapter, our next generation needs to hone their soft skills to prepare them for the future workplace – our job now is to ensure they have the opportunities to develop these skills in their learning with us.

The Curriculum and Assessment Review, started in mid-2024 and it's findings and recommendations coming in late 2025, is seeking to refresh the way we teach and what we teach in schools. This is an opportunity to integrate oracy across the curriculum in a meaningful way.

Curriculum Mapping

Every year, school staff and leaders spend time reviewing their curriculum map for the following academic year. Questions will be asked of the curriculum coverage, such as:

- Which topics worked well this year and which did not? Why?
- Did we cover all the required content and what gaps need to be filled next year?
- Are there any changes needed to make the curriculum relevant and up to date?
- What skills did our cohort struggle to master and how can we adjust our teaching sequence to support them better?

This is an opportunity for staff to collectively reflect on where oracy can live within and across all subjects. Figure 14.2 shows some of the key considerations subject leaders should be exploring when revisiting their curriculum maps.

Tier 2 and 3 Vocabulary
What subject-specific terminology needing explicit teaching?
Are pupils expected to use these words in their articulation?
At which stage in the lesson sequence do we need to share them?

Questioning
What key questions need to be posed and answered by pupils to gauge both prior knowledge and grasp of new learning?
What pivot questions can be used to assess understanding during a lesson?

Collaborative dialogue
Where are the opportunities for pupils to work together on tasks?
How will pupils verbalise their opinions and present findings?
Will pupils have assigned talk roles (facilitator, presenter, summariser?)

Presentation
Are there clear opportunities for pupils to present to others?
How will presentation skills be modelled (e.g. tone, expression)?
What scaffolds (e.g. stem sentences) can support pupils?

Figure 14.2 Oracy curriculum mapping considerations.

Talk-Rich Lesson Design

Over the past two decades, lesson design has evolved considerably away from the traditional 'three-part lesson' of starter, task and plenary to a more dynamic structure; one which builds in opportunities for retrieval practice, class dialogue, ongoing formative assessment, live marking and more. Even before oracy was in the main education spotlight, teaching professionals had started to place far more emphasis upon collaborative learning in lesson design. Opportunities for problem solving, paired work, peer assessment and other shared learning were fed into the lesson sequence.

However, there has not been a consistent approach to embedding oracy and purposeful talk into lessons – at least not consistent enough to be recognised across every classroom. Considering Bloom's Taxonomy, teachers need to be looking at their lesson design to see how they can enable talk for the upper tiers. We want to rebalance the talk so learners are leading the dialogue in the classroom and, therefore, building in talk strategies aimed at the top of Bloom's hierarchy is a positive approach to protecting learner-led talk time (Table 14.3).

If learning is driven by social interactions between fellow learners, the teacher's duty is to put in place the structures and spaces for pupils to collaborate. When lesson planning, it can be helpful to consider how talk is integrated into the sequence through:

- **Consistent talk structures** e.g. Think-Pair-Share, talking chips, placemat consensus
- **Question stems** that align to Bloom's taxonomy e.g. *'I think this because…'* and *'What would change if…'*
- **Discussion checkpoints** are placed directly after new learning is introduced to allow pupils to explore, unpick and ask questions before moving onto the next stage of learning
- **Oracy-based success criteria** is used as part of the formative assessment, whether self, peer or adult led
- **Metacognitive reflection tasks** are included in the learning sequence, not only at the end of a lesson but at any stage where appropriate e.g. *'I used to think…. And now I know…'*

Table 14.3 Enabling talk for Bloom's taxonomy

Bloom's tier	Enabling talk by…	Example prompt	Talk strategies
Analyse	Encouraging pupils to break down ideas, analyse relationships and compare perspectives	What's the difference between….? Can you spot a pattern…?	Odd one out True or False?
Evaluate	Fostering critical discussion, debate and justification of opinions	Do you agree/ disagree? Why or why not? What are your reasons for…?	Ranking opinions Socratic questioning
Create	Supporting collaborative idea generation, creative thinking and imagination	What would happen if…? Can you invent a solution for…?	Pitching ideas Role play scenarios

Stimuli Makes the Difference

As part of their oracy benchmarks, Voice 21 identify the need for teachers to, 'carefully consider the quality of teacher-student and student-student talk' in lessons and to select 'interesting and appropriate stimuli for talk which enables students to develop, apply and consolidate their subject knowledge'. If we want pupils to engage in meaningful dialogue, it is imperative that we provide them with meaningful prompts and questions to stimulate this talk.

Talk stimuli can take many forms, from imagery to music, poetry to artefacts. Finding interesting and engaging stimuli is essential for generating purposeful talk in class. When selecting a stimuli, consider:

- Will it spark curiosity and discussion amongst the pupils?
- Does it link to the current topic and/or to prior learning?
- What type of talk will it encourage (e.g. reasoning, debate, questioning, description)?
- Can all pupils, regardless of oracy and confidence, engage with it?
- Is it open-ended enough to encourage discussion from diverse perspectives?

Assessing Learning through Talk

The UK education system heavily relies upon testing and examinations to assess progress, knowledge and skills. Summative assessments in their many forms, whether National such as GCSEs of Key Stage 2 SATs or school-level such as termly practice papers, are commonplace in the majority of schools. The ability to benchmark pupils against each other using quantifiable metrics can be a useful tool for measuring progress and attainment. However, all too often, schools are driving effort, resources and staff towards these summative outcomes at the expense of other areas of learning that are less measurable. Teachers need the opportunity to work alongside the child to assess what they know (or don't) and where support is needed.

Oracy is one of the most underutilised tools in a teacher's formative assessment toolkit. Providing pupils with opportunities to talk about their learning can be a very effective way to gauge their level of understanding – the caveat is that any oral approaches must be well planned and given the space in the timetable to be effective.

A Culture of Formative Assessment

Formative assessment has risen in stature over the last decade or so. Where historically, summative assessment was the main way schools measured progress and attainment, there has been a substantial shift – in the classroom at least – towards formative assessment. If we consider the metaphor of a chef cooking soup. Adding all the ingredients and only trying the soup for taste at the very end would not be a great way to guarantee a tasty outcome; this is a summative approach in which the chef (a.k.a teacher) is crossing their fingers in hope that the end result is positive. However, imagine a chef who is constantly checking and tasting, adjusting ingredients to improve the taste along the way; this is formative and allows the chef to check progress at all stages of the journey.

Formative assessment brings many benefits to the teaching and learning process, including:

- The ability to **identify learning gaps** for individuals as well as groups
- Happening **'in the moment'** which allows the teacher to give timely, relevant feedback to the pupils
- Allows the teacher to **spot common misconceptions** that need addressing at that stage of learning – avoiding embedding misunderstanding in the long term memory of pupils
- Pupils can **check their understanding** of new concepts by asking questions at the start of the process rather than after completing independent tasks

So, how does oracy fit into this culture of assessment?

If we want oracy to be integral to the way we teach and learn across a school, it has to play a fundamental role in the way teachers assess. This is a cultural shift and, as mentioned earlier in this chapter, can be supported by embedding oracy into the policies and processes of the school.

Recommendations for embracing oracy as part of the way a school assesses include:

1. **Assessment Policy Alignment:** Within the school's assessment policy, ensure oral responses are explicitly identified as valid and expected forms of formative assessment that need to be used daily within ALL lessons and at multiple points within a lesson.
2. **Shared Language of Talk:** Develop a consistent, school-wide rubric of what *'good oracy'* looks like in practice e.g. use of voice, vocabulary selection and application, ability to reason and evidence answers).
3. **Staff CPD:** To be secure, teaching staff need to develop their formative strategies through a blend of CPD, observations of skilled colleagues, shared reflections and feedback loops. It is insufficient to introduce oracy strategies without adequate CPD to ensure staff feel confident in applying them effectively.
4. **Recognition in monitoring:** For teachers to feel confident in deploying formative assessment within their classrooms, they need to feel safe in the knowledge that this is expected and sought out by senior leaders. With the understanding that SLT are celebrating use of formative oracy approaches, teachers are far more likely to use them wholeheartedly and without fear of reprisal.

By considering oral assessment through these multiple lenses, it is possible to gradually shift cultural habits and behaviours of staff and pupils.

Formative Assessment in Practice

With all the good intentions of ensuring the top down approach to formative assessment, the success of any cultural shift comes to life within the four walls of a classroom. Whilst senior leadership buy-in and alignment of policies and processes is important, it is the teaching staff who determine how successful any change can be. If we want teachers to be using oral strategies to assess, we need to equip them with the knowledge, tools and coaching.

To get teachers on side with any changes to in class assessment, it is important to share the potential benefits for both them and their pupils. Without the understanding of how it

Table 14.4 Benefits of oracy for assessment

Benefit	For teachers	For pupils
Time efficiency	Enables quicker checks without the need for lengthy marking through books	Timely, in the moment feedback helps pupils to make immediate changes to their practise
Identification of strength/gaps	Can hear the misconceptions and address them at that time rather than the following lesson	Pupils can verbalise their thinking and discuss what they know/do not know with peers and adults
Depth of understanding	Ability to hear levels of reasoning by individuals, not merely a written answer in a book	Challenged to reason and justify their thinking which helps develop higher order thinking
Classroom engagement	Lends itself to more dynamic and interactive lessons and greater engagement by more pupils	Increased enjoyment and motivation to engage as their voice is being heard
Inclusivity and accessibility	Ability to see a broader profile of learning across all pupils including the less confident writers. Removes judgement solely on written outcome	Pupils with EAL, SEND and/or writing difficulties can engage and demonstrate understanding to a better extent than in writing
Progress tracking	Ongoing dialogue allows teacher to develop a narrative of learning over time for the whole class as well as for individuals	Opportunity for metacognitive reflections because of the frequency of talking about what they know and need to learn going forward

will improve their practice, many teachers will see this as 'another thing for the workload pile' (Table 14.4).

Over the past decade or so, many strategies have been deployed to minimise teacher workload in respect to ongoing assessments. Lengthy, in-book marking has gradually been replaced (albeit not entirely) by more routine use of verbal feedback, live marking and dialogue between teacher and pupil. This change has been supported by a growing evidence base which supports the case for more oral feedback; the EEF Toolkit (Education Endowment Foundation, 2025) ranks verbal feedback positively (+ 7 months progress), stating that feedback, 'should not be limited exclusively to written marking'.

Benefits may sell the need for change but to be effective, teachers need to harness the strategies (see Figure 14.3 which showcases strategies including some from Voice 21 and Kagan). By integrating these strategies into the lesson design, formative assessment using purposeful talk can improve so many aspects of classroom practice.

Embedding Oracy into CPD

Teachers are at the coalface of education, and they are the cornerstone of any changes to be seen in the classroom. For purposeful implementation of oracy, whether policy or practice, the teaching community needs to buy into the vision and feel ready, willing and able to deliver the change. School leaders responsible for continuous professional development (CPD) must avoid bolting on oracy to their existing CPD programme – instead, they should be reviewing how to use oracy as a lens through which to view CPD, ensuring all staff are

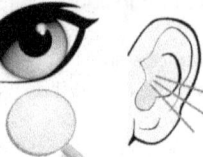

Verbal exit tickets
To catch what has been taught and secured into memory before they leave the classroom

Timed pair share
Equal speaking/ listening time between partners whilst adults 'helicopter' nearby to assess grasp of new learning

Timed pair share
Equal speaking/ listening time between partners whilst adults 'helicopter' nearby

Rally/ round robin
Partners/ groups bounce responses back and forth, highlighting depth of knowledge and recall

Concept corners
Pupils decide by moving to a corner and debating their choices, allowing adults to spot common misconceptions

Figure 14.3 Oral formative assessment.

equipped with relevant skills, sufficient time and frequent opportunities to rehearse and embed new practice.

Oracy as a Lens

Before every academic year commences, senior leaders will be constructing the CPD calendar for the year ahead. Most schools CPD offer consists of weekly staff briefings, some form of coaching/1:1 support, bespoke CPD courses (external, such as the NPQs and school visits/internal, such as visits from experts in a field) and self-directed study. In primary schools, CPD may often be divided by age phase, with Early Years teams focussing upon more age-relevant training versus Key Stage colleagues. In secondary, some training may go school-wide or by age phase, but there will also be far more subject-specific CPD within departments.

In recent years, CPD has moved from being a blanketed, broad-brush model towards more tailored and targeted training that addresses the developmental needs of individuals and groups. The challenge for any school seeking to add oracy into the CPD calendar is that it needs to be a consistent thread throughout the school, not siloed by age, department or specialism. Naturally, some talk strategies may vary by subject but the overarching principles and talk structures for pupils should sit above and across the curriculum. Otherwise, we are at risk of implementing oracy without consistency or shared vision; this could lead to a disjointed implementation through which pupils and staff become confused about the changes expected.

In the *'We Need to Talk'* report (Oracy Education Commission, 2024), they caution that any CPD needs to go, 'beyond inserting general approaches to speaking and listening into teacher development'. They go on to recommend that all teachers need to become *'language-aware'* and grow confident enough to *'grapple with oracy'* as it relates to their specific subjects.

Standalone Oracy CPD

For a school that is coming to oracy completely fresh and with minimal knowledge, explicit oracy CPD will be essential early on to ensure all staff understand:

- The origins and pedagogy behind oracy
- Benefits that stronger oracy can have upon academic progress
- How language is a vital tool for emotional regulation and expression
- The adult's role in modelling and facilitating purposeful dialogue in the classroom

It is just as crucial to provide time in the CPD calendar for staff to be introduced to any identified strategies to be rolled out. For successful implementation, the strategies need to be clearly modelled to staff, practised in class (even possibly starting in pilot classes) and given opportunities for feedback and reflection. With multiple exposures to the strategy, alongside multiple opportunities to trial, reflect and refine, there is a far greater chance of sustainable impact in the longer term.

Oracy as the Thread

Subject leaders are often found competing for space in the overloaded CPD calendar. With such limited and precious time set aside for CPD in the school timetable, trying to fit oracy in as a separate entity may be a challenge, especially when it is fighting for space against core subjects, safeguarding, first aid and other traditional domains. Yet, we can use this advantageously to shift our perspective on where oracy sits in CPD. Instead of being a separate *'thing we do'*, we can begin to examine the CPD on offer through the lens of oracy.

When designing subject-specific CPD, it is useful to consider the following questions to ensure oracy is incorporated into the sequence:

- What **key oracy skills** are essential for pupils to progress in the subject?
- Where are there **opportunities for purposeful talk** within our subject matter?
- What **talk structures** lend themselves well to our subject i.e. Can you debate open questions? Can you unpick misconceptions? Are you able to make informed predictions and evidenced interpretations?
- What **key vocabulary** must the pupils be exposed to, modelled in context and expected to use in their responses?
- How can pupils **demonstrate their understanding** through spoken responses (instead of just written)? How will this aid formative assessment?

By using these questions as a filter, oracy becomes a natural part of how we teach and learn rather than a bolt-on to the status quo. For comparison, consider how retrieval practice has moved from an academic theory to become a widespread practice across all subjects.

The Oracy Education Commission (2024) urge schools to *'avoid a proliferation of tokenistic practice and ill-informed advice and training'* but to ensure subject leaders, CPD leads and classroom teachers have the foundational knowledge to implement the *'active ingredients of high-quality oracy education'* in a way that fits their subject domain. In order to remove the possibility of tokenistic practices, CPD needs to be sustained over a longer period of time and not merely be a standalone, one-off event. To ensure oracy is a thread that runs continuously through our CPD calendar, we can:

- **Pair up** oracy champions (or stronger, experienced staff) with less confident colleagues, to allow for ongoing dialogue, team teaching and shared reflections on any new practices being introduced. If not pairs, consider teaching triads, learning communities or professional learning networks as ways for colleagues to learn from and support each other.
- Build oracy into your **coaching/mentoring** models that exist within your school development structure.
- Find opportunities to **partner with local schools** who may be further along their own oracy journey. Enabling staff to visit, observe and discuss with more experienced colleagues in different settings can be a powerful mechanism for embedding change back at school.

Chapter Summary

- Cultural change starts at the top! Leadership needs to embrace oracy as part of their vision, priorities and efforts in the long term. This feeds into the various policies and structures set up to ensure pedagogy and practice are aligned and consistent across all teaching and learning; oracy needs to be incorporated into these areas, from the teaching and learning policy to the behaviour management policies.
- Oracy is defined (partly) as *'learning through talk'*, so it is vital that any curriculum mapping or review of lesson designs takes oracy into account. By having oracy strategies identified and built into teaching routines, there is a far greater chance of successful and sustainable implementation.
- Formative assessment can be greatly enhanced by purposeful use of talk. It can make *'in the moment'* assessments easier, quicker and less workload heavy for both pupil and teacher.
- Teachers need to feel empowered and equipped to implement oracy in their practice. This is only truly achievable through ongoing CPD and opportunities for rehearsal and reflection of any new oracy strategies. Oracy should become a lens through which staff look at their subject-specific CPD delivery.

Reflection Questions

- How visible is oracy in your school development plan, teaching and learning policies and other policies around your school?
- Reviewing your CPD calendar, where does oracy already feature? If it does not, what opportunities can you identify for oracy to be integrated into your upcoming CPD?

Time to Take Action

Find a current copy of your school's **CPD calendar**. Complete the following questions below:

A   Does oracy explicitly (or implicitly i.e. references made to talk, speaking, listening) appear within the CPD calendar? Are there any dedicated sessions in which oracy is the main or part-focus?

B   Are there CPD sessions that could benefit from adding an oracy perspective? If so, how could you go about discussing this with the colleague leading that CPD?

C   Do you have any mechanisms – such as gap tasks, coaching, team teaching – that you can harness to ensure any new talk strategies are embedded into teaching practice?

References

CIPD (2025) *Organisational Climate and Culture*. Available at: www.cipd.org/en/knowledge/factsheets/organisation-culture-change-factsheet/ (Accessed: 29 May 2025).

Education Endowment Foundation (2025) *Feedback*. Available at: https://educationendowmentfoundation.org.uk/education-evidence/teaching-learning-toolkit/feedback (Accessed: 29 May 2025).

Oracy Education Commission (2024) *We Need to Talk: The Report of the Commission on the Future of Oracy Education in England*. Oracy Education Commission.

15 Taking Action

Building an Oracy-Rich School

Throughout this book, the case for boosting oracy in our schools has been clearly laid out; the benefits for our most disadvantaged pupils, as well as the barriers that come in oracy's absence, have been presented and swell-evidenced. Yet, if we are serious about improving the trajectories of our most language-poor children, theory is not enough. Converting theory into practice is essential to realise the potential of stronger oracy for all young people, regardless of social standing.

Oracy Leads Unite!

Alongside the rise of oracy within educational spheres of influence, we have seen an increase in the number of schools and Trusts designating an Oracy Lead. Responsible for the implementation of new strategies, routines and staff development, these leads are at the coalface of oracy change. Only a minority of schools have already designated a lead for oracy, with many having handed this domain to:

- English leads
- A member of the Senior (or even Middle) Leadership team
- No assigned lead

For oracy to move into the space of *'the Fourth R'*, it needs a leader to drive the change and ensure all stakeholders are ready, willing and able to make the change stick. With the continued squeeze upon school budgets and high levels of workload for staff, finding a dedicated lead can be a challenge. Moreover, finding time to release the lead to spend time on new plans and initiatives can be even harder. To navigate the budgetary and time constraints, there are some alternatives to sole oracy leads, including:

- Forming an **oracy team**, made of a range of passionate colleagues who can share the workload, collaborate on initiatives and own areas of expertise.
- Appoint **oracy champions** to drive change in specific areas, such as: year groups, phases, subjects, key stages. It is wise to get a champion from each main area to ensure any new changes receive feedback and support based on the needs of the different

areas. For example, in primary, appointing a champion in Early Years, Key Stage One, Key Stage Two as well as SEND can give an equitable balance.
- Set up an **Oracy Working Group/Party** that consists of leaders, teachers, support staff and pupils. This group can meet regularly to review initiatives, feedback on progress, suggest new ideas and celebrate successes.
- For schools within a **Trust**, an appointed lead can sit centrally, supported by school representatives. This centralised approach helps the creation and distribution of shared resources, consistent training and collective monitoring; all which help reduce the burden on individual schools.

Establishing a Vision and Gaining Buy-in

A strong commitment to oracy starts with a clear and shared vision that places spoken language at the centre of learning, alongside the core literacy and numeracy fundamentals. School leaders, at all levels but especially the top, must champion their own vision and align it to their school priorities. Establishing oracy as a core priority signals it's importance to staff, pupils and parents; this can help everyone to be *'on the same page'* with the way they plan to implement oracy strategies. When any change lacks a vision as well as the necessary leadership buy-in, it remains shallow and will not have long term sustainability.

Creating a shared vision that brings everyone along on the oracy journey is crucial and there are several steps that can be followed to reach this point early on.

Vision as a School Priority

a   Ensure oracy lives in your **School Development Plan** (SDP) and long-term goals
    i   Currently, is oracy explicitly prioritised in your SDP as an important area of focus?
    ii Is it subtly hidden amongst the broader terminology of language and communication? If so, how can it be more clearly identified as a core pillar of *'what we want to change'*?
b   Draft an **Oracy Vision Statement**
    i   This needs to clearly articulate why oracy is a fundamental part of the school's way forward
    ii Examples include:
- *At [School name], we believe that every child deserves the confidence and ability to express themselves clearly, articulating their thoughts and feelings to others through high quality spoken interactions.*
- *Our vision is to empower every pupil with the confidence and skills to articulate their thoughts clearly, listen actively and engage meaningfully in dialogue, ensuring that spoken language is a powerful tool for learning and connection across all areas of school life.*
- *We strive to create a learning environment where oracy is at the heart of every classroom interaction, building pupils' capacity to communicate effectively, think critically, and collaborate confidently, preparing them for success both in school and beyond.*

c **Engage key stakeholders** in the vision creation process
  i   Construct the vision statement with contributions and feedback from key stakeholders, including teachers, support staff, pupils and parents. This helps to foster a collective commitment to change.
  ii This collaborative process can be achieved through a range of channels, including:
      - Staff meetings, surveys and oracy working groups
      - Parent newsletters, surveys and interviews
      - Governor updates and feedback at regular meetings
d Set clear and measurable **goals**
  i   Establish specific targets for oracy development to ensure tracking and progress monitoring is able to show impact over time.
  ii Examples include:
      - *Increase pupils' verbal contributions in class by c. 20% by XX date*
      - *Incorporate 1 new talk structure into teaching sequence each short term*
e **Launch** the vision
  i   Find an opportunity to introduce the agreed vision to all key stakeholders to ensure alignment and shared ownership of the change about to commence.
  ii Opportunities could include:
      - INSET day/session for all staff (not only teachers)
      - Launch assemblies for pupils, followed by teacher Q&A with pupils to respond to any initial questions
      - Launch video, newsletter and initial communications to families

Opening Eyes Through an Audit

Conducting an oracy audit is an effective way to identify a range of strengths and areas for development within your school. Casting a critical eye over your current practices, policies and processes can allow you to:

- Find areas where language development is already thriving and effectively being supported within areas of the school
- Identify the largest and most significant gaps in oracy across your teaching and learning domains
- Better understand the contextual profile and needs of your families, in terms of their language use at home and pre-joining school
- See where the quick wins are across the school, whether in terms of curriculum design, staff CPD, displays, routines or other areas of pedagogy
- Identify teachers who are already demonstrating a strong grasp of oracy in their practice and whom may be ideal candidates for becoming oracy champions/leads

The auditing process should not be conducted and controlled solely by senior leadership. It should be a collaborative process, through which a range of stakeholders across the school are able to work together to assess the current *'state of play'*. Evidence can be gathered in a range of forms, from learning walks to staff voice, through to surveys and staff interviews. Specific focus should be placed upon identifying the language gap that exists between disadvantaged pupils and their peer groups. Understanding this divide is crucial so any new initiatives can be more targeted for maximum impact where it is most needed.

With this evidence, baselines can be drawn up and used for ongoing benchmarking throughout academic years. Re-auditing can then be utilised to measure progress and demonstrate impact of changes implemented.

Steps to conducting an oracy audit

a   Define the **scope**
   i   Establish clear objectives for the audit by determining what areas of school will be included. Consider curriculum design, teaching policies, staff CPD, environments.
   ii Link it to the School Development Plan to ensure it sits within your key priority areas for the year
b   Collect **baseline** data
   i   Use a set of metrics for consistent data collection. The Oracy Benchmarks from Voice 21 are a good starting point and cover areas including:
      - Shared language
      - Classroom practice
      - Whole school culture
      - Curriculum and planning
      - Assessment and feedback
   ii **Conduct data collection,** using the benchmarks, in a range of formats, including:
      - Learning walks, focused upon teacher modelling, use of questioning, opportunities for structured talk and levels of pupil engagement
      - Lesson observations, examining evidence of structured talk, quality of spoken language, teaching and application of tiered vocabulary and scaffolding for pupils with language needs
      - Pupil voice, via surveys and interview in which pupils can share views on quality of talk, opportunities for them to rehearse and levels of confidence and self-efficacy
      - Staff voice, collecting feedback on staff confidence with new oracy strategies, CPD needs, strengths with talk structures and areas of concern regarding implementation
      - Environment walk, exploring areas where language is *'alive'* (or missing) and accessible in classrooms, shared spaces and outdoor areas
   iii **Analyse** the findings
      - Examine areas of strength that can be refined and incorporated into any new initiatives, ranging from staff expertise/skills to areas of the curriculum that already enhance language acquisition
      - Identify weaker areas in need of change, either whole scale or minor adaptations. This can include areas of the curriculum mapping, lesson design and even policy and procedures
      - Have an equity focus upon the vulnerable pupil groups (i.e. disadvantaged, EAL, SEND) to measure the language gap

iv **Share** findings with key stakeholders
- This is essential for obtaining buy-in from staff, families, governors/trustees and pupils
- Sharing can take place through CPD sessions, newsletters, reports – utilise the pre-existing channels of communication within the school

An audit can very easily become a forgotten, dust-covered document that sits idle on the staff room table or noticeboard. It is important to use the oracy audit as a baseline from which to measure progress over the course of any implementation programme. When action planning for new oracy initiatives, frequent checkpoints should be built in; this will help to establish a culture of continuous reflection against the original audit, keeping it alive and relevant. This feedback loop can take several forms and does not need to be as extensive as the first audit. Using pupil voice, staff surveys and learning walks can be an efficient means to track the effectiveness of any strategies being deployed.

Keeping It SMART!

Any project looking to introduce and sustain change across an organisation needs to have a clear set of goals to aim towards. Too often in schools, leaders can get overly excited about new ideas, introducing them in a rushed manner that leads to shallow implementation that fails to survive beyond the initial enthusiasm. Many businesses deploy the SMART model for goal setting as a means of keeping targets clear, reachable and easy to measure. For oracy changes to effectively embed into a school's culture and pedagogy, it can be useful to keep goals SMART (see Table 15.1).

Ready, Willing and Able

Once a vision has been created, an audit has been conducted and SMART goals have been set, the next step is to ensure all key stakeholders are ready, willing and able to make the change happen. This three-pronged approach to preparing for new changes can help direct resources, time and capacity effectively. With any aspect of this trio missing, stakeholders may put up resistance, lack engagement or implement the changes without the necessary skills to make it sustainable.

Ready

For oracy to successfully embed into the fabric of a school, everyone needs to understand the importance and be prepared for its integration. There are some key steps to take to ensure all stakeholders are ready for change, including:

a   Understanding the **change drivers**
   i   The reasons why oracy is needed should be clearly supported by a trusted evidence base. School leaders should share evidence – whether reports, case studies or real world examples – with all involved or impacted by the change.
   ii Parental engagement in the *'why'* of change is essential as they are a key player in delivering the new initiatives beyond the classroom.

Table 15.1 Setting SMART targets

SMART	Definition	Oracy actions
Specific	Clearly defined goals that identify exactly what is to be achieved	• Aim goals at targeted year groups/subjects (e.g. *Integrate (assigned) talk structure into Year 5 maths lessons*) • Have key oracy skills as a core focus in a phased approach (e.g. using Autumn term to focus on the physical skills of eye contact, tracking the speaker and clear articulation of word)
Measurable	The ability to track progress and measure outcomes against defined criteria	• Identify the tracking mechanisms to be used (including frequency, lead responsible, format), including pupil voice, learning walks • Set numerical targets for each goal (e.g. *Over 50% of class observations to demonstrate use of identified strategy*)
Achievable	Goals should be realistic and attainable, taking into account funding, resources and time commitments	• Establish a staff CPD programme that aligns to the roll-out of new initiatives to ensure all staff feel ready and equipped • Begin with pilot trials in set classes. Choose teachers who are passionate and engaged with the vision as initial pilot champions • Identify support structures (e.g. mentoring, buddy systems) to provide necessary help during implementation
Relevant	Goals need to align to school priorities and oracy vision	• Ensure oracy targets are incorporated into the School Development Plan • Identify the strategies that will focus on narrowing the oracy gap between vulnerable groups
Time-bound	A clear timeframe with built-in milestones	• Set milestones for key phases of the implementation journey (e.g. initial pilot, phased roll out, evaluation stage) • Define the checkpoints (e.g. end of term) and how progress will be assessed against baseline audit

b Space for **planning** and **preparation**
  i Teachers need time within shared planning (individual class, year group, subject or whole school) to explore how oracy strategies can be incorporated.
  ii Pupils will need gradual building of oracy-related skills through practice activities. This helps establish routines and expectations before any official talk structures are introduced.
  iii Parents and families need to be informed and encouraged to discuss the importance of language with their children at home.
c Clear **communication** of expectations
  i The vision needs to be clearly shared with all relevant stakeholders, adjusting the terminology and level of detail according to the audience.
  ii The SMART goals for the change needs to be communicated to all at the start of the journey so everyone is aware off what is trying to be achieved.
  iii Visually mapping the start of the journey, along with the milestones and checkpoints, can help everyone understand the steps in order.

Willing

For change to be successful, stakeholders need to genuinely believe in the benefits that oracy can bring to their school and children. Buying-in to the collective vision is an important necessity for everyone to be singing from the same hymn sheet. Ensuring people are motivated to contribute to new strategies and initiatives will ensure that oracy is placed at the heart of everything that happens in school.

a Motivation through **ongoing shared vision**
  i It is insufficient to only share the vision in the very early stages; to maintain momentum and motivation, the vision should be consistently communicated alongside the core purpose for change. For instance, reminding stakeholders that the most disadvantaged pupils will benefit as a result of the proposed changes.
  ii Supporting the vision sharing with relevant evidence and research from other educational settings can help add a tangible element.

b Sharing **successes** early on
  i Identify any quick wins – the *'low hanging fruit'* – that can be shared and celebrated with staff, families and pupils.
  ii Quick wins can include pupil case studies, specific progress measures against baseline and anecdotal examples from within the school. Seeing these real benefits can solidify buy-in to the vision.

c **Address barriers** to willingness
  i With any change, resistance or scepticism are commonplace, whether from staff, families or pupils. Knowing these potential barriers before you commence can make it easier to mitigate any negativity as early as possible.
  ii Conducting a **pre-mortem** can be an effective way of reverse engineering barriers to change:
  - Assume failure – collectively assume the changes have failed
  - Identify reasons – generate all possible factors (internal and external) that could have led to the failure
  - Develop mitigation strategies – create approaches to address each of the potential factors

Able

Being willing and ready for change is a very important part of the change journey. Yet, without the capacity to deliver the new approaches with fidelity impact will be limited. Stakeholders must be equipped with the right tools and knowledge to deliver oracy effectively. It is the school leadership's responsibility to ensure all parties receive the necessary upskilling and ongoing development to successfully embed the new ways of teaching and learning.

a **Upskilling** teaching staff
  i As mentioned earlier in the chapter, ensure the CPD calendar has some explicit time and space for onboarding staff with new strategies alongside ongoing CPD opportunities
  ii Avoid limiting training just to teachers – other support staff are just as critical in the successful roll-out of oracy, especially those leading interventions and 1:1s

iii Provide the necessary resources to support the new strategies. This can include presentations, templates, guidance videos or quality examples. These resources need to be shared upfront, made accessible through normal sharing platforms and relevant to the context of the school.

b **Pupil readiness**
   i   Any changes introduced into the classroom need to be phased in gradually. As with any new learning, teachers need to take small steps to embed new routines and expectations with their pupils. As a school, it is useful to identify the phases of roll-out and which strategies will be introduced in order.
   ii It is important to be explicit with pupils around the purpose of oracy. If they can understand why talk supports learning, they will feel more engaged and empowered with their own spoken language.
   iii Alongside new routines and structures, teachers should reflect these in their class environments; useful posters, displays and scaffolds can aid recall and embed new ways of learning over time.

c **Parental support** is key!
   i   Parents act as the additional teacher, modelling spoken dialogue with their child beyond the school day. Therefore, it is important that parents are given the necessary support, skills and information to boost oracy at home.
   ii Engaging parents directly can be a challenge, so schools need to be creative and adaptable to support families in ways that best fit their needs and situations. This support for oracy can range from:
   - Online resources – presentations, posters, videos, FAQs
   - Virtual – webinars, online meetings
   - In person – meetings, workshops, stay and learns, assemblies
   - Printed – newsletters, activity sheets, flashcards, flyers, posters

---

Chapter Summary

- A clear vision for oracy needs to be established and co-created with input from all involved parties. This vision needs to be tied closely into the school's forward looking plans and priorities to ensure it is valued as a necessary and positive change.
- Before implementing, schools need to have a very clear overview of their current strengths and areas for development in the oracy space. Conducting a thorough and wide-reaching audit of language can provide this baseline picture; this can help guide resources and support to the most concerning areas for change.
- Implementing change across a school community is a large undertaking that requires clear goal setting. Keeping goals SMART can help school leaders to measure progress, identify successes as well as areas for further refinement.
- All stakeholders need to be *'ready, willing and able'* for a new approach to oracy to embed into the everyday fabric of a school. This means everyone needs to be bought into the vision, understanding their roles and equipped with the required skills to deliver change.

> **Reflection Questions**
>
> - Does your school have a vision for oracy? If so, is it known by all stakeholders? If not, how can you go about creating a vision?
> - If you were to conduct an oracy audit, consider:
>
>   a Who would you involve in the data gathering process?
>   b What methods would you use to collect information i.e. learning walks, surveys?
>   c How much time would you free staff up for conducting the audit, including time to interpret the outcomes?

Time to Take Action

Your task is to create an **Oracy Vision Postcard** in which you will visualise what oracy will look and feel like in your school once your change programme has been implemented (possibly two years from commencing).

Fill in Table 15.2 – it can be useful to ask staff members to also complete their own postcards then discuss collectively to form a shared outlook of the near future.

Table 15.2 Oracy vision postcard

Question	Your response
What does talk for learning look like if we were to walk into a classroom?	
What changes have teachers, pupils and families noticed in terms of oracy?	
How does lesson design feel different?	
Complete the sentence, 'We knew our vision for oracy had become a reality when…'	

16 Case Studies

Oracy in Action

Theory into Practice

Every school has its own individual context, influenced by the community it sits within, the families who send their children into the setting and the challenges facing the area. This means that any implementation of oracy is never *'straight out of the box'* and requires adaptation to meet the specific needs of the school. However, the core principles of ensuring stakeholders are ready, willing and able to change their relationship with oracy still apply.

This chapter shares a range of case studies and interviews with school leaders, including headteachers, oracy leads and subject leads. Their stories explain their oracy journeys so far, sharing lessons learnt, successes and challenges faced along the way.

Why Has Oracy Been Such a Priority for Nightingale? How was the *'language gap'* evident in the school at the start of this journey?
At Nightingale, oracy has become one of the most important pillars of our school development not just because it's an educational buzzword but because our community demands it.

For over a decade, we've served a richly diverse intake, with over 60% of our pupils consistently classified as EAL learners. With this in mind, oracy hasn't been a trendy initiative, it's been a necessity. However, our journey toward embedding it meaningfully across the curriculum didn't start with research or strategy, it began with a hard truth.

In 2016, we faced one of our most challenging moments as a school. Our Year 6 SATS Reading results stood at 46% expected, despite being above the national average in both Writing (79%) and Maths (71%). Most notably, four pupils missed the expected standard by just one mark, and all of them had struggled with vocabulary-based questions. This wasn't merely unfortunate; it was a wake-up call.

We realised that while we had adopted Reciprocal Reading as a strategy to support comprehension, we hadn't fully appreciated the language demands it placed on EAL and disadvantaged pupils. This method assumed pupils had the vocabulary depth, confidence, and oral fluency to navigate the four roles in reciprocal reading. For many of our learners still developing foundational language skills, it led to cognitive overload rather than clarity.

It was at this point that we developed our *'Reading Wheel'* approach, a tool that broke down the seven key reading domains (vocabulary, retrieval, sequencing, prediction, inference, summarising and authorial intent) into concrete, focused teaching points. This became

DOI: 10.4324/9781003607595-17

> **Case Study: A Long-Term Journey towards Sustainable Oracy**
>
> **Name:** Omar Jennings
>
> **Role:** Headteacher, Nightingale Primary School
>
> **Mini Bio:**
>
> Omar Jennings is not just an educator but a visionary who embraced the digital transformation of education during the pivotal years of 2019 and 2020. With over 20 years of teaching experience spanning Canada, Scotland and England, Omar brings a rich international perspective to his work.
>
> Omar has served in various influential roles, including Professional Development Lead for the National Centre for Excellence in the Teaching of Mathematics (NCETM), Numeracy Specialist Teacher and Headteacher Advocate.
>
> Now in his seventh year as Headteacher of Nightingale Primary School, Woolwich, a top-performing institution in one of the UK's most deprived areas, Omar champions innovative strategies to elevate educational outcomes. His leadership is defined by a steadfast commitment to equity, ensuring that every child, regardless of their background, has the opportunity to thrive in an oracy-driven pedagogy and benefit from the transformative power of technology in their learning experiences.

our first real step in building oracy: training staff to teach the language of reading explicitly, and equipping children with the skills to articulate their thinking clearly and purposefully.

To support this, we embedded a vocabulary-rich approach, rooted in the evidence found in *Bringing Words to Life* by Isabel Beck, Margaret McKeown and Linda Kucan. Two strategies we pulled into our practice were:

- Tiered vocabulary selection: being intentional about selecting Tier 2 words (high-utility academic vocabulary) for direct instruction.
- Student-friendly definitions with context: ensuring pupils encountered new vocabulary in multiple rich, meaningful contexts, paired with oral rehearsal.

This worked well for the next 2 years, until 2019, when reading scores again fell, this time to 59%. Upon analysis, we found that the 2019 SATs paper had the highest word count of any test paper since 2016, clocking in at 2,128 words. Our pupils simply hadn't built the stamina to handle such dense texts.

This led us to explore John Hattie's research, particularly his findings on repeated reading and close reading strategies, which emphasised the importance of fluency and depth. We integrated structured repeated readings, fostering not only fluency but also oral phrasing and intonation, which are key elements of oracy development.

Over time, the goal has shifted beyond improving test scores. The SATS simply provided us with clear, sometimes painful, evidence to help us recalibrate our thinking. The real goal has been to elevate the quality of teacher instruction, which in turn raises the level of pupil oracy, especially in a school where English is not the first language for the majority of our children.

We now understand that reading comprehension, vocabulary acquisition and oracy development are inseparable. They are three strands of the same rope, and if one is weak, the others can't hold the weight.

How has the local context and demographic influenced your approach to language development?

Our pupils come from one of the most deprived areas in the UK, which has significantly shaped our approach to language development. According to the 2019 Index of Multiple Deprivation (IMD), SE18 7JJ was ranked 7,478 out of 32,844 Lower Layer Super Output Areas (LSOAs) in England, placing it within the top 25% most deprived areas nationally (GOV.UK). This level of deprivation often correlates with limited early language exposure and fewer opportunities for rich oral interaction outside school.

In response, we place a strong emphasis on developing oracy across the curriculum. High-quality talk is essential not only for building vocabulary and comprehension but also for fostering pupils' confidence, reasoning, and ability to articulate their thoughts clearly. By embedding structured speaking and listening opportunities, through strategies such as oral rehearsal, sentence stems and dialogic teaching, we aim to close the language gap and equip our pupils with the communication skills they need to thrive academically and socially.

What initiatives and strategies have you implemented to narrow this language gap? What challenges did you face along the way?

At Nightingale, narrowing the language gap has never been a one-off intervention, it has been an evolving journey grounded in both high-level pedagogical reform and the deliberate, consistent development of classroom talk. As a school serving a richly diverse community, with over 60% of our pupils identified as EAL learners for more than a decade, addressing language development has been not only a priority but also a necessity.

While shifts in reading instruction and curriculum design have certainly played a vital role, we've also made a deliberate effort to embed structured classroom conversation into the fabric of our pedagogy. One of the key approaches we've implemented is the Kagan Cooperative Learning structure, specifically routines like Talking Chips, where pupils take turns contributing to discussions. This ensures that all voices are heard and that pupils are explicitly taught how to listen, take turns and respond respectfully and meaningfully. It also allows teachers to assess the quality of pupil dialogue in real time and intervene with targeted language prompts.

Alongside this, we have drawn heavily from the book *Making Thinking Visible* by Ron Ritchhart, Mark Church and Karin Morrison, using teaching routines such as '*See, Think, Wonder*' and '*Headlines*' to help pupils articulate their ideas, deepen their understanding, and share their thinking with others. '*See, Think, Wonder*' encourages students to closely observe, reflect and question, helping them engage in meaningful discussions while articulating their thoughts clearly. '*Headlines*' asks students to summarise their thinking in one impactful sentence, honing their ability to communicate concisely. These strategies provide structured frameworks for pupils to verbalise what they're noticing and how they're processing information.

To ensure consistency, we've introduced visual cues for silent communication in class, including Agree, Build and Challenge signals. These are supported by stem sentences that scaffold language for discussion, helping learners, especially those new to English, engage with academic discourse. These routines have now become a staple of how we talk and learn across the school.

Of course, maintaining fidelity to these approaches isn't without its challenges. The transient nature of staffing in schools means that a great deal of onboarding is required for new teachers and support staff. Embedding these strategies so that they don't feel like add-ons, but are integral to classroom culture, takes time and persistence. There have been moments when consistency has slipped, something that happens in any real school environment. Still, because these strategies are deeply embedded in our whole-school pedagogy, we can recalibrate quickly when we notice a shift.

Ultimately, our work on oracy is not just about *'doing'* a set of routines, it's about building a shared language of learning, one that empowers pupils to be articulate, thoughtful and confident in expressing their ideas. It's a journey we are still on, but one we believe is worth every investment of time and effort.

How have you changed the culture and ethos of the school to value oracy more?
At Nightingale, shifting the culture to place greater value on oracy hasn't been about declaring it as a standalone priority. Instead, we've taken a more nuanced, embedded approach, focusing on the specific learning needs of our pupils and identifying which strategies will help them communicate and comprehend more effectively across the curriculum.

We've always recognised the importance of early intervention, with *Early Talk Boost* being a longstanding staple in our EYFS provision, well before my time at the school. However, it was in 2019/20 that we saw a clear opportunity to build on this foundation when we participated in the EEF's NELI (Nuffield Early Language Intervention) trial. This initiative provided us with a structured approach to further support the development of language skills, particularly for our younger pupils. NELI is designed to improve oral language skills in reception-aged children by providing targeted, small-group intervention sessions. The programme focuses on enhancing vocabulary, sentence structure and listening skills, giving children a stronger foundation in oracy that supports their broader academic progress. By joining the trial, we were able to incorporate evidence-based strategies into our practice and develop more targeted interventions, ensuring that our pupils had the language tools they needed to succeed academically and socially. Participating in that project deepened our understanding and gave us the confidence to believe that no single programme holds all the answers. Instead, a layered approach is needed, one that adapts and responds to what pupils show us through their learning and progress.

One of the pivotal developments we introduced around that same time was the implementation of strategies to improve **reading fluency**; specifically *words correct per minute* sessions. These weren't just about improving speed, but about developing accuracy, expression, and ultimately, a love of reading. Initially piloted in Years 3 and 4, these sessions are now a core component of our lower Key Stage 2 approach to ensure pupils transition into UKS2 with the fluency needed to access, enjoy, and discuss increasingly complex texts.

We've also become far more rigorous in how we *review and refine* our teaching of reading and writing. Rather than making broad, unsustainable declarations like 'we are now an oracy school,' we zoom in on specific practices, refining and adapting based on what we learn through trialling, workshops and class-based inquiry. If a strategy proves its worth, we scale it. If it doesn't, we return to the evidence base or consult with others to challenge our thinking.

This iterative approach, coupled with careful use of formative and summative assessments, has helped us steadily shift the culture, from one where oracy was something happening incidentally, to one where purposeful talk, expressive reading, and vocabulary-rich interactions are becoming the norm. And perhaps more importantly, we've nurtured a staff team that's not afraid to question what works, seek feedback, and remain agile in the face of change.

So, while we may not always say *'we're working on oracy'* explicitly, almost everything we do, from reading instruction to classroom discussion protocols, has that thread running through it: helping children find and use their voice with confidence, clarity and purpose.

What has the tangible impact been upon academic progress as well as pupil wellbeing?
Over the past three years, Nightingale has consistently achieved strong academic outcomes, particularly in Maths, where we have been proud to maintain *results of 88% or higher at the expected standard since 2018*. Our Reading and Writing results have also remained *above national averages*, a reflection not just of curriculum delivery but of the thoughtful, structured shifts we've made in how pupils access and engage with language across subjects.

These outcomes are not just numbers, they tell a deeper story of how our focus on oracy has begun to bear fruit.

A key driver of this impact, particularly in Maths, has been our whole-school adoption of *Number Talks*, a strategy first developed by Sherry Parrish. Number Talks offer short, daily opportunities for pupils to develop mental math fluency, communicate their reasoning, and listen to and critique the strategies of others. we saw early on how this aligned beautifully with our oracy goals, teaching pupils not only to calculate but also to *articulate their mathematical thinking* with precision and clarity.

From Nursery to Year 6, this practice has become part of the rhythm of our classrooms. We placed strong emphasis on introducing and modelling *tier 3 mathematical vocabulary*, a shift that has elevated the depth of classroom discussion. By giving pupils the language to express themselves mathematically, we not only improved their confidence in reasoning and problem-solving, but also helped reduce the anxiety often associated with maths.

And while academic outcomes are significant, we've never let them become the sole driver of our practice. We see outcomes as one lens for evaluating the impact of teaching, but our wider goal has always been to support children in *feeling successful, heard and capable* in their learning.

The oracy-rich environments we've created across the curriculum, whether in Reading through fluency work and vocabulary teaching, or in Maths through Number Talks and shared reasoning, have had a real impact on pupil well-being too. We hear it in the classroom: pupils are more willing to share their ideas, challenge one another respectfully and feel pride in their thinking. They're not just learning to *'get it right'*, they're learning to *explain* and *understand*, which gives them a stronger sense of agency.

We don't claim to have solved everything, and we know that sustaining this takes consistency and reflection. But the progress we've seen, both in outcomes and in how our pupils approach learning, tells us we're on the right path. It's not just about improving oracy for oracy's sake; it's about *equipping pupils with the tools to thrive academically and emotionally*, now and in the future

Reflecting back over the whole journey, what are your three main lessons learnt to share with other schools?
Looking back on our oracy journey at Nightingale over the past 9 years, it's clear that real, sustainable change takes time, humility and a clear-eyed view of what works for *your* pupils. While we've seen encouraging signs of progress, we're very much still on the journey, because oracy isn't one initiative or programme. It's a collection of practices and principles woven into the fabric of excellent teaching.

Here are three key lessons we'd share with other schools considering a similar path:

1 **Oracy is not one thing, so don't try to fix it with one solution.**
   One of our earliest realisations was that treating oracy as a single strand or bolt-on strategy would never work. Instead, we approached it as a complex, layered skillset that cuts across subjects, ages, and developmental stages. Whether it was Early Talk Boost in EYFS, the introduction of word count per minute fluency lessons in lower Key Stage 2, or embedding *Number Talks* and structured vocabulary instruction into Maths, each step focused on specific facets of oracy relevant to that phase or subject. We've learned to *prioritise a few key elements at a time*, rather than chasing a complete overhaul all at once.

2 **Map the journey, but don't be afraid to adapt it.**
   We've become strong believers in the power of a mapped journey. Having a clear sense of what we're trying to improve and *why* has been essential. But just as important has been knowing when to pivot. For example, when reciprocal reading strategies didn't meet the needs of our EAL learners, we shifted to our in-house *Reading Wheel* approach, built around clarity and concrete comprehension strategies. Each time we've trialled an idea, we've done so *in practice first*, piloting it in a year group or with a specific staff team, before rolling it out school-wide. That readiness to reflect, test and refine has helped us avoid initiative fatigue and build deeper buy-in over time.

3 **Change the practice first, then the culture follows.**
   Cultural change is a big, abstract aim. What's worked for us is *starting with practice*. We've built oracy not by declaring *'we are now an oracy-focused school,'* but by making small, deliberate shifts in how teachers teach and how pupils think, speak and interact. From Kagan structures like Talking Chips, to sentence stems, silent communication signals, and Making Thinking Visible routines like *'See, Think, Wonder,'* we've embedded oracy practices across lessons. It's been through this repeated, consistent modelling that we've seen a deeper cultural shift, one where children are more confident speakers, active listeners and reflective thinkers.

Interview: Embedding Oracy across a Department

Name: Peter Munroe

Role: Head of Chemistry at Uckfield College

Mini Bio:

Peter is Head of Chemistry at a large state secondary school where he champions the use of oracy and dialogic teaching, both in science and across the curriculum. He is passionate about equipping teachers to use talk effectively in the classroom, sharing practical strategies for oracy. Peter has a research interest in the attitudes of teachers towards dialogic teaching, and finding ways to overcome barriers towards it.

Q: How have you integrated oracy into the pedagogy of your Science department?
A: Initially, we developed some resource packs to share oracy strategies within the team. However, realising this was too passive to become embedded, we adapted to focus upon short and engaging oracy strategies that teachers could use as part of their lessons. We didn't want oracy to be seen as an 'add-on' but tried to make sure it became a routine part of the lesson sequence.

We also wanted to avoid reinventing the wheel. Instead, we reviewed existing structures (like the Frayer model) to see how purposeful talk could replace elements of the task. The adoption of simple questioning phrases such as 'So what...?' and 'What if...?' by pupils and staff helped to deepen the discussions with minimal resourcing or preparation required.

Q: How did you develop CPD to equip your staff for implementing oracy in the classroom?
A: Our main priority was to get staff onboard and bought into the purpose of oracy in Science. This required extra focus on the WHY – why does oracy benefit learning and understanding? – as well as explaining the long term benefits of oracy for a pupil's future prospects.

Alongside this mindset shift, we also directed the oracy strategies in Science towards tangible outcomes, such as use in problem solving or structuring thoughts. This made it easier for staff to understand how oracy could become a tool in lessons.

Q: What barriers have you faced with staff so far?
A: Science is a content-heavy subject, especially at secondary school for exam classes. Asking staff to fit in oracy, which can often be perceived as a lengthy process of debate and discussion, into a busy lesson is a difficult sell. This is particularly challenging in Science, where many of the answers are black or white. Explaining the need for oracy in such a fact-based subject is not easy.

Many staff already deploy some forms of talk structures in their practice but might need support with developing deeper dialogues or consistently using talk in lessons. Therefore, we wanted to adapt our approach so that oracy became short and engaging, and supported the progress of learning within the existing curriculum"

Q: What success stories can you share about your oracy journey?
A: From learning walks, I have seen further embedding of simple talk structures and prompts. Teachers are clearly more engaged with oracy and this is evident in how they use the tangible resources and structures built into the slides.

Staff have also shared their eagerness to engage pupils in richer discussions. This positive feedback shows that the change is slowly becoming something our staff want to use.

Lastly, we are seeing increased pupil participation which is due to a change in our expectations in class. For example, applying a 'No Hands Up' rule is helping more pupils to share.

Interview: Championing Oracy

Name: Emma Howe

Role: Assistant Headteacher and Oracy Lead, Temple Hill Primary Academy

Mini Bio:

I'm Emma, and I've been an Assistant Headteacher for over ten years at Temple Hill Primary Academy, a busy, four-form entry school. In my role as the English and Oracy Lead, I guide pupils in finding their voices and excelling in literacy. I am also Lead Practitioner for English across our trust, supporting and enhancing teaching practices. I am deeply passionate about driving social mobility, which, to me, is about empowering individuals with the choices and opportunities to shape their own futures. This commitment to creating equitable opportunities is what inspired my journey into education, and I am dedicated to making a meaningful impact on every child's life.

Q: What were your key drivers for introducing oracy as a priority?
A: In recent years, we have seen our writing outcomes at Key Stage Two fall below National levels, with more children not reaching the 'Expected Standard'. We spent some time examining this trend and analysing contextual data in an attempt to identify the underlying symptoms of this concern within our writing. As part of this exploration, we clearly identified the correlation between our high levels of disadvantaged children and poorer writing attainment.

Children from disadvantaged backgrounds were often coming from home environments that were language-poor, lacking in access to quality literature and missing the high quality talk every child needs. In essence, our children were experiencing 'word poverty', and this hindered their progress and confidence with writing. As a result, we then viewed our data across the school through the filter of *'disadvantage'*; a key trend was the worryingly low levels of our reception children. Only 28% of disadvantaged children reach GLD at the end of reception – I think this is crucial to add as our focus on how we can support disadvantaged pupils played a key factor in implementing Oracy

Q: So how did oracy become a part of the solution?
A: If you can't say it, you can't write it!

As a team, we recognised the integral connection between language and writing. Our children's writing, as well as all the other areas of development, would benefit from stronger levels of oracy. In September 2024, I led our Staff through a CPD session in which we dived into:

- What do we understand by the term *'oracy'*? – many initially say oracy as *'talk'* but we came to collectively realise the wider scope of oracy beyond just speaking.
- Where would oracy benefit learning in all year groups? – we identified many areas in the curriculum, from EYFS to Key Stage 2, where language development was vital for learning to progress.
- How can we start to make oracy part of what we do?

Traditionally, our school had relied upon PowerPoint slides to guide a lesson. This limited opportunities for learner-led talk so we recognised a need to shift the way we teach to give children more chances to use their voice. Since September, we have been on a journey to integrate oracy into our pedagogy and practice, but we are still at the early stages.

Q: Tell me more about your Oracy Champions and their role?
A: As a new member to the Voice21 community, we were advised to have an Oracy Champion. However, as a four-form entry (with an SRP provision for complex needs), I knew it was important to have wide representation across the school if we had any chance of effectively implementing change.

Therefore, we structured our approach to have four champions:

- EYFS champion
- SRP champion
- A Key Stage 1 and a Key Stage 2 champion

Our champions are all outstanding practitioners, and they were tasked with supporting and leading staff CPD sessions, inviting other staff in to observe their oracy practice and being available to support staff with any oracy-related questions. So far, they have done an amazing job of establishing good practices and embedding change in the way our staff perceive oracy.

Q: After your first year of oracy, what is your vision for the coming academic year?
A: I want oracy to be our *'bread and butter'* across the school and embedded in everything we do. Up until now, we have focused upon oracy for academic progress as well as its influence upon behaviours. For the coming year, I want our oracy champions to help review and embed oracy into the wider school curriculum and daily routines. From interactions at the lunch table to the ways we engage our parents, oracy should be at the heart of our school.

> ### Interview: A Phased Approach to Implementation
>
> **Name:** Katie Ridgway
>
> **Role:** Whole School Literacy Lead Practitioner, Belmont Community School
>
> **Mini Bio:**
>
> With 14 years of experience as a Secondary English teacher, Katie has developed a passion for embedding Oracy into the classroom. As a Whole School Literacy Lead, she champions reading, writing, speaking and listening across the curriculum. Her keen interest was sparked in 2018 when she started the Voice 21 Oracy Pioneers Programme and was reconfirmed after the COVID-19 lockdown periods, making her keen to promote high quality talk in education: both within the classroom and wider school environment. Katie believes that Oracy is key to unlocking student confidence, empowerment and academic success.

Q: In your school, what gave you the impetus to embed oracy in your pedagogy and practice?
A: My personal focus on embedding Oracy within my own classroom pedagogy and practice came from attending the Voice 21 Oracy Pioneers Programme in 2018. I already held growing concerns about the decline in Oracy skills since the removal of the speaking and listening tasks required for GCSE English and the course only served to highlight the major implications of this, especially for disadvantaged children.

The decision to make Oracy a whole school focus was made by governors who had become increasingly aware of the need to embed Oracy across the curriculum and the real life benefits of developing Oracy skills.

Q: How did you initially plan and design the implementation of oracy strategies (considering staff CPD, planning, resourcing, policies etc)?
A: Initial planning for the implementation of Oracy strategies started between the T&L lead and myself in the Spring of 2021. I recognise now even more the importance of this timing being post COVID-19 and the lack of opportunities during the lockdown periods for children to communicate in a range of scenarios.

We decided to start small with the basic expectations for meet and greets and answering the register at the start of lessons so that we could focus on formal register and building back up high expectations for this post-lockdown. We then wanted to reintegrate rigorous questioning expectations which linked to our whole school ethos of contribution and build students ability to communicate their ideas, questions and answers fluently.

Q: Did you phase implementation (i.e. pilot and trial first)? If so, why and how successful was this approach?
A: In terms of implementation we phased this down to starting with the basics and we designed *'Oracy: The Belmont Way'* to align with our already existing whole school T&L strategy so

that it linked clearly with other elements already embedded into teaching practice. This, we acknowledged, allowed staff to see Oracy as interwoven with existing practice; something that would not create additional workload and something that was not simply a *'tag on'* practice.

Q: What range of strategies did you decide to implement first? Can you explain your reasoning behind the chosen strategies?
A: Firstly, we focused on very small basics: formal meet and greets and answering the register. We then phased this up to no opt out and format matters which were existing questioning practices before lockdown and allowed us to tap back into established questioning routines and expectations.

Q: How did you ensure staff were knowledgeable and supported? What mechanisms were in place to provide targeted support where necessary?
A: To ensure staff were knowledgeable and supported, we provided a document with expectations e.g. model formal greeting sentences and examples of student responses that met the format matters criteria. Secondly, I identified good practice through learning walks and shared recordings. We also reinstated an open door policy whereby staff could come to observe good practice if needed.

Q: What has the impact been so far? How has it benefited the disadvantaged pupils in their learning?
A: The most notable impact has been student's confidence which has improved greatly, especially for disadvantaged students. They know to formally meet and greet teachers at classroom thresholds and around school which is always commented on by visitors to the school in a positive way.

Knowing expectations and routines around questioning has been helpful for all students but especially disadvantaged children – they know that they can be cold called and that *'I don't know'* is not an accepted response. Teachers provide scaffolds such as sentence starters or prompts as simple as *'because...'* to help these children structure their responses and explanations to questions. The aim particularly in relation to the questioning strategies is that to build confident communicators for life beyond education, we need to build confident speakers.

Case Study: A Long-Term Journey towards Sustainable Oracy

Name: Catherine Gardner

Role: BEAM Facilitator, Barnet Early Autism Model (BEAM): Specialist Inclusion Services

Mini Bio:

Catherine has worked with children across schools, nurseries and the NHS since 2012. She currently works as a Facilitator within the Barnet Early Years Autism Model team (BEAM) in the London Borough of Barnet. Her role and that of her skilled team is to support young autistic children and their families predominantly at home and also joint working with nurseries and schools too.

Q: How may young autistic children communicate differently to their neurotypical peers?
A: For some autistic children, they may prefer or will use non-verbal communication. This may be all of the time or at specific times especially when it may be harder to vocalise their needs. From my experience, some autistic children may start using verbal language later in the early years and beyond. Therefore, it is important that these children need to be accessing different forms of communication, whilst at the same time the supporting adults are looking for their attempts to communicate and responding accordingly.

There is also another way to language acquisition called 'Gestalt language processing'(not solely linked to autism) whereby some children may acquire language by learning scripts and 'chunks' of language, which they repeat immediately or later on, known as echolalia. This can be somewhat shown in how autistic children may copy phrases from TV shows, songs or books and repeat these in other contexts. For example, with one child I supported, they had a keen interest in football and would sometimes say 'welcome to match of the day!'

It is good practice to reflect upon the ways children maybe language processing and for staff to access any available training and resources to further support these children develop their language in a way that suits their learning style.

It is also important to bear in mind that a child's use of verbal language does not necessarily represent their ability to process and understand language; we must be mindful of making assumptions here. There can also be differences in a child's social communication and how they navigate play with their peers.

Q: What language development strategies from SEND can transfer into mainstream early years?
A: Visuals are key. Visual processing can be a strength for many autistic individuals. These could be photographs or symbols to represent activities or toys. Also, they can be accompanied by vocal words and Makaton sign language too. Makaton can be naturally incorporated into songs and everyday scenarios to support dual coding.

For those children who may become frustrated where they cannot verbalise or clearly express their needs yet, having exposure to signing is great. Visuals and symbols also last much longer, as words disappear as these are concrete sources. They are also highly beneficial in helping a child understand transitions, which helps the child to know what is coming next and can bring a sense of calm.

Furthermore, it is good practice to be reflective on the amount of information being given to a child at any one point. We can simplify language to key words especially when giving instructions. Visuals can scaffold new language, such as having 'open door' placed on the door so it can be modelled verbally and visually for the child to see every time it is used.

For those children using phrases, it may be that they need support with language around play and social situations. Therefore, adults need to provide scaffolded support such as modelling language, providing visual language scripts to help equip the child to engage in play or creating social stories to help them understand.

Lastly, where adults may naturally over-help, taking a pause can be a simple but effective strategy to allow time to see if the child may make a request; this creates opportunities for shared communication and joint attention.

Q: What language skills are the first ones to focus on with young children?
A: A good foundation for general communication is joint attention; this does not necessarily equate to direct eye contact or back-and-forth conversation but rather both adult and child attending to a shared moment or activity. It is an opportunity for shared enjoyment with the child's interest at the forefront.

We incorporate and model an approach called Intensive interaction into our sessions, where we follow the child's lead and interests which fosters natural and joyful exchanges. I have seen firsthand how this has built joint attention and a connection with a child therefore increasing opportunities for communication to flourish. Using song and rhythm can be a great method of gaining a child's attention and pausing to see if they will join in with familiar words or respond with an instrument on cue.

The main thing is for it to be fun and child-led, it is great when the child notices your interest in their world!

17 Conclusion

The Reality of the Oracy Divide

The Social Mobility Imperative

As explained by Major and Machin (2018), social mobility has remained stubbornly *'sticky'* at both ends of the social class ladder, with the most disadvantaged communities finding it increasingly more difficult to become upwardly mobile. In recent years, post credit crunch and pandemic, the United Kingdom has become an even less mobile society, in both absolute and relative terms. Disadvantaged pupils often enter school with a language deficit – up to 30 million words in some studies (Hart and Risley, 1995) – which creates barriers to learning that only widen as they progress through school. Academic achievement can be correlated with language capacity as well as social background – in essence, a child's social status and language has a significant influence upon their success (or failure) at school.

Oracy has the power to narrow the growing divide, providing more pupils with a voice that can be heard, valued and celebrated. The benefits of oracy for social mobility have been well documented by numerous bodies, from Voice 21 to the Oracy Education Commission. Oracy is not a *'nice to have'* or an optional extra; it is a matter of social justice that should be central to any discussions around equitable access to education and life opportunities.

Schools play a crucial role in providing pupils with the opportunities and skills to find their voice and develop their oracy skills. Schools are not unfamiliar with their social responsibilities and have been core pillars of communities for many decades, supporting families in many non-academic areas (i.e. housing advice, early help, access to local services and more). Yet schools will have to play an even larger role in raising social aspirations and opportunities through oracy initiatives. However, converting idealistic visions for oracy into reality is not straightforward. Boosting social mobility for our most disadvantaged children requires many barriers to be overcome.

Barriers to Change

As with any change, whether cultural, procedural or both, implementation will always face obstacles to overcome. Implementing new approaches for oracy is no different. Schools are increasingly under more pressure in regards of budgeting, staffing, crammed curricula and workload; introducing new change amongst these challenges can often lead to a failed or shallow implementation that lacks any longevity.

Schools are prioritising their areas of most concern, including cost-saving initiatives, staff retention/recruitment and trying to stay on top of the growing SEND crisis. This means oracy is often pushed further down the list of priorities and requires a brave and forward thinking leader to ensure it is resourced and funded sufficiently. New programmes are often underfunded and under-resourced, with staff asked to launch new strategies without the time or training to make the change effective.

As this book has revealed, the benefits of oracy are well documented. Getting oracy effectively embedded can have wide-reaching impacts upon academic success as well as improving the well-being of pupils and staff. These potential benefits should act as the catalyst for change and the arguments to provide sufficient funding and capacity within the school. If everyone - teachers, pupils, parents, governors - can visualise the benefits, it can make the resistance to change easier to overcome.

It is important to consider the most disadvantaged pupils who we support in schools; the impact of weak language skills upon their life chances are substantial. Oracy is a vehicle for social mobility, and it is our collective responsibility, schools and families, to provide the best opportunities for oracy - especially for those who need it the most.

A Sense of Hope

Evidence Showing the Way Forward

There is a growing evidence base being established across the UK and internationally that supports the benefits of oracy interventions in schools. Organisations, from Voice 21 to the Education Endowment Foundation to Oracy Cambridge, are helping guide schools and educators through the oracy journey. Their solidly reliable and extensive research studies, along with their ongoing pilots and trial programmes, provide a well-rounded overview of oracy in action. School leaders need to utilise this collection of quality evidence when establishing their vision and strategies with their stakeholders. If teachers can understand the pedagogy behind oracy, connecting it to their existing practice, they are more likely to buy into the need for change.

Certain schools around the country have already started their journey in recent years. As with any new pedagogical strategies, observing fellow educators deploying new techniques in a real class setting is an effective way for teachers to understand the nuts and bolts. School leaders looking to introduce oracy interventions should be seeking to take their staff - oracy leads at minimum - to visit these pockets of excellence. Establishing collaborative relationships with such schools can help build an ongoing dialogue between teachers that acts as a support mechanism.

Looking at the bigger national picture, policy makers have placed oracy at the forefront of their priorities in the past 18 months. The establishment of the Oracy Education Commission is a clear indicator that oracy needs to be recognised as a key driver of equity. The Curriculum Review delivered it's recommendations in late 2025, with oracy featuring in it's report. For national change to effectively happen, the Government needs to continue working in close partnership with oracy organisations and school leaders to ensure policy matches schools' demands.

Sustainable Change Matters

Oracy needs to be woven into the fabric of a school; it should be a central and overarching feature in policies, practices and routines. It needs to be an integral part of CPD, curriculum mapping, lesson design and assessment cycles – not a *'bolt-on'* or a *'nice to have'*. Changing a school's culture and value of oracy is not a quick fix. Yet, incorporating oracy into the many aspects of school life is a helpful starting point for change.

Too often, new fads and initiatives are introduced in one academic year and fall out of favour by the next. Running on an annual cycle can make long-term change trickier to implement. New staff, new leaders and new pupils rotating in and out of school each Summer can make embedding new approaches very difficult. School leaders need to consider how best to shift one-off oracy initiatives towards longer-term strategies that focus on consistency and small steps.

The long term vision needs to place the child at its centre – especially those disadvantaged pupils who lack the language to thrive. A useful way to ensure change lasts beyond the short term is to constantly refer back to the vision and remember those pupils who will benefit the most from sustained change. If oracy is partly defined as *'learning through talk'*, there is no reason why it shouldn't be an ever-present part of school.

A Collective Call to Action

Schools are complex ecosystems, inhabited by many different people. However, because oracy is a tool for pupil agency and mobility, we all share a collective responsibility for ensuring oracy is championed. Each stakeholder has a responsibility in this change journey:

- Government
    - To listen to the education community for better understanding of the challenges they face in terms of funding, staffing and resourcing
    - To design and introduce policies that provide the guidance, but also freedom, for schools to embed oracy
    - To collaborate with oracy organisations to ensure policies are supported by research and solid evidence bases
- School leaders
    - To work with their stakeholders to create a vision for long-term change
    - To use an evidence-informed approach to change, ensuring staff buy-in and family engagement are high
    - To prioritise oracy across teaching and learning, providing opportunities for CPD and time to collectively reflect as a teaching body

- Teachers
    - To develop a stronger understanding of the pedagogy of oracy, through self-study and curious exploration of research
    - To work with school leaders to trial new strategies, providing constructive feedback and ideas for more effective change that fits the school's context and community
    - To be consistent with new approaches, trialling them effectively in class and providing feedback for improvement
- Parents
    - To better understand the importance of early language upon a child's life trajectories
    - To engage with school initiatives, from parent workshops to reading newsletters, supporting the school with their own child's development
- Pupils
    - To learn new strategies in class as well as understanding the reasons why oracy matters to their own development and future opportunities
- Trustees/Governors
    - To engage with school leaders, asking questions and challenging new initiatives in a positive manner
    - To develop a more secure understanding of the pedagogy and benefits of oracy, especially in relation to the community they serve

Improving social mobility must be a collective endeavour, as change on this scale stretches beyond education and across the whole of society. Schools have a very important part to play in this mission because they are the consistent presence in children's and families lives. Whilst schools have a wide remit for supporting pupils and families, it is clear that oracy and language development can play a much larger role in this support set up.

The optimism around the increasing value and prioritisation of oracy as a lever for change needs to transfer into tangible action – otherwise, it risks becoming *'just another fad'* that could be left aside. Oracy is both learning to talk and learning through talk; language is the key to unlocking the future for our most disadvantaged learners.

References

Hart, B. and Risley, T.R. (1995) *Meaningful Differences in the Everyday Experience of Young American Children*. Baltimore: Paul H. Brookes Publishing.
Major, L.E. and Machin, S. (2018) *Social Mobility and its Enemies*. London: Pelican Books.

INDEX

0-3 years 29-33
3 Rs of Reading, wRiting and aRithmetic: oracy as fourth 101; tracking 74
30 million word gap 31-2

ABC (Agree Build Challenge) approach 122-3; signals 181-2
absolute mobility 20-1
academic outcomes: measures 74-5; oracy goals, and 183-4; oracy outcomes, and 74; poor oracy, and 47-8; school focus 151; school readiness, and 47; shifting 152; workplace preparation 137
accent bias 140-1; definition 141
actual development 7
adults: child dialogue gap 53; interactions with child 40, 132; skills required 30; workplace, in *see* workplaces
Alexander, R. 10
articulacy 151
artificial intelligence (AI): equipping pupils 153-4; workplace changes 152-3
assemblies 133-4
audit 172-4; conducting 173-4
autistic children 189-91

baby stage 29-30
Barnet Early Autism Model (BEAM) 189-91
behavioural influences 12
belonging 127-8; definition 128; sense of 113
benchmarking: academic outcomes 74-5; oracy audit 173; social mobility 21-2
books: access 36, 54-5; cultural capital, as 69-70
Britton, J. 9
Bruner, J. 8

buddy system 128-30; benefits 129-30; set-up 129; structuring 128-9

case studies: autistic children 189-91; championing oracy 186-7; department embedding of oracy 185-6; impact of NELI 63-5; lessons learnt 184; next generation challenges 145-7; oracy gap 81-3; oracy-rich environment 179-84; phased approach to implementation 188-9; vocabulary divide 95-6
champions of oracy 13, 186-7
child development: assessing 44; cognitive 9, 47; decline 46-7; domains 44-5; environment, and 33; funding, and 26; Government recognition of impact 24-6; language, and 67; level 46-7, 109; school readiness, and 43; socio-economic status, and 25, 33-7; socio-emotional 11-12, 45, 48
child-directed speech (CDS) 38-9
Children's Literacy Charity 81-3
classroom facilitator 81
clubs 134
code switching 141-2; definition 141
cognitive load: barriers to expression 89; impact on learning 73; limits 96; questions 69; scaffolds 127
collaboration 127-8
confidence 112-14; boosting 132-4; definition 113; job interviews 138-9
conflict resolution 125-7; oracy, and 126
continuous professional development (CPD) 165-8; calendar 166, 169; oracy as lens 166-8; oracy as thread 167-8; standalone 167

COVID pandemic: impact 23-4, 62; oracy, and 99-100; special educational needs (SEND), and 83
cultural capital: cultivating 56; definition 56, 70; gap 56; examples 70; reading books 69-70; strategies for 57
cultural change 4, 158; barriers 192-3; ready, willing and able 174-7; recommendations 194-5; sustainable 194
culture: language development 6-7; leadership 157-60; risk-taking 121-2; shift 4 see also cultural change; strategic vision for change 157-8; valuing oracy 182-3
Curriculum and Assessment Review 101-2; teaching profession, and 102-5

debating: private schools 112-13; skills development 134
demographics: changes 73-4; language development, and 181
dialogic teaching 10-11; definition 9; principles 78-9; strategies 78-80
disadvantaged children: barriers to oracy 50-1, 82, 86, 192; cognitive overload 179; confidence 132, 139, 189; definition 75; digital divide 24; emotions 48-9; funding 25; gap 29-31, 63, 74-5, 99-100, 172-3; home environment 1, 33-8, 58, 186-7; mental health 116; outsiders, as 127; receptive language 88; school readiness 46; The Matthew Effect 52, vocabulary 87, 95; wellbeing, and 108, 112-16; workplace, in 140, 143-4, 146
disciplinary knowledge 94

early interventions: caregiver role 37-8; importance 36-7; need for 62
early years: baselining 52; closing gaps 58-9; development domains 44-5 see also child development; goals 108-9; learner's voice 68; reassessing priorities 49; receptive gap 88; social mobility opportunities 110; SWOT analysis 60-1; wellbeing 108-10
Early Years Foundation Stage (EYFS) Areas of Learning 109; early learning goals 43-4; Profile 44
economic capital 18
Education Endowment Foundation (EEF) 14, 62, 76, 193; advocates for change, as 2, 99; Key Stage One Literacy Guidance 74

educational gap 21, 24
emerging cultural capital 18
emotion wheel 124
emotional development 45, 48; oracy, and 11-12
emotional expression 123-7; opportunities 123
emotional regulation 116, 123
emotional vocabulary 124-5; definition 125; strategies 126
employability: next generation 151, 154; oracy, and 2, 150
English as an Additional Language (EAL): demographics 73; emotions 124; improving oracy 74; language gap 179, 181, 184; outcomes 74; school readiness 47
English Speaking Board 76
exploratory talk 9
expressive language 9
expressive vocabulary 87-8; definition 89; milestones 89; receptive foundation, and 88
extra-curricular oracy 132-4

formative assessment 163-5; benefits 164; oracy, in 165; practice, in 164-5
free school meals (FSM) measure 46
future workplaces: challenges for young people 145-7; changing expectations 151-2; impact of AI 153-4; preparing next generation 150-4; soft skills as priority 150-1; technology 152-4

gap and strength analysis (GSA) 53
good level of development (GLD) 46-7; areas of deprivation, and 47; social and emotional skills 109
government reviews 2-3
Great British Class Survey (GCBS) 18-19

headlines strategy 181
highbrow cultural capital 18
home learning environment (HLE): disadvantaged families 1, 33-8, 58, 186-7; key aspects 40; strategies for oracy 39-40

income inequality gap 1, 19, 22-3; impact 25
Initiation, Response, Feedback/ Evaluation (IRF/ IRE) 76-7; definition 77
inner speech mechanism 12

jargon 142
job interviews: confidence, and 138-9; opportunities to practise 139; oracy in 138; skills 137-9

Kagan talk structures 77, 181, 184

language: acquisition *see* language acquisition; development *see* language development; education in 3; enabler of learning, as 3, 71; focus, as 40; interpretation 12-13; learning, for 9-11; life chances, and 1-2; social mobility divide, as 142-4
language acquisition: conditions 29, 31; process, as 67; vocabulary, and 94 *see also* vocabulary
Language Acquisition Support System (LASS) model 8
language development: academic goals, and 31, 86; babies 29; confidence, and 139 *see also* confidence; culture 6-7; disadvantage, and 63, 181; early years importance 37; environment 53, 131; gaps *see* language gaps; language exposure 31, 73; mental health, and 116; milestones 89; pre-formal education 8
language gap 1-2, 29-32, 39, 62, 100; addressing 37-40; strategies needed 144-5
language-poor environment 32
language-rich environment 31-3; building 53-4; definition 32; quality of language 32-3; strategies for 54
learning: developmental domains 44-5; language for 9-11; locked door, as 72-4; readiness to engage 44; talk, through 10, 67-9, 71 *see also* dialogic teaching; talk, to 10
lesson design 162-3
Leuven scale 48-9, 110
lexicon 143; definition 142
life chance indicators 24-5
literature: access 36, 54-5; vocabulary, as gateway 91-2
lower class 18

Makaton sign (reference) language 190
Marmot Review 36-7; 10 years review 37
Maslow's hierarchy of needs 33-5; early years disadvantage 48; impact on oracy development 35

mental health in children 115-16
middle class 18

National Curriculum: lesson design 162-3; mapping 161; talk, for 160-3; topics 70
National Literacy Trust 14, 114; surveys 36, 40
Nuffield Early Language Intervention (NELI) 62-5; barriers 65; impact 63-5; reflections 64-5

Oracy Cambridge 14, 76; advocates for change, as 2, 99; Oracy Framework 3, 13-14, 108-9
oracy concept: building blocks 30-1; conceptual model 10-11; definition 1, 6; foundations 3-5; integral 3-4; listening 11; model 10-11; need for 1-3; omnipresent 3; origins 6-8; predictive power 30-1; redefining 13
Oracy Education Commission 100-1; recommendations 102
Oracy Framework 3, 13-15; areas 108; strands 14-15; wellbeing 109
oracy gap 1-2: addressing 81-3; call to action 194-5; closing 53; evidence of way forward 193-4; hope, sense of 193-5; reality 192-3; sustainable change 194; widening 52
oracy impact: academic 47-8; child-directed speech 39; classroom, in 72-4; confidence, on 114; cultural capital 57; early years development 45; language-rich environment 54; non-academic 11-13, 108-12; outdoors learning 59; play 58; skills and learning 67-8; social and emotional 48; socio-economic barriers, and 38; storytelling 55; wellbeing 109, 111
oracy implementation: ability 176-7; absence 99-100; barriers 105; change drivers 174; culture change, and 158-60; designated leads 170-1; monitoring 160; national call for change 100; phased approach 188-9; pre-existing within classroom 102; prioritising 103; ready 174-5; school audit 172-4; School Development Plan (SDP) 158; school environment 119-21; school systems 159; school vision 171-2, 178; SMART goals 174-5; willingness 176
oracy readiness 47-9; academic impact 47-8; social and emotional impact 48
oracy-related organisations 13-14, 76
oracy strategies 76-81

outside learning 57-8; role of adult 132; strategies for 59; talk opportunities 131

personal, social and emotional development (PSE) 109
Piaget, J. 6, 8-9
play 56-7; importance 110-12; role playing 111-12; strategies for 58; talk, and 130-2
playground 130-1; role of adult 132; talk 131
poetic language 9
potential development 7
primary emotions 125
pupil premium funding 25

rally robin strategy 78
reading: fluency strategies 182; power of 34, 36; statistics 36
reading wheel approach 179-80
receptive vocabulary 87-8; definition 89; early gap 88; milestones 89
reciprocal reading strategy 179
relative mobility 20-1
repeated reading strategies 180
restorative conversations 126-7
roundrobin strategy 78

safety: environment 119-21; psychological 121; sense of 119
schema 7, 56
school development plan (SDP) 157-8; oracy, in 171
school readiness: decline 46-9; defining 43-5; gap 46; UNICEF definition 43
schools: equalisers, as 2; events 133-4; oracy-rich change programme 170-8 see also oracy implementation; social responsibility 192; values 120-1
secondary emotions 125
see, think, wonder strategy 181
self efficacy 112-14; definition 113
self-regulation 109
SMART goals 174-5
social awkwardness 115
social capital 18
social class: evolution 18; gap 20, 22-3; new model 18-19; traditional system 17-18; vocabulary, and 89; workplace, in 144

social connectedness 114-15; definition 113, 128; oracy as protective factor 127-8; strengthening 127-32
social constructivism 6-8
social interactions: adult-child at baby stage 29; barriers 116; learning, and 8
social interactionist theory 8
social mobility: audit 27; class, and 17-18; concept 17-21; definition 17; early years opportunities 110; gap 33, 58-9; imperative 192; ladder 19; language divide 142-4; outcomes, and 24-5; stickiness of ladder 20, 23, 144, 192; UK, in 21-3
societies 134
socio-economic barriers 33-7; academic success, and 2; impact on oracy 38
Socratic questioning 79
soft skills 152; definition 151; prioritising 150-1
special educational needs (SEND): COVID pandemic, and 83; crisis 2; emotions 124; improving oracy 74; language development strategies, and 190; outcomes 74
speech, language and communication needs (SLCN) programmes 62
storytelling 54-5; strategies for 55
structured talk strategies 76-8; definition 77
substantive knowledge 94
summative assessments 163

talk stimuli 163
talking chips strategy 78, 181
talking points 79-80
taxonomy of learning 71-2; enabling talk 162
teachers: barriers to oracy 105; mistake modelling 121-2; oracy current practice 102-3; prioritising oracy 104-5; talking see teacher-talk
teacher-talk 68; control, and 81; questions 68-9; three types 77
technological developments 152-4
tertiary emotions 125
The Change Wheel 106-7
The Communication Trust 14
The English Speaking Union (ESU) 76
The Matthew Effect 52
think pair share 78
thinking aloud 80
time poverty 33-4
transactional language 9

UK: Government initiatives 25-6; economic troubles 23; Labour government election 100-1; nationwide approach 24-6; post-pandemic impact 23-4; public perception 22-3; recent drivers 23-4; regional variations 24; social mobility comparison 21-2
understanding 69-71
UNICEF 43
upper class 17-18

visual learning 190
vocabulary: complex, exposure to 36; cultural capital, and 70-1; definition 86; development strategies 94; dimensions 87-91; emotional 124; explicit instruction 91-2; expressive 87-90; gap *see* vocabulary gap; lexical bar 91; literature, and 91-2; poor progress, and 87; pyramid 97; receptive 87-90; rich approach 180; social class, and 89; three tiers 90-1; wider curriculum, across 93; workplace 148
vocabulary gap: bridging 91-6; narrowing 95-6; oracy gap, and 86

Voice 21 14, 76; advocates for change, as 2, 99; benefits of oracy 193; Commission on the Future of Oracy Education 100; Oracy Benchmarks 173; Oracy Framework 3, 13-14, 108-9; Oracy Pioneers Programme 188; teachers 163, 165
Vygotsky, L. 6-8, 12

well-being: definition 109; disadvantage, and 112-16; domains 113; early years 108-10; gap 108, 112-16; language, through 108; oracy impact 109, 111; virtuous circle 119-20
Wilkinson, A. 6
word-learning strategies 91-3
work readiness gap 154-5
workplaces: attributes to flourish 30; employer priorities 151, 154; fitting in 140-7; job interviews 137-9; language in 140-2; next generation challenges 145-7 *see also* future workplaces; preparation 137; social mobility, in 142-4

zone of proximal development model 7

For Product Safety Concerns and Information please contact our EU representative GPSR@taylorandfrancis.com
Taylor & Francis Verlag GmbH, Kaufingerstraße 24, 80331 München, Germany

www.ingramcontent.com/pod-product-compliance
Lightning Source LLC
Chambersburg PA
CBHW080805300426
44114CB00020B/2838